The
LOVE PIRATE
and the
BANDIT'S SON

The
LOVE PIRATE
and the
BANDIT'S SON

MURDER, SIN, AND SCANDAL
IN THE SHADOW OF
JESSE JAMES

LAURA JAMES

UNION SQUARE PRESS
An imprint of Sterling Publishing Co., Inc.

New York / London
www.sterlingpublishing.com

STERLING and the distinctive Sterling logo are registered trademarks of
Sterling Publishing Co., Inc.

Library of Congress Cataloging-in-Publication Data

James, Laura.

The love pirate and the bandit's son : murder, sin, and scandal in the shadow of Jesse James / by
Laura James.

p. cm.

Includes bibliographical references and index.

ISBN 978-1-4027-6069-3

1. Wilkins, Zeo Zoe. 2. James, Jesse, 1875-1951. 3. Murder—United States—Case studies. 4.
Crime—United States--Case studies. I. Title.

HV6529.J36 2009

364.152'3092--dc22

2008042434

2 4 6 8 10 9 7 5 3 1

Published by Sterling Publishing Co., Inc. / Union Square Press
387 Park Avenue South, New York, NY 10016
© 2009 by Laura James
Distributed in Canada by Sterling Publishing
c/o Canadian Manda Group, 165 Dufferin Street
Toronto, Ontario, Canada M6K 3H6

Book design and layout by Chris Welch

Sterling ISBN 978-1-4027-6069-3

For information about custom editions, special sales, premium and
corporate purchases, please contact Sterling Special Sales
Department at 800-805-5489 or specialsales@sterlingpublishing.com.

CONTENTS

Part I
ZEO ZOE

Part II
THE SON OF JESSE JAMES

Part III
THERE COULD BE BUT ONE END

LIST OF ILLUSTRATIONS

AUTHOR'S NOTE

This is a work of nonfiction that attempts to present the strict truth about everything and everyone it describes. Details were gleaned from many sources, public and private, which are listed in the bibliography at the end of the book. Any information that appears in quotation marks is the verbatim report of at least one reliable source.

Prologue

A Terrific Fight

On March 15, 1924, snowdust coated staid Park Avenue in Kansas City, Missouri. The street was quiet for a Saturday night. There were no wild parties on this frigid evening. Around ten p.m., an exceptionally beautiful woman unlocked the front door of her home at 2425 Park.

She must have known him. She let him in the house. But before long something alarmed her. It could have been the late hour or the reek of alcohol, though she was a stranger to neither. She numbed herself that night, as she usually did, with most of a bottle of Jamaica Ginger. Did she see the man lock the door as he turned to face her? Maybe a snarled threat or a flash of steel warned her that he was not there to make love to her. Instead, her premonition of a violent death was coming true. She surely thought—if she could form a complete thought—of all the friends and lovers to whom she had turned for help in her last few days. She told them someone wanted to murder her. She'd even said it would happen that weekend.

No one was there to help her. Nobody believed her.

She fought for her life. She threw every object within reach. She eluded death with "a terrific fight." At five feet eight and a hundred and thirty pounds, she could have held her own for a while. But the man was stronger. He chased her into a corner, punched her in the chest, and knocked the telephone from her hands. Chairs were smashed in their duel. In her desperate resistance she got the worst of it. He pummeled her and tore at her plaid dress and underwear. If she cried out in pain and terror, the only one who heard her screams was the man killing her.

It must have been a thunderous blow that sent her spinning into a metal stand. She struck her forehead and collapsed onto the oriental carpet in her living room.

The man grabbed her slender throat and squeezed. He gouged her left eye, blackening it and nearly severing her eyeball from its socket. Perhaps she fainted. But she rallied at the last when he brandished a small, rusty pocketknife. As she held out her hands to protect herself, he slashed them. The face that had aroused the passions of so many men now felt the sting of the blade. He sliced open her cheek and jammed the point of the knife into the side of her neck—once, twice—the deep stabs slitting her jugular. Blood gushed forth. Within a few heartbeats she was dead.

The blood-drenched killer dropped his knife. It fell onto the rug a few inches from her dead hand. He assured himself she was irretrievably dead.

Without pausing to wipe himself off, he strode to her dining room. He lifted a large metal strongbox onto the dining table, opened it, and tore through her personal papers. Her blood dripped from his hands onto her letters and documents as he rifled through the box for what he sought.

Papers, books, clothes, and bags were heaped onto the floor as the killer ransacked her house, plunging through the closet, roving through the kitchen, smearing blood on drawers and cupboards, leaving crimson tracks on the stairs between the first and second floors, in the hallways, in all her rooms. He pulled up the tacks holding down the corners of her carpets. He tore letters from envelopes. He searched most of the closets, chests, and shelves.

And yet he did not touch many pawnable items, such as her designer clothes and household items. This man was after particular valuables, things he knew she kept in her home. Nothing less was worth even a moment.

The murder scene. *(True Detective Mysteries)*

His search completed, he entered a downstairs bathroom and washed away her clotted blood. He found a hand towel and dried himself on it as he returned to the living room. Standing near the dead woman, he threw the towel onto the rug. He wadded some papers, put a flame to them, and started a fire near her head. He stuffed a strongbox filled with treasure under his arm.

Maybe he looked at her one last time.

Then he yanked open a window, crawled through, leapt several feet to the ground, and fled the scene of his perfect murder.

It was perfect not because of how he did it. He was an amateur killer. He left bloody prints everywhere, and the fire never caught. It was perfect because of the woman he killed. For no matter who cut down Zeo Zoe Wilkins, no matter why, newspapers across the country declared on moral grounds that her brutal death was a fitting end for a vampire. They proclaimed that the case would never be solved, officially or otherwise. Their wishes were granted. A lot of folks would come right out and say it: the bitch had it coming to her, and by golly, she sure got it.

Part 1

ZEO ZOE

Hoggie! Hoggie! Hoggie!

Again, if two lie together, then they have heat [zeo]: but
how can one be warm alone?
— *Ecclesiastes 4:11*

The Greek word "to be zealous" (zeo) means to boil,
sizzle, to be hot.
— *North American Dawn Ministries*

The first skirmish she fought in her war on men took place in a
hog pen. Zeo Zoe Wilkins was six years old and bored. She commanded her brother Arthur, who was seven, to play her favorite game
with her.

But he said no. She could bat her eyes, toss her dark brown curls,
stomp her feet, and cry all afternoon; Arthur wasn't budging this time.

Zeo marched to the hog pen. "You do it, Arthur."

"No."

She made as though to enter the pen and screamed, "You do it, or I'll
let the hogs eat me!"

Like all farm children, they knew better than to mess with hogs. Losing
your footing in a pen where swine were kept in numbers could earn you
a certificate that read "Cause of death: Attacked by hogs." They'd heard
the stories. When Zeo was seven months old, a tale crossed the country
of a little girl from North Carolina who tried to slop the hogs and was
devoured alive. Another story, circulating on Zeo's first birthday, told
of an old woman in Illinois whose kinfolk found nothing but bits of her
cotton dress underneath a snarling, squealing drove of hogs. Despite the

gruesome stories and parental warnings, Zeo thought less of the danger than she did of her desire to dominate her brother.

When Arthur still refused to play her game, Zeo stepped into the muck, threw herself bodily into the manure, and called, "Hoggie! Hoggie! Hoggie!"

The stunt curdled her brother's blood. Arthur yielded to her demands.

"After that," she later wrote in her diary, "I never had any trouble making Arthur bow to my will."

If only Arthur hadn't crumpled, if only he or someone else had put a paddle to his sister's bottom, perhaps the series of scandals and tragedies that lay ahead might have been avoided. But discipline was a luxury the Wilkins household could not afford.

John and Mary Wilkins trekked from Pennsylvania to northern Ohio after the Civil War. Like so many others, they thought a westward journey would improve their lives. But they were unsettled for several years, moving from one homestead to another. They proved themselves to be more fertile than the dirt they farmed. By 1884 the Wilkins Bible listed ten offspring from their union: a baby who died unnamed, William, John, Margaret (who died at age eleven in 1878), Mary Blanche, Horace, Charles, Mary Gertrude, Harriet Irene, and Arthur. Those who survived were more than John and Mary could feed, let alone clothe, and the Wilkins clan—"call it a family if you wish," one child would later remark—stumbled through crisis after crisis. The children fended for themselves for every need. Sometimes they begged for meals from the neighbors, and they weren't above pleading with strangers for a bite to eat. At times the only way to fill their bellies was to steal food. At school they were among the poorest, and the other children were as mean as children can be. The Wilkins kids stood back to back to fight for one another. Then they'd return home and, as a Wilkins boy would one day describe it, "just about slit each other's throats."

When the umpteenth (officially, the eleventh) baby Wilkins opened her pretty blue eyes for the first time on October 17, 1885, the other children must have grumbled. Mary Wilkins was by then forty-six, and she promised this baby would be her last. In a romance novel Mary found an unusual name that began with Z, the traditional initial of a large family's "caboose" in some parts of the country, and adorned her child with Zeo Zoe.

If the name wasn't enough to distinguish Zeo Zoe Wilkins from the rest of the brood, the family soon noticed—when the din of her squabbling siblings ebbed enough for them to hear her—that their prettiest little one showed signs of tremendous intelligence. As the baby grew into a toddler, then a child, they reckoned she was gifted beyond their experience or ready explanation. In that time and place, such smarts would seem a waste, especially in a girl. Nineteenth-century rural poverty had a cruel way of shrinking the world and diminishing opportunity.

When Zeo was still a small child, her family lived in a shack on thirty acres in Huron County, Ohio. The farmhouse was two doors down from the B&O railroad tracks. After a day of aimless play, Zeo often went to bed hungry. Listening to the trains singing late into the night, rattling the windows and spewing the smell of coal smoke and hot metal, she'd no doubt wonder where the tracks might one day take her. When she was bored, Zeo could walk a few miles along the tracks to the nearest hamlet, little Havana. There she could pop inside the dinky Geo. Van Horn Grocery and General Store, but the Wilkins name probably preceded her. Desperate children who stole to eat were hardly welcome in a grocery store. In Havana she could scrounge up playmates. Maybe they'd kick rocks or find a swimming hole uncontaminated by manure and leeches or put some bent nails on the tracks so the trains could flatten them into interesting shapes.

Other than the thunder of passing freight, there were few outside influences on Zeo in her early childhood. As Dayton Williams, another Huron County farm boy who grew up in the same era, would later reminisce:

For the general atmosphere of our life, I should say that it could be called <u>solid</u>—no wars or threats of wars, no sudden wealth, no sudden poverty, no threat of inflation, no fear that the reds would sneak in while we were not looking. . . . In our family there was not much loose money. But that was the accepted, usual and natural condition of affairs. At Christmas time a bag of candy and an orange were enough.

Conditions for the Wilkins kids were similarly spartan. They wore dingy, faded, hand-me-down clothes and shoes with little life left in them. There wasn't enough "loose money" for food, let alone medical attention or literature or trips out of Huron County. Being so poor gave John and Mary Wilkins plenty of chances to use the same line that has aggravated the children of rock-bottom America for generations: wish in one hand, shit in the other, and see which fills up first.

Since the old homestead was a desert for the budding genius, Zeo directed her mental abilities at family and friends. Her temperament suggested that her gray-haired mother and father had exhausted all their parental energies long before her behavior called for a firm talk or a switching behind the barn. Her propensities for dominating others with her personality alone likely began as a series of little rebellions and attention-seeking misbehaviors that went unchecked until her strength of mind was such that she took charge of her siblings and playmates, to the point of "incorrigible willfulness." Having her say would have been about her only entertainment.

He'd have said she was going to hell in a handbasket, but even Arthur didn't know that Zeo would, through sheer native force of will, lift herself up from the muck of poverty. Born into a family of thieves, she would out-thieve them all. Along the way, she would commit sins never heard of in all the history of Havana, Ohio. Her mother would have paled to learn that the name borrowed from a sentimental novel would come to stand in the nation's imagination for an uncontrollable libido, expensive divorces, and scandalous tragedies. Only a Bohemian fortune-teller would have guessed that the youngest child of a peasant family from the sticks, hungering for something, but so long starved of ideas that she had barely a notion as to what that something ought to be, would one day accumulate unimaginable riches that in the end would cost her everything.

2

Someday I'm Going to Be Rich, Rich, Rich

There are no new types. A certain social condition produces
its particular people wherever that condition prevails. Among
the pioneers, there were probably a negligible number of
gigolos—and not many gold diggers. They do not fit in with
that life. It takes leisure and a moneyed class to
produce social parasites.
— *Allene Sumner, "The Woman's Day" (1930)*

f Zeo Wilkins had matured in Havana, some hapless farmer would
have had himself a remarkable teen bride. At the turn of the century, girls in rural Ohio often settled their marital affairs the moment they legally could. Maybe Zeo would have slept with the same husband every night for the rest of her life. As it turned out, a list of men awaited the privilege.

It's impossible to say what finally made the Wilkins family go haywire, but something did. By 1900 John and Mary Wilkins had moved to yet another Huron County farm. Arthur was the only child who went with them. Arthur didn't like his older brother Charles and didn't care much for his little sister Zeo, either. He loved her, of course, like any brother would, but he hated her too. He couldn't help it. She came along and she was the treasured little red caboose, which made him a common freight car. Arthur alternately suppressed and nurtured a grudge he'd carry all his days.

The older Wilkins kids married young and took up the plow on their own farms, but the younger ones buttoned up their old shoes for a ride on the B&O. They joined a stream of migrants drawn from the farmlands to the industrial center of Cleveland. Zeo left Havana before she reached adolescence and surely thanked the stars for her escape from a rural purgatory. She would never talk much of her childhood. On occasion, when newsmen sought a quote from her, she made up a story that placed her beginnings far from Havana, Ohio. There's reason to think she left hating her parents and begrudging a world that threw her a brick instead of a rope when she nearly went under in Huron County. Perhaps she wasn't alone in rejecting her parents. Two of her sisters were named after their mother, but Mary Blanche and Mary Gertrude both dropped their first names and went by their middle names for the rest of their lives.

Once they arrived in Cleveland, two of Zeo's siblings took on the roles of Pa and Ma in a cheap rental house at 1580 Central Avenue in a Bohemian immigrant neighborhood. To anyone else the place might have looked sorry, but to the Wilkins offspring it boasted the twin miracles of running water and an indoor toilet. The city also offered the sort of high-paying work on which even a young, uneducated man could support a family or, if need be, rescue his siblings from misery. Charles Wilkins worked as a machinist and made enough money to support three of his sisters. Blanche kept house for them, Zeo attended school, and Irene found work at a homeopathic college.

Zeo found a father figure in Charles, eleven years her senior. A recurring character in her lurid drama, he would flit in and out of her life up to its end. In Cleveland, though, a crushing schedule as a two-dollar-a-day man in a machine shop kept him away from home. He detested the work and his employers. He lost all interest in God or family life. His religion was the IWW, the Industrial Workers of the World, a militant, Socialist-influenced, American labor powerhouse with membership in the six figures that advocated the progressive notion of a forty-hour workweek. Charles became an agitator for the union and, under the guise of a barber, would one day travel the country's labor camps and other hellholes to shill for recruits.

While her siblings stood *in loco parentis,* Zeo roamed. The twelve-year-old Zeo might have gone window-shopping, a popular pastime in the city. She must have stolen glances at the homes and wardrobes of the wealthy. The poor farm girl who scrounged to keep alive surely stared in culture shock for weeks before she began to declare to her family, "Someday I'm going to be rich, rich, rich. I don't give a damn what I've got to do to get it, but I'm going to have everything."

Zeo stole up to the school where Irene worked, Cleveland Homeopathic Medical College. There, she met a very old man, Andy the caretaker, who treated her to some adult attention. Zeo began paying the old man visits. A diligent mother would never have let her little girl near the place alone. The city of Cleveland was still whispering about the faculty and staff of the college who were prosecuted years before for furnishing their dissection labs with fresh cadavers unearthed from local cemeteries. By one account, Andy's predecessor as caretaker led the grave-robbing gang.

But it was Andy who should have worried. Andy didn't know it, but the cute little girl was tormenting him for sport. Her brother Horace was a witness to it. One day when Horace Wilkins left his own farm in Huron County to visit Cleveland, Zeo took him for a walk to meet Andy. Knocking on Andy's door, Zeo called out, "It's Helen! Let me in!" Andy warmly greeted them and invited them on a tour of the school. He even let Zeo touch the skeletons.

After Horace and Zeo took their leave of the caretaker, Zeo told her brother to watch her do a trick. She knocked for Andy again. "Let me in!"

"Who is it?"

"It's Zeo."

"Go away—and stay away," Andy barked. "I told you last week I'd never let you in again!"

Zeo explained to Horace that she had persuaded the old man that she and "Helen" were twins, one good and one bad. Andy loved Helen but hated the naughty, taunting Zeo. It was a sophisticated stunt for a little girl, but it was more than a child's game. She learned from old Andy's reactions. She was a tiger cub toying with half-dead prey.

By that point, Zeo thought of herself as two different people. "Helen was the better self, Zeo the evil," she wrote in her diary. "My family always liked Helen the better, but Zeo developed so readily that I soon grew too fond of her, and Helen found less and less welcome in my mind." Many children dream up playmates, even twins. In Zeo's case, the fictional twin was the good girl; her *genuine* self was the evil one. Perhaps her parents told her so. Maybe her siblings chastised her even as they capitulated to her whims. *Alright, Zeo, have your say. But you're a naughty little girl.* Regardless, she decided while still a child that being Zeo the Evil was much more fun than being Helen the Better. Something in the psyche of Zeo Wilkins had come unlatched.

Irene Wilkins's work at the homeopathic college spawned intriguing thoughts. Women, she learned, were welcome to study in some branches of medicine. Irene shared the discovery with all her sisters. Like many of her siblings, Zeo's sister Gertrude also wound up in Cleveland. She attended high school and business college, obtained a teacher's certificate, and found work as a bookkeeper and stenographer. Gertrude liked Irene's idea and decided to pursue a medical career. Zeo, then fifteen or sixteen, got caught up in Gertrude's enthusiasm. Zeo never mentioned having any noble calling to heal the sick, but practicing medicine would put her in touch with men of wealth.

The Wilkins sisters investigated medical schools. Together they pored over a brochure from the American School of Osteopathy in Kirksville, Missouri. It included photographs of a dissection amphitheater and a microscopy laboratory. Female students were pictured prominently. Handsome male students, too. The brochure specified that "women are admitted on the same terms as men," unlike the stodgy medical schools in the East. A degree in osteopathy did not at that time require as much education as did an M.D. Practitioners could dispense limited medical treatments and add D.O. to their names. They could not perform surgery or prescribe drugs, but they could practice medicine in some states. The school required prospective students to have "good moral character" and a high school diploma or a teacher's certificate. To graduate, students had to complete two years of study and had to be twenty-one years old. The tuition was three hundred fifty dollars plus the "dissection fee, twelve dollars and a half," but the school would allow students to finance this amount at seven percent interest over three years.

In the summer of 1903, Gertrude decided it was time to try medical school. She was old enough and held a teacher's certificate. Zeo was only seventeen and was still in high school, but she found a way to meet the requirements. In her request for admission, Zeo Wilkins claimed she was nineteen years old. As she didn't have a birth certificate—John and Mary never bothered to register their children's births—nobody could prove otherwise. Zeo solved the remaining admissions challenge by borrowing a duplicate of her sister's teaching certificate and forging her own name on it. As to the requirement of "good moral character," well . . .

A few weeks later, Zeo Wilkins received a letter in the mail. The American School of Osteopathy had accepted her as a student. She headed west by train to conquer more than medicine.

3

I Will Let Him Kiss Me

If we are going to be wicked, we might as well
make a good job of it.
— *Jesse Woodson James*

The first epithet the vivacious Zeo Wilkins earned was "queen among the coeds." Several heads surely swiveled to take in the sight of her and her sister Gertrude as they entered an auditorium on their first day of medical school in Missouri. Many students at the American School of Osteopathy were wealthy and brilliant; the Wilkins sisters were poor and brilliant. Almost all of the osteopathy students were unmarried. And Zeo was stunning: slim, tall, and shapely, she wore her thick, curly hair piled on top of her head. She looked much older than she actually was. Her features were perfectly even and delicate. She had an immaculate complexion, one rarely seen except on babies. Nary a freckle appeared anywhere on her face. Even when judged against all the other lovely young women in the room ("attractive coed" being an almost redundant phrase), Zeo was an extraordinary beauty. She was prettier than her sister Gertrude, who had small, deeply set eyes that were perhaps a bit too close together. When the single young men of means cast appreciative glances toward the Wilkins sisters, their gazes would have been drawn to the younger girl, and Zeo returned the favor with her electric blue eyes.

That's not to slight the institution. The American School of Osteopathy (now the Kirksville College of Osteopathic Medicine) was a moral and medical triumph. Its founder, Andrew Taylor Still, M.D., D.O., took the podium during the opening exercises. In the fall of 1903, his audience was the incoming class of '05, about one hundred and forty students from across the Midwest, nearly sixty of them women. The ratio slightly preferred men, so Zeo was introduced to a predominantly male milieu for the first time. It would later be said that Zeo distracted her fellow students, that the "budding osteopaths were more impressed by her glamor and daring than they were by the lecturer to which they listened." But no one who heard the founder speak could help but be impressed by the tragedies that marked his life. Some of them must have wondered how he remained standing.

Dr. Still watched helplessly as his first wife died after childbirth. Three of his children died in a meningitis epidemic, and another died of pneumonia. He served in the Civil War on the bloody Missouri front as a Union field surgeon. These cruel losses inspired Dr. Still to undertake a comprehensive study of the healing arts. He applied himself as few other scientists of his time to develop his own medical theories. He coined the term "osteopathy," and, in 1892, Dr. Still opened his own medical school. In only a decade, he built a great demand for a new curative approach that did not rely on the drugs available at the time, which he believed, quite correctly, were often more harmful than helpful. His pioneering theories on the musculoskeletal system, overall health, and preventive medicine propelled his institution from a small frame house to a grand brick building with several stories. Hundreds came daily for osteopathic manipulative treatments; often they presented desperate cases. The railroad companies added ever more passenger trains on the route to Dr. Still's growing infirmary.

Of course it is possible that Zeo didn't hear a word of Dr. Still's opening remarks because she was too busy returning stares. On her very first day, sometime between lectures—or during, though one doesn't want to think their eyes met in the dissection amphitheater—a young man caught her attention. His face was plain but his clothes were fancy, and he introduced himself as Richard. Before long, she elicited from him the fact that his father was a banker. She batted her eyes and smiled at Rich, always a close-lipped smile—dental care was nowhere on the list of necessaries in Havana—but inside she sneered at him. He had probably never missed a meal in his life, never gotten chased out of an orchard or a general store, never faced the risk of death slopping hogs. Maybe she saw him throw away an apple after two bites, as the sons of bankers will. Either way, he had something she wanted: tuition.

Later that night Zeo wrote in her diary, "There are some lovely boys going here. I met one today I am going to marry. He is not very clever and isn't handsome, but his father is rich and he soon will have lots of money. He is almost 21 now. He is going to take me to a party tomorrow night and I will let him kiss me." She went to that dance with the Devil on one shoulder and Cupid on the other. Once Rich bussed Zeo on the cheek, she knew she had snared him. "I shall get enough money to finance my start in osteopathy," Zeo bragged to a friend, "and then divorce him."

This—at *seventeen*. This at an age when a normal girl, saturated in the chemistry of late adolescence, is doe-eyed in her devotion to romance. Zeo Zoe, still not quite a full-grown woman, pegged Richard as her first ex-husband from the very moment they met. The legal age for marriage in Missouri at that time for men was twenty-one; for girls, eighteen. Marriages between students were common at the school. Zeo's sister married a student from Kentucky and became Gertrude Wilkins-Clements. Young, innocent Richard, hanging onto the edge of twenty, whimsically engaged himself to a girl he barely knew, a girl with a heart of arctic ice. Mere weeks into their term—she turned eighteen in October—they eloped.

Neither her family nor any journalists agreed on the details of the wedding or even on how Richard spelled his last name. It was given variously as Dryder, Dyer, Dryer, etc. Zeo's brother Arthur could only recall that she was "married 'oncet' or twice before she got that diploma in her hand." Some said they went to Texas. Others said the groom's parents bestowed three thousand dollars upon the couple, then Zeo told him she didn't truly love him, and he attempted suicide. By some accounts, he succeeded.

Despite some doubt, most versions of her wicked career counted this mysterious young man as the first of many husbands. Did she indulge in a weeks-long marriage, as she confessed in her diary? Was her story of the banker's son fact or fiction? It's one secret she took to the grave.

Whatever the details, Richard did not continue medical school. Zeo returned alone to the ASO with a greenhorn gold digger's haul. Then she promptly forgot all about Richard. Her first husband, first vows, first wedding night, first honeymoon—she reduced it all to a few lines in her diary and cast aside her memories of Rich. Meatier prey had strayed into the domain of the vampire in bridal lace.

4

Dr. G. Just Adores Me

[It's] the only really surefire tool a gold digger can pack—an'
that's a wedding ring . . . that's the one weapon that gives you
your sucker right in one hand and lets you put your fingers up
at the law on the other.

— *Jack Lait, "The Gold-Digger's Spade" (1923)*

harles Kittredge Garring came to the study of medicine by
a roundabout trail. The Ohio native traveled southwest along
the railroad lines in search of business opportunities and in the 1890s
opened a jewelry store in the oil boomtown of Denison, Texas. He leased
the offices above his shop to a medical man named D.D. Crawford, D.O.,
a graduate of Dr. Still's American School of Osteopathy.

They became fast friends. Dr. Crawford's attestations about osteopathic medicine impressed Charles Garring. "He showed so much ear-
nestness and enthusiasm over his work that I began to investigate the
subject," Garring said. "It seemed a rational and scientific method of
treating disease. I watched very closely the patients treated and in every
case found perfect satisfaction and results that could not be obtained by
use of medicine and drugs." Dr. Crawford's rapid prosperity inspired
Garring to sell his jewelry store and enroll himself in the ASO in 1902.

As one of the older students, he had a quick mind and earned excellent
grades. In his final term of study, he met incoming student Zeo Wilkins.
The serious, studious Charles Garring fell in love with the willowy, dark-
haired, underage girl. Their romance raised a few eyebrows even in the
let's-get-hitched-and-practice-together atmosphere of Dr. Still's school.

Zeo wrote only two sentences about him in her diary: "Dr. G. just
adores me. I wonder if I could put up with him very long."

They were wed on July 16, 1904, before a justice of the peace in Cleveland. He was thirty-six; she was eighteen. Both denied having had prior marriages on their license application. Zeo gave a false address: 1076 First Avenue, Havana, Ohio. Havana has never had a First Avenue. That month Zeo made her first payment of one hundred dollars on her tuition bill.

Her brother Charles would later tell Kansas City authorities that Dr. Garring was the jealous type who held fixed ideas about working wives—he believed they shouldn't—so he pressured his bride to abandon her training in osteopathy. He failed, however, to keep her from returning to medical school in the fall. Meanwhile, Dr. Garring decided to set up a medical practice in an oil boomtown. He moved to Durant in the Indian Territory, near the northern border of Texas, and sent many letters to Zeo Garring. His correspondence infected her with Southern easy-money fever.

Around that time, a massive black-gold rush engulfed the Indian Territory. Rumors of rich strikes spread into neighboring states. Oil towns sprouted overnight along the railroad tracks. These towns were wild places dominated by the drilling crews. The young, hale roughnecks made exceptional wages and were in dire need of a decent place to buy a drink, have a tooth pulled, and get some help for a stiff back. Businessmen catering to the oil workers minted their own money. The boomtowns hurt so badly for medical professionals that the Indian Territory passed one of the earliest laws permitting the practice of osteopathy in 1903. The first doctors were all women, despite the territory's reputation for fostering marauding cutthroats and the general depravity of life on the frontier.

Dr. Garring joined the rush in 1904, and his medical practice became his gusher. Young men lined up for his services. Though he had far more patients than he could handle alone, he wasn't inclined to advertise for a partner. He waited for his true love to join him, apparently oblivious to the effect an oil rush atmosphere might have on his beautiful young wife.

As Zeo continued her studies in Missouri, no one could have guessed from her performance that she was as young as she really was. She earned her highest grades in anatomy classes. She had an incredible memory for the functions of the human body. Some of her lowest marks were in hygiene, perhaps a reflection of a childhood spent in dire poverty. Her grades in obstetrics and gynecology were poor as well. Evidently she lacked any interest whatever in maternity. Zeo graduated from the American School of Osteopathy on June 21, 1905, with an average grade of eighty-one percent. It was not nearly as high as her sister Gertrude's grade point average, but not bad for a high school dropout. She would always brag that she was the youngest member of her class; apparently no other teenagers cheated their way into the medical school the same year she did.

At nineteen years of age, she was a certified doctor of osteopathy. The newly anointed Z.Z. Wilkins-Garring, D.O., promptly joined Dr. Charles K. Garring in the Indian Territory. They began to practice medicine together, and the townsfolk of Durant would long remember the Garrings and the house on North Fourth Avenue where they lived until the troubles came.

Though her husband tried to lavish Zeo with jewelry, he could not hold her attention. Within months Zeo was going out auto riding after dark with another man. By some accounts, several different automobiles and their accompanying male drivers captured Zeo's imagination. The marriage was doomed from the moment Zeo set foot in Durant, and so, nearly, was Dr. Charles Garring. Every day she met male patients. In an environment where men outnumbered women dozens to one, she must have heard every compliment and come-on known to mankind. She met as many men as she was willing to accommodate, though from an early date she was choosy in whom she'd see as a patient. Her ministrations were usually expensive; she always charged by her own unique formula for services rendered. In her version of osteopathic practice, she came across at least an occasional exceptional specimen of manhood she longed to see again.

Within months of her move to Durant, a man wooed Zeo away from her marital home. She began going out auto riding after dark with him regularly, because an automobile was a bed on wheels for Zeo and her lover. Her husband would soon learn of her "auto rides."

The day came that she could no longer bear her husband. By happy coincidence, his life was heavily insured in her favor.

One night she took opportunity and a loaded revolver in hand. Zeo waited inside their house clutching the gun. She heard her husband mount the front steps. When he opened the door, she shot him point-blank. As he fell, she shot him again.

Zeo later told the police she fired two bullets into her husband in mistaken self-defense. "I heard noises downstairs and saw a shadowy figure moving about. I thought it was a burglar and I fired."

Her husband was not badly wounded. For a while, he believed Zeo's story. Zeo dutifully attended him as he recovered. Her brother Arthur would one day reveal, however, that Dr. Zeo Garring's ministrations to her husband included rubbing her hands in horse manure before changing the dressings on his wounds. His good luck and robust constitution finally defeated her murder attempts. But the truth had by then dawned on him.

One account of their official unhitching summarized Dr. Garring's complaints: "In court he stated his wife had disavowed all relations with him; that she had repeatedly gone riding with other men; that she kept a separate mail box in which to receive her many billets-doux in secret; and finally offered evidence that she was conspiring to kill him." He was granted a decree of liberation. If Dr. Garring ever resented being the object of an attempted insurance murder and receiving lousy treatment at the manure-tainted hands of his temperamental teenaged wife, he had only to consider the gifts of blood, treasure, and freedom that others would lay at the foot of the love pirate.

5

Poor B.B.

Three types of men help to maintain The Gold Diggers Union.
They are the old man, the young man with the inferiority
complex, and the sporting young man who likes a girl
with kindred tastes.

— *Beatrice Fairfax, "Girls Men Should Shun" (1933)*

D r. Zeo Zoe Wilkins liked her maiden name, and she also liked
the Indian Territory, where rarity elevated women. The laws
of supply and demand gave even a homely woman a shot at a well-to-do
mate, and Zeo was far from homely. After shooting her way out of her
Garring marriage, she took up prospecting in a promising congregation
of budding Rockefellers: the oil town of Sapulpa, part of the Indian Territory, the Creek Nation. Around 1905, fervent wildcatting led to an oil
strike and Sapulpa found itself smack dab in the middle of the Glenn
Pool. A newsman would later describe the transformation:

Imagine a waste of hilly land, partly bare and partly wooded with
stunted oaks, three miles wide and five miles long, inhabited only
by a few Indians who tilled but little patches just around their
shacks. Let the curtain drop, and after the space of three years
raise it again in the present. That fifteen square miles of waste land
is laid out into avenues 400 feet wide, defined at intervals of 400
feet by towering derricks. Between the first scene and the last lies
the romance of the Glenn Pool, the richest and the most wonderful
petroleum field ever found.

Experts agreed there was nothing like the Glenn Pool in the history
of oil strikes in the United States, never an oil pool as large and produc-
tive, never so much instant wealth.

What followed was something they called "reflex prosperity." Sapulpa's
population swelled until it boasted tens of thousands of oil workers and
the businessmen who loved them: pharmacists, doctors, dentists, bankers,
and an occasional woman with the appetite of a man-eating hog.

Death himself was a frequent visitor. With the riches came street
fights of awful intensity. The law of the oil towns was "every man for
himself and the Devil take the hindmost." Sapulpa had trigger-happy
policemen and shootings galore, justified and not. So corrupt was the
police chief that his own men turned against him. A brave patrolman
disclosed his boss's misconduct to city officials. The chief did not take
his termination well. He tracked the turncoat to the police station and,
before a room full of witnesses, kicked him to death. In addition to frequent murders and manslaughters, certain criminal activities had to be
tolerated. If they'd closed the casinos and whorehouses, there would've
been a riot.

The most common man in Sapulpa was the crewman, and he had
bloodthirsty tastes. The boxing arena was barred to women and drew
the largest crowds. So much money was made off these pugilistic con-
tests that towns like Sapulpa started putting in bids to host the most
anticipated fights. It bid high on an important match around the time
Dr. Wilkins hung her shingle in town. The city promised to build an
arena for fifteen thousand spectators, half the population.

All those men, all that money—a gold digger found her element in
Sapulpa, I.T. Even an ugly gal had only to stroll the boardwalk and giggle.
Before she could say grace, she'd have herself a free lunch. These oil
field hands could offer a divorcée a wild night on the oil town, but most
owned little besides their spending money, and they kept busy earning
it. They weren't the sort to appeal to Zeo. Not for very long. Amidst the
lawless oil mania, past the fields full of brawny lads, was Main Street. It
offered a more attractive target.

His name was Bates B. Burnett. Zeo and everyone else called him B.B. If he weren't already married, she might've become ZZ. Burnett. She had to settle for being his mistress. B.B. was handsome and moneyed. He was also a man with whom she shared an affinity for adultery, audacity, and unconscionable theft.

B.B. was married to a Cherokee woman and had fathered two children. That's not to suggest his wife and kids were chucks under his wheels. He had a Winton Six touring car. Its six-cylinder engine had only been out for a year, and if there was any truth in advertising, the public clamored for that Winton Six. It was made in Cleveland and cost a whopping three thousand dollars. B.B.'s new automobile was a convertible model with enough heavily upholstered seats for several passengers. At a time in Sapulpa's history when "to go riding with Zeo became the objective of the masculine elite of the town," B.B. had just the vehicle by which to win the attention of the town belle. Zeo probably first met him on the street. Maybe B.B. screeched to a halt when she strolled the boardwalk.

B.B. Burnett loved showing off his Winton Six. When the Grand Secretary of the Odd Fellows visited Sapulpa, he was foolhardy enough to accept a ride. "A few strenuous hours were passed in Burnett's Winton Six," wrote the newsman who witnessed the ride. "Mr. Burnett has one of the finest cars in the southwest and he is not afraid to make it go. While rolling over the finely asphalted streets the car went so fast that Captain Chauncey couldn't see the town and they had to go round and round hundreds of times." At one point, B.B. got his machine going fifty miles an hour down the street. The town had no speed limit, and neither did a bad businessman named B.B. Burnett. Zeo never mentioned the Winton Six in her diary, but B.B. surely showed her wildly bouncing turns on roads rutted by wagon wheels. Within minutes a town of thousands was a spot on the horizon. In the shadows of the oil derricks, far from human detection, Zeo could treat B.B. to more pleasurable bouncing in the Winton's generous rear seat.

Before long, Zeo went to his place of business, where she regaled him with a story of her desire to be an emancipated businesswoman. B.B. and his brother Birch clerked in a bank founded by their father in Sapulpa, the Farmers' & Merchants' Bank. In 1905 a local paper described the Burnetts' bank as a nice place to sashay into:

> Last year the bank built the prettiest building in this city on the corner of Main and Dewey. The building is 26 by 120 feet, two story, pressed brick, trimmed in white stone and cost $10,000. The inside fixtures are beautiful. All the woodwork is of rich mahogany. An extra large vault and a Mosler Tribble Timer screw door safe, with safety deposit lock boxes for private use, are among the fixtures.

Alas, B.B.'s father passed away. He should have ordered the sale of the bank in his will. Instead he mistrusted the bank to his sons. B.B. secretly withdrew other people's money. The Burnetts used the bank's assets to fund their own schemes in oil and real estate. By one account, they wiped out deposits of ten thousand dollars. Dr. Zeo Zoe Wilkins was a recipient of some of these diverted funds, as she confessed in her diary; she took out a loan of one thousand seven hundred dollars from B.B.'s bank "without the scratch of a pen." The amount was considerable; she could have paid for medical school four times over with her paperless loan from the Farmers' & Merchants' Bank.

But it was a crime. All three committed felonies. All three used the money to buy oil leases in the hope that a good return would cover the losses at the bank. It was pure robbery, nothing less. No, it was worse than the typical bank robbery. When the Jameses and Youngers took a bank, there was no deception about their purpose. If criminals were snakes, members of the James Gang were rattlers: war-hardened, trained in insurgent tactics, they struck hard and slithered away. B.B. Burnett was a boa constrictor. He wrapped himself around his victims and got in close for the kill.

To garner more funds for his businesses, Burnett found work at the county courthouse as an appointed guardian for orphans and the elderly, most of them members of the Creek tribe who owned land in the oil fields. The local judge let B.B. plunder their assets and invest the money of his many wards in his own ventures in crude. The judge was B.B.'s brother-in-law. A statute barring judges from ruling on matters involving relatives daunted neither man, nor did a string of lawsuits.

These criminal efforts to drum up investment capital resulted in a windfall. B.B. spent some of his haul on Zeo and gave her free advice on the purchase of oil leases. With no income tax to bother them, and with no accountability to anyone else, they raked in and spent oil riches.

Eventually gravity had its say. They gambled all the assets of the bank and lost. The ordinary folk who'd placed their savings in the bank—including, by some accounts, a group of miners who had just sold a valuable gold claim after years of working the earth—lost everything. And so the nineteenth-century gold digger yielded his fortune to the gold digger of the twentieth century.

Had they done it years earlier, they might have gotten away with it. But the law caught up with the Burnett-Wilkins Gang. After the discovery of oil, the Indian Territory became a part of the State of Oklahoma in 1907. A judge in Muskogee entered a judgment against B.B. for the $48,895 he stole from Creek children. Another child sued him for a million dollars. Days later the bank collapsed. The state bank commissioner seized the building and locked the doors. Oklahoma's attorney general filed a suit demanding the accounting books and records for all the deposits and loans made at the bank.

The Burnett boys found themselves on the horns of a dilemma. If they told the truth, they would provide critical evidence for a criminal case against themselves and Dr. Wilkins. They could all wind up in prison. The potential financial penalties were staggering. They could lose their oil investments. B.B.'s pretty young mistress might go to jail. He decided to take his lumps like a man.

The brothers were hauled to the courthouse. Said the judge: "Come forward, Mr. Bates B. Burnett and Birch C. Burnett. You have been heretofore directed by this court to produce certain described books and papers of the Farmers' & Merchants' Bank of Sapulpa, or show cause why you did not produce them. You have filed an answer. You failed to produce them, but you filed an answer, saying you did not know where they were. Your answer has been held to be insufficient by the court. Have either of you anything further to say why you should not be punished for contempt of court in failing to obey the order, Mr. Bates B. Burnett?"

"No, sir."

"Mr. Birch C. Burnett?"

"No, sir."

The judge—not their brother-in-law this time—read them the riot act, parts of the banking act, and a sermon on the need to compel strict adherence to the orders of an official court of the State of Oklahoma. Weeks later, the justices of the Oklahoma Supreme Court unanimously cleared the way for their arrest, remarking that "the contumacious conduct and acts of these defendants, as officers of said bank . . . were well calculated to embarrass and obstruct the court . . . and constitute a contempt of flagrant character. . . . [T]hese delinquent defendants must realize that the law is not so lame, helpless, and impotent that craft, intrigue, and subterfuge, or bold defiance, can defeat the due administration of justice." Bates and Birch Burnett were held in criminal contempt.

"Poor B.B.," Zeo wrote in her diary. "He had to go to jail for ninety days."

Zeo kissed B.B., Sapulpa, and the Winton Six good-bye. Leaving her bankrupt lover in jail, she moved on to the next man-filled boomtown.

It took B.B. a while to wriggle out of the mess completely. It cost him much of his fortune. Later an unnaturally sympathetic jury acquitted the Burnetts of embezzlement on "legal technicalities," a local paper reported. But his reputation as a banker was justifiably ruined. That might've been a stroke of luck for him, because he fell back on the oil business, which made him a millionaire by the age of thirty. He built a mansion in 1914, more than six thousand square feet, on Sapulpa's Main Street. It boasted a solid mahogany staircase, Tiffany stained glass windows, and a third-floor ballroom. He kept building his wealth until it catapulted him all the way to Park Avenue, Manhattan.

Crooked bankers like the Burnetts destroyed the public's trust in banks, and as a consequence most people found it both easier and safer to spend than save. Many wildcatters in towns like Sapulpa indulged in lavish parties and immoderate habits, tossing dollars into the air for the pleasure of seeing them vanish. "If I'd put my money in savings it would have been lost," said Max Meyer, an early Sapulpa merchant. "The banks in Sapulpa failed and everybody lost their savings."

This lesson was not lost on Dr. Wilkins. Never did she keep anything in a bank. She always stored her valuables close at hand. It would one day cost her. In the meantime Zeo brought to bear all the skills she learned in the Indian Territory, such as how to take a banker for a fortune without ever pulling a gun.

6

The Cigar Girl

Should you meet one of these sparkling bits of femininity just
emerging from her favorite beauty parlor, you might, thinking of
employment, ask her what she is doing this winter. "A steel mag-
nate, my dear," she will reply with a shrug. And that is the Gold
Digger! Oh, yes! This has been going on for some time! It isn't
just a new fad, like an appendicitis operation. From Cleopatra
down the ages, ladies have specialized in this line of business.
And from all reports it looks like a grand old game.
— *Louise Fazenda, "Famous Gold Diggers of*
History and How They Dug" (1923)

As Dr. Zeo Wilkins roared through her twenties, the dark-haired
vixen continued to roll men, and practice made her perfect. In
1910 she was a fortune hunter on the trail in the oil boomtown of Tulsa,
which struck high-grade crude in 1904. To Zeo and many others, Tulsa
looked like a treasure map marked with a big, red X. Literally, for some,
as rumor had it that the James Gang once buried a fortune in gold on the
face of Lost City Mountain, six miles west of Tulsa. Zeo rented a home
in town and headed her own household at twenty-four. She convinced
her brother Arthur to move to Tulsa with her, and she probably provided
the financing when he went into the bootlegging business. His specialty:
"Taos lightning," a cheap whisky, or anything with a "good kickapoo,"
as Arthur liked to put it.

The city's newspapers described her as a widow, since she claimed
Dr. Charles Garring had died and left her a fortune. They also described
her as "a brunette of dazzling beauty" who lived in luxury in Tulsa
and had many male friends.

Arthur Wilkins, bootlegger. (*Colorado State Archives*)

Zeo advertised for patients in the business pages of the city phone book and practiced her medical arts out of her home. She soon became known around Tulsa for what her brother called her famous rubbings. "She was a helluva good actress," Arthur said. "She really thought she was one good doc." He took to calling her Doc, and the nickname made her "proud as a peacock," he said.

Many men in Tulsa would remember Dr. Wilkins not as an osteopath but as a cigar girl. Eager to meet more rich men, Zeo took a job running a cigar stand in a new, five-story professional building in downtown Tulsa, the First National Bank Building at Second and Main, which featured the city's first elevators. Despite the incongruity of a doctor selling cigars, Zeo met many businessmen who liked flattery, a good smoke, and a long rub. Selling cigars gave her opportunities to exchange flirtatious innuendo with lawyers, bankers, salesmen, and businessmen. Maybe that's how she met her next luckless mate.

Grover M. Burcham was a twenty-eight-year-old furniture dealer originally from Missouri. He was addled by her beauty and managed to make a nuisance of himself, so she married him. Just "to get rid of him," she told Arthur and her friends. But she probably married him for his furniture.

What was this furniture man thinking? Perhaps Grover believed she was a widow. He probably did not know the true outcome of her last marriage. Arthur apparently did not do him any favors. If Grover did know the truth about Dr. Garring's fate, he might have taken comfort in the fact that she was a bad shot. Thanks to her remarkable ability to put men at their ease, he overlooked a few things in his haste to make her Mrs. Burcham.

The longest available account of the marriage describes a man who soon regretted entering into wedlock with Zeo. Her materialistic nature soon emerged. He left with what portable assets remained and took a westbound train to escape her.

Dr. Wilkins ended up leaving Tulsa rather hastily herself. Zeo agreed to watch her sister Irene's three-year-old son Horace for a little while because her sister was quite ill. Zeo told her friends in Tulsa that Horace was her son. They accepted the story until Zeo's sister appeared to demand her baby back.

Zeo refused. Irene was forced to file a lawsuit against her. Judge Lewis M. Poe awarded custody of the boy to his mother and set a date and time for Dr. Wilkins to bring the child to the courthouse.

Zeo fled with the boy to Kansas City. It would appear that she wanted the child so desperately, she stole him. Perhaps Helen the Better emerged, along with a deeply buried maternal instinct.

Irene Wilkins passed away on December 10, 1910. One can only hope she saw her child before she died.

Zeo ended up adopting Horace, though the family was never quite clear on whether it was a formal, legal adoption. In either event, she soon hustled him off to a boarding school. So much for maternal instinct.

Free again, she headed south once more into gold digging country.

7

Goodbye Zoe, Forever

A fool there was and he made his prayer
(Even as you and I!)
To a rag and a bone and a hank of hair
(We called her the woman who did not care)
But the fool he called her his lady fair—
(Even as you and I!)

. . . .

The fool was stripped to his foolish hide
(Even as you and I!)
Which she might have seen when she threw him aside—
(But it isn't on record the lady tried)
So some of him lived but the most of him died—
(Even as you and I!) . . .
— *Rudyard Kipling, "The Vampire"*

Oklahoma could be glad there was only one of her, for Dr. Zeo Z. Wilkins, "osteopath to the wealthy," tore through Oklahoma like a statewide twister. She set up a mantrap in the town of Claremore, thirty miles from Tulsa, circa 1911. To gold diggers of the less metaphoric sort, it was a bit off the map. It had been tapped years before, and the only thing that had bubbled up so far was the smell of rotten eggs. Still, Claremore had made the most of its geology and become locally known for its artesian wells. The mineral-laden water supplied bathhouses where one could take a long, hot soak courtesy of the Claremore Radium Wells Company. The brochure promised that Claremore's "magic mineral Radium Water has more miraculous and wonderful cures to its credit than any other known agency. . . . Hundreds are being cured to its credit. . . . It cures quick." That statement, of course, was hogwash. Even if radium held curative properties, a chemical analysis of the smelly miracle water reportedly showed no radium. Maybe Zeo felt at home among the charlatans in Radium Town as she brewed her own blend of medicine. The one condition her remedy surely could cure was low blood pressure.

Leonard Smith came to Claremore from Kansas City, where he worked in a drugstore. Maybe he came for the radium water. Somehow, somewhere, he fell into orbit around Zeo. For Leonard, Dr. Wilkins beat every drug in the pharmacoepia. She provided her special ministrations to the young man. He showered her with fifteen thousand carefully saved dollars, lavishing upon her every cent he had. At some point he discerned that she repaid him with a counterfeit love. He was very angry with her, but not as angry as he was with himself.

Destitute, heartsick, Leonard Smith walked into an alley behind a bank in downtown Claremore, took a pistol from his pocket, and fired a fatal shot into his own skull.

The Claremore police questioned Dr. Wilkins. She said she didn't know the man. She did not even attempt to explain the note they found in Leonard's pocket. The wire services would one day run its contents in newspapers across the country:

Leonard Smith's suicide note, illustrated by the *Lima News*. (*Lima News*)

In Zeo's diary, Leonard's life and death merited a mere line. "He gave me all his money and went to get more . . . poor man."

But it was her next marriage that would make Zeo Wilkins, for about a year, the most infamous woman in the West.

8

The Old Man's Darling

It is because men do not understand women that a woman
can take in even the shrewdest man and put across any kind
of propaganda about herself that she desires. The flapper gold
digger can make the aged millionaire believe that she is marrying him for love of himself alone; the hard-boiled woman
can make a man believe she is a clinging vine; the woman
with a lurid past can make a man believe that she is an angel
at heart and is the unfortunate victim of circumstances. Even
a moron can roll her eyes at an intellectual man and make him
think she would be a congenial companion.
— *Dorothy Dix, "If Men Understood Women" (1930)*

The putrid stench of crude oil finally struck the nostrils of Claremore, Oklahoma, when its wildcatters struck black gold in
1912. The rush was on. Sudden wealth filled the air. But it was the
radium cure that lured Thomas W. Cunningham to the door of an
exclusive medical clinic in Claremore in 1912. Had he known what
was good for him, he would have dropped his bags at the threshold
and run shrieking in another direction. But he was a tame, sixty-eight-
year-old man, too infirm to make a quick getaway, and the proprietress
of the nicely furnished house was a beautiful, glib, twenty-six-year-old
osteopath.

"What do you do?" would certainly have been among Zeo's first questions. His answer would likely have included the word "business" and
the phrase "Cunningham National Bank." The last syllable would have
strummed the spider's web. Cunningham's bank in Missouri was one
of the most famous financial institutions in that section of the country.

As Dr. Wilkins learned the extent of his assets, the three-time marital failure knew she might never want for anything again.

In 1912, the average American was more likely to meet someone with six fingers on one hand than a millionaire. There were only about forty thousand of the latter in a population of more than ninety-two million. Most of them lived in New York and the Northeast generally. But the millionaires' map was changing rapidly. Zeo had the good fortune to find on her medical table a man whose holdings were worth upwards of two million gold-backed United States dollars. His bank alone was worth more than $1.2 million. And he was all alone in the world: widowed, childless, and unaccompanied by friends, business partners, or servants.

Cunningham, a farmer and dabbler in commercial ventures, entered the banking trade in Joplin, Missouri, with a mere five thousand dollars in start-up capital in 1882. Jesse James had been killed in April of that year, so it was an ideal time to start a bank. Though he established his business in an age when the average metropolitan newspaper contained a story virtually every day about failed banks and defrauded depositors—witness the sufferings of the unfortunate Sapulpans—Tom Cunningham was an honest, generous man. He was also fond of women. He hired female cashiers to work at his bank, to take deposits and to make loans, a practice which was unheard of in that day. His thrift and smart investments were duly rewarded. The lucre poured in and stayed put.

Cunningham could have afforded a horde of servants and a mansion with Tiffany windows, but rural-minded frugality compelled him to live as a boarder, while he chose to share his vast wealth with the people of Joplin. He donated his farmland for the creation of the city's first public playground, Cunningham Park. He also made it known that he intended to bequest his vast estate for the expansion of the public roads in Jasper County. The city fathers rewarded him with a stint as the mayor of Joplin. He was easily one of the most respected businessmen in the region.

As he neared the threescore and ten mark, the old banker had begun to suffer. He had locomotor ataxia, a degenerative neurological condition that causes uncontrollable spasms. The affliction is amenable to osteopathic treatment. He suffered another condition easily recognized by anyone with medical training, a condition related to his ataxia or simply old age: the banker was growing senile.

According to her diary, Zeo ambushed him with her trademark gingham. Perhaps plaid appealed to his penny-pinching nature. Maybe his departed wife once had a figure as fine as Zeo's. Maybe he was a ladies' man. The attraction was mutual, if asymmetrical. It was no sofa cushion romance, either. Later developments would suggest theirs was a consummated love, aided perhaps by her osteopathic knowledge of male anatomy. With money her highest aim, she found it easy to waste herself, her beauty, and her youth kissing her old frog. She threw aside the last speck of decency that stubbornly clung to the hem of her favorite gingham dress, along with the dress, perched herself on his knee, and became what they used to politely call an old man's darling.

She closed up her rich-man trap in Claremore. She persuaded the doddering millionaire to settle himself against her bosom as they traveled to a larger community, somewhere they could be anonymous. Oklahoma caught its last whiff of Zeo's expensive perfume. She must've left thinking the Klondyke had nothing on Claremore.

But where does one go when a boldly sinful dalliance-cum-larceny is on the agenda? Zeo would have known which city in America was more open to the possibility than all the others, a good fellow to all its friends. She had visited it a time or two. She was comfortable in the naughty old cow town. The place was called the Paris of the Plains. The nickname had nothing to do with water fountains and architecture. It was well known as the Devil's American lounge, sin-soaked on a Parisian scale, second runner-up after Singapore as a world-class center of corruption and nasty doings. Booze, drugs, gambling, brawling, naked wonders, all were easy to find in Kansas City, Missouri. The dead voted in great numbers. Money was the highest power. One measure of its depravity in the hectic days of Zeo's early gold-digging career was a crackdown in 1911 when, in a city of 250,000, 7,089 tickets were issued for public drunkenness. Under pressure from reformers, the police arrested several brothel owners and prostitutes and charged them with "keeping a bawdy-house"—all 957 of them. "This evil," said one reformer, "is deep rooted."

Zeo the Evil put down roots at 2226 Tracy Avenue, Kansas City, by using Tom Cunningham's money to buy herself a little house. As she settled in with her new old man, she still took a listing in the city telephone book as an osteopath. What better way to meet other men in numbers? She also dragged Tom downtown to shop, where she treated his wallet worse than cotton treats soil, "leading him at a rapid pace," as some would say later. "Doc was twenty-nine and on the loose with all that money," her brother Arthur said. "She was real good lookin' and was greedy as hell. She was always looking for more men and more cash." Tom Cunningham didn't mind how she spent either his money or her time. Under Tom's rheumatic eye, she could take any lover she pleased, just about anywhere, do just about anything she wanted and with whomever.

The arrangement satisfied both of them for more than two years. Before long, Zeo boasted in her diary, her sugar granddaddy had bestowed upon her $200,000. She could have sent nearly six hundred people through Dr. Still's medical school for that kind of money. She used the gift to buy corporate and government bonds that she stashed in a strongbox—a gold digger's retirement fund. She'd never have to work again unless she chose to do so. Hers would be a life of Sundays. Or Saturday nights, anyway.

By and by, she thirsted for more. Old Tom was pliant. Zeo decided she would try to marry the old man. She sent an accessory—a guess: her brother Arthur—to Gallatin, Missouri to rob the Daviess County recorder of a marriage license. The clerk heard a story about the bride and groom coming on the next train. It was quite a ways from Kansas

City. Anyone with sense would have gone to a closer county marriage office. Maybe it took a few tries to find one who'd accept an affidavit instead of the personal appearance of the bride and groom as Missouri law required. The sworn statements said Mr. Cunningham was past the age of twenty-one (without specifying just how far past it he was); Miss Wilkins was past eighteen; they were unrelated; and neither had other spouses. As a local paper would one day explain to its readers, "It has developed that the license to marry Thos. W. Cunningham and Zeo Z. Wilkins, both giving Kansas City as their residence, was issued here on Nov. 21st, 1914. This was while D. E. Cope was in charge of the recorder's office for Mrs. Cashman."

Reverend Walter Tennant McClure received a phone call on the afternoon of November 26, 1914, from a woman who asked for his nuptial services at her home at eight that evening. She explained that she wanted a wholly private wedding without any publicity. Reverend McClure agreed to carry out the ceremony of holy matrimony even after meeting the prospective newlyweds, insisting there was "nothing to excite my comment or suspicion."

Dr. Zeo Wilkins, twenty-nine, and Thomas Cunningham, seventy, were thus wed. Reverend McClure would later admit the proceeding was a tad irregular. Tom was silent during the whole evening. "He did not say over half a dozen words," the minister noted. "I didn't realize until several days later that he was the Joplin banker," added Reverend McClure. "Miss Wilkins did all the talking." It was a strange account, odd enough to make one wonder whether Cunningham, elderly or not, actually managed to mutter the two most necessary words, "I do," and why, when he married his doctor, he seemed so unemotional, so . . . sedate.

To toast their troth, Zeo took her fourth husband to the nicest local establishment available, the brand new Muehlebach Hotel in downtown Kansas City, where the West's banking, land, livestock, and oil millionaires congregated. The new Mrs. Cunningham sashayed into the lobby of one of the most luxurious hotels in the country wearing a gingham

Mrs. Zeo Cunningham.
(*Jackson County [Mo.] Historical Society Archives*)

dress and carrying a shovel, by one account causing "extended, if not explosive, comment." She later wrote in her diary that she made such a spectacle of herself "just to please Tom."

Cunningham's new bride lavished herself with even more of his assets after their wedding. She systematically transferred his property into her own name and sold it. In one transaction, she swapped a hundred city lots he owned in Joplin and nearby towns, valued at about a quarter of a million dollars, for six thousand acres in rural Lake County, Michigan worth about three dollars an acre. In this curious transaction, of which little more was reported, she somehow managed to keep the difference.

But his friends back in Joplin were beginning to miss their beloved captain of industry. They found it quite unusual for the city's most well-known figure to absent himself so long. He was suddenly gone from Joplin for several months at a time, only returning for a few days here and there. His friends starting asking around. No doubt they looked her up in the Kansas City telephone directory and pounded on her Tracy Avenue door. Finally they found Mr. Cunningham and his new companion holed up in a suite at the Muehlebach Hotel. They questioned Zeo. She explained that they were married. Tom couldn't remember the ceremony. His friends declared the marriage a fraud.

Spooked by the confrontation, Mrs. Cunningham and her brother Arthur, prize in tow, beat it to Colorado Springs. Zeo took a nice home at 21 East Willamette Avenue and worked with her brother to devise a plan to shore up her legal claims. Arthur would one day confess that Tom Cunningham was misled into believing Zeo was pregnant and he was the daddy. It was the "damndest setup," Arthur admitted, but he still agreed to talk to the "old boy" about it. "I knew he knew I had a gun in my pocket."

On December 5, 1916, old Tom was again groom to Zeo's bride in a shotgun wedding in Pueblo, Colorado. It would soon become apparent why she felt it necessary to wed Tom Cunningham a second time. She wanted a wedding present from him.

The day after the ceremony, she finally coaxed Tom into assigning her all of his stock in the bank. He cheerfully transferred his most significant asset into the name of his bride, the woman whom he believed would soon bear his first child, never suspecting her intentions—or the fact that she wasn't actually expecting a baby.

Zeo had long known that other bankers in the region were keen to acquire the assets of Cunningham National Bank. She contacted a number of them.

The day after she wed Tom for the second time, Mrs. Cunningham, now the sole owner of Cunningham National Bank, took a train ride to Denver. There, she met with Amos Gipson, president of a rival institution in Joplin.

Before the ink was dry on her husband's wedding present, Zeo sold all the stock in her bank to Gipson. She received $307,000. Amos Gipson might've gotten a gut full of guilt. A few years later he killed himself in Mexico. His suicide note said he was "all worn out."

But in the meantime Gipson returned to Joplin, where the newspaper advertisement announcing the sale of Cunningham National Bank was an almighty thunderclap that had the whole town bellowing. The greater shock still lay in store. News of the marriage of the most eligible bachelor in Joplin broke in January 1917, when a Sunday edition of the *Joplin Globe* reported that Tom Cunningham's wife arranged the sale.

The city fathers felt cheated of the promised inheritance of road funds. But one Joplin resident in particular was more aghast than anyone. Her dismay soon turned to anger, and she stomped her way down to her lawyer's office as fast as her old feet could move. Her name was Tabitha Taylor, though she preferred to be called Mrs. Cunningham. It would soon be her turn to deliver some shocking news along with lawsuits that accused both Tom and Zeo of bigamy. The woman scorned would touch off a national sensation that bared Zeo Wilkins's catalogue of sins to every Midwesterner who read a newspaper.

9

Plucky Old Mrs. Cunningham and the Siren

The millionaire pays with what he has to pay—money, reputation; the girl pays with what she has to give—character, youth and her future. Only the vendors in the marketplace, the merchandisers of youthful beauty and aged folly, collect—all others pay.
— *"Behind the Curtains of the Slain Butterfly,"* Lima News *(1923)*

Tabitha Taylor appeared in the offices of the law firm of Walden & Andrews in January 1917 to tell a pitiful tale. The old woman said she had lived with Thomas W. Cunningham for years in the furnished rooms above his bank at 405 Main Street in Joplin. For decades, Tabitha said, she'd carried on a sexual affair with the millionaire.

Through her tears she gave this account: "Eighteen years ago, the day after his first wife died, Mr. Cunningham came to me and told me we would live together the remainder of our lives. 'Honey,' he said, 'we'll live together and this place shall be yours. In a year or two we will be married.' When a year had passed I reminded him." But he breached his promise because she had children by a prior marriage that ended in divorce, and he thought her children would be upset if she remarried.

Despite his frivolous excuses—would a sane person object if Mother married an heirless, elderly millionaire?—Tabitha stuck by him. "I have lived in [his] building twenty-eight years and have worked and toiled for him. I am the one who has cared for him when he was ill, who has shared his troubles. I have even done janitor work in the bank when they were without a janitor. No one would have done by him as I have."

To others she would remark, "If that woman is worth $300,000, I am worth $600,000."

Her attorneys took her tale on faith and ran to the courthouse with it. *Cunningham v. Cunningham* was on its face a divorce petition (much later, such a claim would be called a palimony case). They sought an order to freeze Tom's assets and asked the court to award alimony immediately. It was claimed that Tom and Tabitha cohabited as man and wife from 1899 to 1917, during which time she "looked after his every want, wish, and desire" as a "faithful, obedient and helpful" wife and housekeeper. These facts, asserted her lawyers, amounted to a common-law marriage and entitled Tabitha to the "rights of a wife under the law of Justinian."

Tabitha's lawyers had to reach back to the laws of Justinian, an emperor of ancient Rome, because the laws of Missouri certainly did not help her cause. Under the state's most recent marriage act, a man and woman could, in peculiar cases, become man and wife without a license; the rules on common-law marriage required a mutual pact, consummation, and cohabitation, and to be valid, the couple had to behave as though they were properly wed. Tom and Tabitha's relationship, whatever its nature, did not meet all of these criteria. Tabitha alleged but couldn't prove she lived with Mr. Cunningham for eighteen years. For one thing, if any credit is to be given the census-takers, Tom Cunningham wasn't living with Tabitha in 1900 or in 1910. He had been with Zeo since 1912. What did she do with his slippers during all the time he spent with Zeo?

Once court jurisdiction was invoked, the press caught wind of the May-December-December love triangle. The lawsuit caused a sensation throughout the region. The press responded with tabloid zeal. The litigation Zeo aroused, proclaimed the *Kansas City Journal*, was "one of the most spectacular legal battles ever written in court history" with "climaxes [that] followed in kaleidoscopic array." The sexual metaphors flourished. Zeo Wilkins was a made-for-page-one woman.

In the 1910s and 1920s, virtually every newspaper in the country was a scandal sheet. Editors routinely sent reporters to the courthouse to write stories about divorce cases and civil "heart balm" lawsuits for personal torts with euphemistic legal names like "alienation of affections" and "criminal conversation." Translation: adultery. Divorces were so out of the ordinary at the time that even the divorce of wholly private persons who'd been faithful during the marriage merited a few lines on an inside page. This piece was typical of such courthouse reporting:

> William Spencer Adams, traveling salesman, said his wife, Daisy Adams, left him in 1918 and four years later he found her with a carnival. In the meantime, he went on, she acquired the habit of smoking cigarettes—not a cause for divorce, the court observed— and when he rented her an apartment in Springfield, Mo., she continued her nagging, spent all his money, and refused to let him talk with the children. He was given a divorce.

Few people enjoyed or could reasonably expect privacy in their personal lives. Every detail of every known affair was bared for inspection by friends, neighbors, coworkers, and family. A case with a good strong whiff of sex—particularly when third parties were named—always made page one, sometimes with illustrations or photographs. Even an affair several states away could earn a slot above the fold. Readers enjoyed stories about old-fashioned sexual misconduct replete with proper names and details. Sex sold newspapers.

Zeo Wilkins's amorous career drew much attention. Four marriages! It was truly astonishing, especially for a woman under thirty. It was virtually unprecedented. Zeo and her series of weddings amazed the yellow press, as she "stirred Southwest Missouri" and the greater Southwest as well. Reporters painted the Cunningham episode in vivid colors, calling Tom a "love prisoner" and never suggesting that their "amours" were anything other than sensationally funny. The details of her entire campaign against the stronger sex were bared in scarlet letters for all of America to study. Zeo, meanwhile, clipped the articles and put them in her strongbox.

The headlines alone give off the aroma of scandal. From the *Fort Wayne Sentinel* in Indiana:

TWO CLAIM TO BE
WIFE OF RICH MAN;
ONE ASKS MILLION

The *Sandusky Herald* in Ohio capped its piece with:

"ETERNAL TRIANGLE" BARED
WHEN HOUSEKEEPER, 71,
SUES AGED MILLIONAIRE
AFTER HIS MARRIAGE
TO KANSAS CITY BEAUTY

And from the *Chicago Daily News*:

A DASHING YOUNG OSTEOPATH
COMES INTO LIFE AND LUCRE
OF CINCINNATI [*sic*] MAN

Given the intensity of public interest in the story, reporters in several states were eager to ask Tabitha Taylor for quotes and evidence. She told them she had written proof of her relations with the banker in the form of a bundle of more than a hundred letters from him that she kept under lock and key. "A few months ago he ceased to write," she said, which is how she learned "something was wrong." She let a reporter for the *Joplin*

Globe see her collection of correspondence and made a show of kissing the letters as she stored them. "They're all from him, and are precious to me," she said.

"Half of Tom Cunningham's estate is due me and I'll get it," she continued. "Nothing less will satisfy me. I am 71 years old and am ready to fight this case to the end. I have been heartbroken for weeks over this matter."

The *Joplin Globe* sent its staff to Colorado Springs to find and interview the banker. Visiting the home on Willamette, a reporter found Tom and Zeo "surrounded by servants." When he met the younger Mrs. Cunningham, the reporter could not help but remark that she was "an exceptionally beautiful woman" as well as "the center of a spirited social set."

Both Cunninghams spoke to the newsman at length. "At first this story was a great shock to me," Zeo Cunningham remarked. "But when I investigated and talked with Mr. Cunningham, it straightened itself out. This woman's story is false."

Zeo confirmed reports of her marriage to Tom, though she refused to produce a license. When asked if she had been married before, her only answer was, "I was a doctor, not a Mrs."

"I never was married to this woman," said Tom of Tabitha Taylor, "and I never lived with her in any such relation as charged. She is mostly after my money, but she won't get it. You will notice she hasn't claimed that she was legally married to me. She doesn't dare."

Added Zeo: "Mrs. Taylor's story is ridiculous."

They were asked to describe their plans for the future. "My wife and I will make our home in Colorado Springs," Tom said, "but we expect to travel a great deal."

Said Zeo: "Tom and I are very happy with each other and always have been. Mr. Cunningham is not well and the strain of this affair has been heavy upon him."

After the interview, Zeo and her brother thought it prudent to hire a lawyer. It also seemed a smart idea to avoid journalists for the time being. In her search for representation, Zeo returned alone to Kansas City and took a suite at the Muehlebach while Arthur took Tom Cunningham to Chicago and secreted him in the downtown Blackstone Hotel.

But she could not avoid the reporters. The *Joplin News-Herald* followed Zeo to Kansas City and reported that she was alone; Tom Cunningham had apparently disappeared. The *Herald* asked for the missing banker's whereabouts, but she refused to answer the question. All she would say is, "I will help my husband fight the suit brought against him by Tabitha Taylor. All of his money is now in my name."

Zeo consulted with the Kansas City law firm of Prince & Harris, which declined to take on her interests but agreed to represent her husband in the divorce case. Zeo kept shopping for lawyers. She wanted the best attorney her husband's money could buy. By and by she got him: Frank P. Walsh. He happened to be one of the best known lawyers in the United States, widely considered a giant of the bar. Walsh was a labor lawyer, Democratic Party activist, and crusader for working children. He was particularly noted for his defense of Jesse James Jr. in one of Missouri's most famous criminal trials. His name was also attached to the largest personal injury judgment to date in the entire state of Missouri: a verdict of thirty-five thousand dollars.

Zeo met with Walsh in Kansas City on January 30, 1917. Reporters outside the building timed their conversation at three hours. Missouri's best trial lawyer agreed to come to the defense of Zeo Cunningham and charged in accordance with the facts of her case. Several accounts said Walsh demanded fifty thousand dollars for his fee, though Walsh would neither confirm nor deny the astounding figure. If correct, it was the most lucrative legal case of the storied lawyer's career.

A few days later, a man from the *Kansas City Post* pounded on the door to Zeo's suite to ask her again to prove she was married to Tom Cunningham. "She tilted her chin," his account read, reporting that she'd refused to say where or when the wedding took place. "Why cannot a young woman love an old man?" she asked. "And why should they kick up such a row about it all?" In response to her question, the *Post* noted what it termed "the white slave aspect" of the matter.

On the heels of the *Post*, the *Kansas City Journal* found her at the Muehlebach and asked her about a rumor that she had kidnapped her sister's child a couple years back. She explained that she nursed her sister Irene before her death and legally adopted Horace in Kansas, but she refused to say where the boy was.

Such questions may have surprised her. Tabitha and her lawyers, as it turned out, were digging into her past and sharing what they learned with the press. As the rumors flew and Tabitha learned more about her rival, her attorneys changed strategies. They filed a second lawsuit, this one against Zeo, demanding a quarter of a million dollars on the grounds that Zeo had alienated the old man's affections with a bogus wedding.

The lawyers for Tabitha argued that such a mockery of a marriage ought to be declared illegal as well as immoral. Public sympathy favored the old restraints, and there was something wrong in many an estimation with the casual way in which they had been disregarded. Her "love adventures," as the newspapers put it, trivialized a sanctified institution as critical to the security of women as it was to the privileges of men. The protections afforded wives and the bonds of marriage were diluted when those protections applied to harlots and scamps, when licenses were issued to couples sight unseen, and when divorce was so readily granted that one woman could rack up four marriages in ten years. It was well understood for generations, for centuries, that certain taboos about marriage were in the best interests of the race. A few centuries before, women like Dr. Wilkins were burned at the stake.

Missouri grew a little too warm for Zeo. She headed for the white lights of Chicago with her lawyer. When they arrived, they discovered that the Chicago tabloids had found Tom at the Blackstone. Reporters had quizzed the hotel staff. They described the old man as perceptibly ill and said he had not left his room for two weeks. Frank Walsh removed him to the St. Regis Hotel. Arthur Wilkins called it "a dingy, crummy place."

It was an untenable situation. Reporters circled constantly. Tom wanted to take Tabitha by the horns himself. He decided to return to Joplin. Zeo talked him into letting her brother accompany him; one journal identified his escort as "C.C. Wilkins." It seems Arthur Wilkins was reluctant to have his full name publicly connected to his scandalous sister.

Both men were in for a great surprise when they attempted to transfer trains in Kansas City. Tom's influential friends back in Joplin had formed a citizens' committee and convinced a probate judge to issue a court order to take him into protective custody. Waiting in the train station for them was the sheriff of Jasper County, the city attorney for Joplin, the chief of police, and several officers. When the old man was helped off the train and saw those awaiting his arrival, he managed a soft "hello." It was said he did not recognize men he'd known for decades.

In a five-year span, Zeo Wilkins had reduced a respected businessman and civic-minded millionaire to destitution, unemployment, disability, and arrest on an insanity warrant.

When Tom Cunningham came back to Joplin under police escort, the city held an impromptu parade. The newsboys shouted as people poured into the streets to witness their beloved banker's safe return.

Frank Walsh caught wind of Tom's arrest and immediately went to Joplin. He was forced to cool his heels outside the county jail while Tabitha Taylor spoke to Tom in the presence of several reporters and city officials.

"Tom, are you glad you're back?" Tabitha asked him.

"Yes, honey, I am."

And yet Tom still refused to speak much of his marriage to Zeo or his money. He would only say that he remembered marrying her "a long time ago" in a small town in Colorado. He did not lament the sale of his bank. He did not know it had been sold, he said, but he didn't mind. "She had a right to sell it if she wanted to. It belonged to her."

In a later interview, Tabitha Taylor declared that she was "happy as a lark." Reached in Chicago for a comment on Tom's reunion with Tabitha, Zeo gave the *Kansas City Journal* a brief quote. "Bosh, rubbish, otherwise pish and tush. That's what I've got to say."

She would face a series of harder questions soon enough. Tom's bags had been packed hastily. As they were unpacked for him, out came a slip of paper on which were written curious notes mentioning various substances. The press identified them as "poison recipes." Much later, a lawyer for the old man would testify that he had uncovered evidence that Dr. Wilkins was, in the lawyer's words, "experimenting with a slow poison."

Back in Chicago, Zeo settled into a luxury room at the Hotel Sherman, the city's premier nightlife destination, and made no effort to avoid the tabloids. At the height of the scandal, she received several newspaper reporters at once in her suite. She was scantily clad for the occasion. The reporters were guided to her bedroom and offered seats surrounding her as she reclined on the bed "that she might," explained the *Kansas City Post*, "with more propriety, enchant them with glimpses of her bare arm." The prurient *Post* duly noted that her arms were "rosy with the tints of youthful femininity."

One of the newsmen asked her if she thought Tabitha's lawsuit was an effort to blackmail the old banker.

"Blackmail?" Zeo responded. "Of course. What else can it be? But she'll never get a cent."

They informed her during this interview that her husband had been arrested in Kansas City, declared incompetent by several alienists, and was at that moment being held as insane at the home of the Jasper County sheriff. As the *Kansas City Star* relayed to its readers:

Even these extraordinary tiding[s] failed to perturb the equanimity of Mrs. Cunningham. She smiled amusedly and dabbled her long fingers in a finger bowl on the breakfast tray beside her. "What next, I wonder," she mused, drawing her fingers on a napkin. "I've grown so accustomed to hearing all manner of frightful things about me that nothing can startle me now."

They kept trying to startle her. They gave her the news that she was accused of drugging her husband. Her response:

She laughed merrily. Her dark eyes sparkling, she sat up in bed with a kittenish movement, swept her heavy hair back from her brow with a swift movement of her bare arm and exclaimed, "That certainly is the most ridiculous thing yet. . . . We're awfully happy together, even if he is twice as old as I am. Why can't people leave us alone?"

She continued lazily, her eyes half veiled by her long, dark lashes. "It is mirth provoking, is it not? To think that grandmotherly old woman who ought to be at home darning stockings for her grandchildren, [is] chasing after my husband and trying to extort money from him.

"But anyway," concluded Mrs. Cunningham, snuggling into her downy pillow, "she's too old to think of love. Love is not for such as she."

As finely as Zeo played the part of a blissfully happy wife, Tom Cunningham's ardor cooled when he left Chicago. His lawyers brought an action on his behalf to annul his marriage to Zeo. In the lawsuit, they brought up the name she least wanted to hear: Grover Burcham.

Tom and Tabitha's lawyers had discovered her marriage to Grover. But they could not find a divorce file.

Zeo told them Grover was deceased—that he was shot and killed in Houston, Texas while burgling a home.

It was a clever lie. Maybe she feigned shame when she told it.

The State of Texas has never issued a death certificate to anyone named Grover Burcham, not to mention the fact that weeks after Zeo declared him dead, Grover Milburne Burcham registered for the draft in Los Angeles.

The fresh sensation made new headlines nationwide as the correspondents in their excitement mixed up all her marriages. From the *Mansfield News* in Ohio:

WAS YOUNG GIRL'S SLAVE SAYS AGED MILLIONAIRE

Joplin, Mo., Feb. 24 – Thomas W. Cunningham, 72-year-old multi-millionaire and former president of the Cunningham National Bank, put a new twist on the old line about "an old man's darling," in discussing his suit for divorce today.

Pretty young Zoe Wilkins Cunningham, the dashing osteopath, whom the multi-millionaire is suing for divorce, didn't become an "old man's darling" when she entered Cunningham's life, he said. Instead the aged capitalist declares he became a young girl's slave.

It wasn't the first marriage for Zoe Wilkins by any means. Two of her husbands had died suddenly and a third, a man of wealth, became a bankrupt and a wandering derelict. Cunningham declares she plotted to marry him as part of a conspiracy to wreck his health and powers of resistance and acquire his wealth. She obtained more than half a million dollars, he alleges, sold his bank and disposed of his real estate, all the while keeping him a "love prisoner." Now, he says, she refuses to account for the money or to give him the comfort of her society.

Then the scandal culminated with the most sensational coverage of all, found in a supplement to the *Washington Post.* It gave the affair this headline:

PLUCKY OLD MRS. CUNNINGHAM

AND THE SIREN:

HOW THE TOIL WORN WIFE

OF 72 WHO SCRIMPED AND

SAVED TO HELP MAKE

HIS MILLIONS WON BACK

THE BANKER FROM THE

BEAUTY OF 30 WHO

SPENT HIS

MONEY ON

LUXURIES

The piece quoted both ladies at length and ran their photos. Said "Mrs. Cunningham" (a.k.a. Tabitha Taylor):

> That woman will never get my Tom again. He never had a chance in his younger days to sew the wild oats every man must harvest. It was right, perhaps, that he should wander away, just to learn that the old love is always better than the new.
>
> We will both forget the other woman. We can't begin over again—we've lived through our younger days.
>
> We'll just begin where we left off, and when Tom wants sympathy, or taking care of, or when he is worried or needs a hot flannel to ward off a sore throat, he'll know he has me at his side to turn to.
>
> There is more virtue in a hot flannel cloth when the throat aches than all the kisses in the world.

And the quote provided by Zeo Zoe:

> They say my husband has returned to his old love. Pish-pish—and also pish tosh! When I want him here with me, here where I can

snuggle my bare arm around his neck, where I can perch on his knee and call him the endearing names that only young love can invent—when I want him here with me again I shall call to him. And when I call he will come—even though he has to break every bond with which human ingenuity can fetter him.

How did I win him? How did I make of him a willing slave, eager to pamper my every wish?

Ah! That is one of the secrets of young love that only an old man can understand. Where old love reminded him of his advancing years—of the nearness of death itself, I reminded him of youth and beauty and gayety and drove his cares away and brought him back from contemplation of that which is hidden beyond the grave.

The *Washington Post* spread on the Cunningham scandal. (*NewspaperArchive.com*)

What a conundrum the cases presented to the judiciary of Jasper County. Where should the old banker's fortune go? Which of his "wives" was less deserving of the title? Both of them were as crooked as bedsprings.

The litigation progressed rapidly, and Zeo was ordered to appear at the Joplin courthouse to answer questions under oath. This she could not do, particularly if the subject of her undissolved prior marriage arose. She knew from the newspaper coverage that the many lawyers involved in the case were prepared to quiz her extensively about Mr. Burcham. A settlement was Zeo's only hope of avoiding a charge of either perjury or bigamy.

To resolve the cases, old love and young love struck a deal. Zeo's marriage to Tom was annulled, though she was awarded all the money from the sale of the bank, the houses she acquired in Kansas City and Colorado Springs, plus roughly a hundred thousand dollars more, as well as all the tens of thousands of dollars' worth of furs, jewelry, and clothes she'd given herself. Tabitha Taylor got to keep Tom. The outcome must have elated them both. One wants to think that during their settlement talks the two gold diggers, craning for a sight of each other between all the lawyers, exchanged little winks. With all the lawsuits resolved, Zeo Zoe's ship came in, as they said back then, and she would live the rest of her life like a sailor on perpetual shore leave.

10

Love Makes Time Go, Time Makes Love Go

For years, the amazing story of Zoe Wilkin's [*sic*] marriages,
her divorces, her successes in persuading her husbands to
endow her, actually as well as nominally, with all their worldly
goods, and the tragedies in which some of her affairs ended,
has been printed in the newspapers and written into the court
records of Missouri, Colorado, Oklahoma and Texas, as one
mid-westerner after another walked into the web already so
well advertised and found there just what
they might have expected.
— Frederick *(Maryland)* Post

In the spring of 1917, Zeo Zoe Wilkins Dryder Garring Burcham Cunningham, Doctor of Osteopathy, had nearly half a million dollars stuffed in her strongbox with the approval of the law. She didn't know it yet, but she had only seven years left to spend it. "I've got money now," she wrote in her little brown diary, "and I've decided to have my fun." She just had to decide where and with whom to have it.

Because of the publicity brought on by Tabitha Taylor's lawsuit, men by the score studied the pictures in the newspapers of the pretty and now very rich lady doctor. She inflamed the imaginations of dozens of men, rich and poor, and they mailed endearing offers to lay themselves on her altar.

But one well-formed figure was uppermost on her mind. He was a businessman, and he was too handsome for words. To add to his appeal, he lived in the one city that could match Zeo for wealth and awesome impiety—a nonjudgmental, soaking wet, discretion-assuring town that revered new money, indulged the sinful secret wishes of the millionaire class, and sold liquor behind the counter in every drugstore.

Colorado Springs it was, then.

In the 1870s, railroad men turned their gazes on the famous pinnacle in the Rocky Mountains called Pike's Peak and decided that the beautiful chunk of granite thrusting itself skyward ought to stand for something greater than itself. They overcame rattlesnakes, "Indian troubles," and wind-driven winter weather featuring long freezes and sudden blizzards in spring and fall.

But the summers! The newly minted city of Colorado Springs offered virgin, spruce-scented air and infinite mountaintop views. By the 1880s, it was one of the earliest health resorts in the country. Wealthy tuberculosis patients spread word of the mile-high air, and, before long, the town boasted several luxury hotels for lungers who could afford envigorating pleasure trips. Among many famous visitors were Oscar Wilde, President Harrison, John D. Rockefeller, Marshall Field, William Jennings Bryan, and Jefferson Davis. To Colorado Springs, morality took a back seat to money; thus the town welcomed a visit from Rev. Henry Ward Beecher, the most famous clergyman in the country, even after a scandalous extramarital affair with Elizabeth Tilton destroyed his reputation elsewhere.

And then in 1893 came *another* lucky strike. The high-stakes town went through a gold rush, one of the last large rushes in the West, which added more tycoons of the overnight variety. Tales were told of men who became filthy rich through land, oil, silver, zinc, lead, and gold—and *then* learned to read and write. Thus "no one [in Colorado Springs] ever frets himself over how a person acquired his fortune," the correspondents reported. "The main question asked by the exclusive set is not how did he get it, but has he got it?" The city soon bragged that it had "more millionaires, acre for acre, and population for population, than any place."

And what a naughty town these old capitalists created—so accommodating, but so good at keeping up a respectable "health farm" front. The nation's travel writers pointed out that the "millionaire's paradise" didn't have any "establishments where liquor is sold." That was strictly true, since the booze-swillin' red-light district was just outside the official town limits. Liquor was never hard to find in Colorado Springs before or during Prohibition. In all of 1913, more people were ticketed for letting their chickens run at large (three) than for violating the local liquor law (two).

The mountains proved to be fruitful grounds for gold diggers of every variety. Upper-class matrons from the Midwest and as far away as Britain brought their daughters on the long train ride to Colorado Springs to make whoopee in the rich man's play town. And wherever there were ladies, there were men eager to serve their every impulse. "A high quotient of quality playboys has always been a feature of club life in Colorado Springs. At the turn of the century, the volume soared," wrote one historian, adding delicately that some men "came to win the heart and purse of any rich widow or any wife of social eminence who might yearn for a change of pace."

One man in particular kept his gaze on the horizon between Zeo's visits to Colorado Springs. He was a member of the vast fraternity of businessmen who'd laid early bets on the city and were perfectly poised to cater to a swelling caravan of automobile travelers. Not one of them was more perfectly poised, even under moments of distress, than Albert Marksheffel.

Albert, or Al to his many friends, was the self-made son of Kansas settlers, and he devoted himself with German fervor to contraptions. He was married twice but only briefly; both wives divorced him. Ah, well, bicycles were mechanical and thus more *verständlich,* or understandable. Then it was electric vehicles. In 1899 gasoline-powered machines spluttered into the mountains, frightening the horses and burros, and the bike shop manager finally found a lifelong passion.

Always ahead of the curve, Marksheffel raced autos professionally in his spare time. He managed a parts shop, then a dealership, sold car after car, and bought the shop. He became a prominent, popular businessman in the city: president of the Automobile Club and committee man for the Chamber of Commerce and Rotary Club. In less than a decade, the bike shop boy bought out the competition, edged out the horse stables, and cornered the market for automobiles in the millionaires' heaven.

Al spent his evenings with his wealthy clients in the guise of a "chauffeur," spiriting around tourists in Cadillacs, Fords, and REOs, offering them driving lessons and stimulating tours of gay times and heady nights in the Rockies. His life was comprised of new cars, long rides, vistas, champagne, and an occasional dotted line. As Al learned, "women buy cars very largely by color." They may also have been persuaded by the color of the salesman's large, languid blue eyes or his thick blond hair.

In the winter of 1916, Dr. Zeo Wilkins made her first trip to Colorado. She stayed only long enough to remarry Tom Cunningham. When she picked up the telephone and requested number 238, she reached the Marksheffel Garage. She ordered a car and a chauffeur to take her to the shopping district. Albert Marksheffel, four years her senior, came with the car.

At first, they met on the sly. She kept the affair a secret from her husband and brother. Then she threw caution to the wind and took Albert shopping. The pair of them were seen for days around Colorado Springs, flaunting Cunningham's wealth in jewelry shops, in clothing stores, and at Rotary Club entertainments. Al sold her a roadster that they enjoyed on motoring trips through the mountains. The Kansas City press called Marksheffel "a dapper companion, appearing in evening clothes and escorting her to theatre parties with friends." Marksheffel knew exactly where the money was coming from. He was the sole witness to the transfer of Cunningham's city lots.

But that, in the spring of 1917, was in the past. Zeo had settled her marital affairs in Joplin, and she was soon back in town. The city would welcome her, cater to her, and would not gossip about her in the paper. The *Colorado Springs Gazette* never spared one column inch for the details of Zeo Wilkins's fraudulence while she was alive, even when they knew she was a resident there, even when other editors gave her gallons of ink and the news wires nearly melted with details of her exploits.

The *Gazette* hadn't always been quite so willing to overlook the sins of Al Marksheffel. Maybe that's why he embraced Zeo Zoe on her triumphant return to Colorado Springs with her Cunningham prize. He had no reputation to lose.

A decade earlier, on September 16, 1907, as tourist season was winding down, Albert Marksheffel spent a night of revelry at the Elks Lodge with his friends. Then he talked them into taking a ride in a brand new race car of Henry Ford's creation. The tiny machine boasted forty horsepower and a six-cylinder engine. Marksheffel and eight friends motored the Ford into the red-light district over the town line and into Colorado City. After whiling away forty-five minutes of their evening, some of the slowpokes as long as an hour, all nine climbed back into the Ford for a downhill ride on a mountainside street known as Colorado Avenue. They opened up the race car all the way.

The Ford got up to the city speed limit—twelve miles an hour—and passed it. Then it got up to the country limit—eighteen miles an hour—and passed it.

The car flew down the hill. Near the bottom, the Ford sped by a parked police patrol car.

The patrolman said he saw the machine go by at "a mile a minute." Men were hanging out all sides of the car. The officer shouted a useless warning and began to give chase when before his horrified eyes the Ford hit a set of streetcar tracks and overturned into the intersection of Huerfano Street.

Al Marksheffel's Ford rests in pieces. (*Pikes Peak Library District*)

Everyone was thrown from the car. Three were killed at the scene. A fourth suffered fatal injuries. Said the *Gazette:* "Those who arrived at the scene soon after the accident tell a sickening tale of picking up dead bodies while brains oozed out through the hands that supported the heads."

Marksheffel walked away without a scratch, but the law could not let him off so easily. In one of the first fatal drunk-driving prosecutions in the West, if not the very first, and certainly among the first to involve so many fatalities, Marksheffel was charged with manslaughter and speeding. The crash involving the race car made news across state lines and was featured on front pages as far away as California. Throughout the region newsmen devoted considerable coverage to Marksheffel's accident, dwelling in shock and horror on the "sickening thud which ended three human lives."

The paper that mattered most to Al—the local *Gazette*—gave the fatal accident its own issue:

NEWS SPREAD RAPIDLY

GAZETTE EXTRA GIVES DE-

TAILS OF ACCIDENT.

Large Crowds at Scene of Disaster
All Day—Wrecked Machine Re-
Moved to Garage.

News of the frightful automobile accident, with its death harvest of three lives, spread rapidly through the city yesterday morning. Within a short time after the issuance of the Gazette extra edition, the details of the tragedy became generally known, and large crowds flocked to the scene of the disaster on West Huerfano street during the entire day.

There was little to see of the night's carnage except the once powerful racing machine, demolished and wrecked, with its wheels broken off, its steering gear twisted out of place and the body battered and beat out of shape. The track that the wild car took after it swerved from its intended path was marked by broken cross pieces . . . The fence of the corral and the ground in spots were stained with blood.

The police attached a rope around the machine, to keep the overcurious at a safe distance. After some time what remained of the machine was removed under the direction of the Western automobile company, to its garage. It took eight men to lift it into the transfer wagon.

Al Marksheffel was arrested within hours. The *Gazette* took the further, unusual step of railing against him on its editorial page and was undoubtedly not alone in heaping shame and abuse on him for his fatal stunt. The *Gazette* editor wrote:

It is hard to find words of condemnation serious enough for the chauffeur, whose crazy recklessness caused the disaster. It seems

to be pretty clearly established that this man Marksheffel is a speed lunatic of an extremely dangerous type, one of the wild-eyed variety who take a 'smart aleck's' delight in imperiling their own necks and those of everybody else concerned, either passenger or pedestrian. No man who possessed a shred of common sense would try to descend the Huerfano street hill [*sic*] at such a terrific speed as Marksheffel's machine was going when seen by Policeman Cornell . . . it was sheer lunacy.

The outcome of his criminal case depended largely on how well Al could hold himself together during the proceedings, since the lack of precedent made the law's role in responding to the tragedy unclear. The exact criminal charge proved to be a matter of legitimate debate. Marksheffel was called to testify at a coroner's inquest into the accident and gave a statement that suggests he was very well prepared and projected a calm defense despite weeping onlookers.

Said Marksheffel:

I was perfectly clear-headed, and had control of the machine at the top of the hill. I had one or two drinks during the evening, but certainly not enough to affect my ability to run the machine in any way. I have taken this hill, on almost this identical turn, a hundred times, and never before have I had the slightest trouble. It is simply one of those unaccountable accidents. It was fearful, and no one better appreciates the gravity of the calamity than I.

I can't explain how it happened. We were coming down the middle of the street between the two car-tracks. I know I had the brakes on.

At the top of the hill, I turned to cross the right-hand track. It seems to me that I felt the rear wheel slip against the rail . . . before I could make the second turn onto the road, we were in the ditch.

At the most, we could not have been going at a greater rate than 35 miles an hour. It has been stated that we were going at the rate of 75 miles an hour, but the maximum speed of the machine was not over 35. This is shown by the fact that the best mile I made at Overland during the Labor day race was in 1:04.

There was a speedometer on the car, but we could not see it in the dark. The machine had not been working well during the day, and this fact made an exceptionally high rate of speed impossible.

Perhaps Al Marksheffel was the first drunk driver in the West to use the "one or two beers" defense. His intelligence and skill at prevaricating served him well. The criminal litigation dragged on for two years, and, by the time Marksheffel's name appeared on the trial docket, nobody supported the case against him. Sure, he killed several of his friends that night, but Colorado Springs would forgive him for his error. When the prosecutor "accidentally" failed to prove that he was the man actually driving, all charges were dismissed.

Two weeks later, Al Marksheffel ran over a five-year-old child with his car. The boy wasn't hurt badly. The *Gazette* reported that the boy darted out into traffic.

Ten years after the fatal night, Al Marksheffel knew his reputation would never fully recover. What could wield a greater blow to a man in auto sales and rentals than being that young German race car driver who killed several passengers at once? Maybe it had something to do with his decision a decade later to yoke himself to a woman some of his friends privately called "the scarlet harlot."

He was at least honest with her about it. "I don't love you Zeo," Al told her, "but we can be pals."

May 7, 1917, found Zeo Zoe Wilkins and Albert William Marksheffel gazing into a camera after exchanging vows before the justice of the peace in Pueblo, Colorado. Zeo's fifth husband wore a small, one-sided smile. She wore fur. Both wore huge diamonds.

Mr. and Mrs. Albert Marksheffel. (*Pikes Peak Library District*)

And what did he hide with his little smile and rigid spine? Did he think he could introduce discipline to the Devil's pet daughter? Was there a discussion or only assumptions on the question of monogamy?

Maybe she only wanted to show off Albert, to don him like a fur stole. But maybe the calculating queen of the sirens said "I do" with new intentions. Perhaps true love, refreshing, invigorating love, finally pierced that thickened heart. She must have truly loved him. For the first time in her life, she let her emotions get the better of her business judgment. Of Zeo's six known marriages to five husbands, the Marksheffel deal was the only bad bargain she ever struck.

Al wanted to avoid the draft at a time when marriage made men eligible for deferment. He also wanted money and quite a lot of it: seventy thousand dollars to build the biggest motor car garage in the country. Zeo said yes. Then he wanted twenty-five thousand dollars more to spend on a traditional bridal trip to the West. Zeo said yes to that too. She bought a Cadillac touring car for the occasion, and they went motoring through several states. Al took plenty of pictures of Zeo in the desert wearing a relaxed smile. They posed together for several photos in California. Her extended honeymoon with Al may have given her the happiest days of her life.

The news of their marriage traveled faster than they did. Coming so soon on the heels of her sensational Cunningham annulment—she married Al only a month later—the regional press delighted in reporting that DIVORCED WIFE OF TOM CUNNINGHAM WEDS AGAIN.

Then she took him to Kansas City, back to the Muehlebach Hotel. Zeo loved the atmosphere of wealth and privilege to be found there and must have relished the contrast in her circumstances since her last visit. A few years before, she'd taken the train and walked into the Muehlebach wearing gingham, holding a shovel, and bearing a tottering old Tom on

The Marksheffels in California. (*Pikes Peak Library District*)

her arm. Now she arrived by Cadillac and wore mink, diamonds, and Albert.

One-time Kansas City resident Ernest Hemingway once remarked on the joys of a stay at the Muehlebach, which had by his estimate "the biggest beds in the world" and let ordinary people "pretend that we are oil millionaires." Zeo Wilkins didn't have to pretend anything. On her Marksheffel honeymoon, she took an extended stay in the Muehlebach's presidential suite for a hundred dollars a day and ran up a bill of five thousand dollars. It may well have taken the biggest bed in the world to accommodate the passions of Zeo Wilkins. There's no greater aphrodisiac than money, as Oscar Wilde said. Her fifth honeymoon also featured long dinners at the orchestra hall next door to the hotel. She loved to listen to the orchestra play and became a favorite of the musicians. On more than one occasion, Zeo tipped the conductor a fifty-dollar bill to play "Barcarolle" from the Jacques Offenbach opera *The Tales of Hoffman,* the song of the Venetian gondoliers (*"Belle nuit, o nuit d'amour"*), which drips honey. It was always her favorite piece of music.

It wasn't only wine and roses with Al on her sojourn to Kansas City. Shortly after she got her Cunningham fortune, she enjoyed a rendezvous at the Muehlebach with her old friend from Sapulpa, B.B. Burnett. His brother Birch also came, and the Burnett brothers relished Zeo's company for a time. The three scoundrels swapped stories of quick riches and the thrills of playing hunches in the oil business. In her diary she noted, "They thought I was drinking too much and gave me a lease they didn't think much of for $5,000." The land was near (of all places) Paola, Kansas.

B.B. had drilled in the four corners of the property and come up dry. Zeo financed another hole and told the crew to drill in the center. Sure enough, it was a gusher. Zeo's first payout was one hundred ninety-five thousand dollars. Everyone remarked on her "super-gambling instinct." With a single bet, she struck enough oil to buy Al a new garage and a fleet of Cadillacs. But she celebrated the oil strike with B.B., enjoying the all-natural stimulant of overnight riches with the man who made them possible. The most lyrical passages of her *quelle belle nuit* in Kansas City surely echoed in the Cadillac all the way back to Colorado Springs.

Once Zeo Wilkins had everything in life she could have wanted, she worked to be rid of it as quickly as possible. She began with her fortune, throwing it around like she thought she'd never spend the last penny, no matter how many vacations she took or how many diamonds she bought. There was a trip to Palm Beach, then another to New York. In Miami, she hired two yachts, one just for her servants. In Colorado Springs, she became well known as "one of the most lavish spenders in recent years here in a city of lavish spenders. She bought fine motor cars and jewelry, entertained on an elaborate scale and was the talk of the town."

Al moved into Zeo's home at 21 East Willamette, which she had outfitted with the best in linens, dishes, and silver. She stocked their house with the finest wines and champagnes. Damn the liquor laws; they weren't enforced anyway. She bought forty thousand dollars' worth of diamonds for herself and another fifteen diamonds that she gave out as treats to her friends. She added to her holdings a four hundred-acre ranch on Turkey Creek south of Colorado Springs and allowed her brother Arthur and his new bride Laura to manage the property. Zeo also brought her adopted son Horace into her Colorado Springs home for a time, insured her life for his benefit, and then returned him to boarding school. Al and Zeo spent their spare time in pleasurable pursuits, fishing and motoring through the mountains.

She didn't forget her promise to Al. Zeo financed the construction of the Marksheffel Motor Company garage at Cascade Avenue and Kiowa Street. At forty-six thousand square feet, it was the largest concern of its kind in the United States.

She bought him nine Cadillacs and at least seven more for herself. Arthur's wife, Laura Wilkins, said she had twenty brand new cars. Once the fleet of Cads arrived, Zeo ordered the drivers who worked for Al to pick up all the poor children they could find in town and buy them

The Marksheffel Motor Company Garage. (*Pikes Peak Library District*)

anything they wanted. But she was smart enough with the loan to Al's business to have it reduced to a formal written agreement. Maybe she was inspired by the inscription Al had placed around the face of the clock over the front door of the world's largest garage:

Love makes time go, time makes love go.

After she became Mrs. Marksheffel, Zeo again gave up her medical practice. A real marriage was a damper on her brand of medicine, and she didn't need the money anyway. But nothing could have been worse for Frau Marksheffel than boredom. She started drinking in such quantity that she bought her liquor wholesale. Arthur Wilkins once spoke of some bootlegging he did with his sister. He described a trip they made to Kansas City circa 1918:

> We took 2 Cadillacs and on our return trip, loaded down, we stopped in Junction City for lunch. Doc wanted to drink, so she sent one of us to the car for a bottle.

Several interested people were standing around, looking at the shiny new Cads and wondering why they were so low in the back. After Doc poured several drinks out of the bottle, the law showed up and we were invited to go down to the police station.

Because of their conspicuous consumption they were in a peck of trouble, but still she managed to sweet-talk her way out of Junction City.

Of another round trip to Kansas City, Arthur said:

Boy, oh boy, do I remember that trip. Al Marksheffel, Laura, and me went with her. He was driving a new Cad. I was so geed-up I sang all the way over there.

Somewhere around the Colorado-Nebraska border we got ourselves lost. It was a nightmare.

Suddenly we saw lots and lots of eyes in the dark. Al reared up and bellowed, "Jesus Christ, what is that?" By God, we were in the middle of a herd of antelope.

Al and Zeo at the summit of the Rocky Mountains, September 11, 1917.

(*Pikes Peak Library District*)

On the same trip they also drove through a U.S. Army installation, Fort Riley. Arthur thought he was being clever when he piped up with, "four thousand soldiers and Doc. Let's get the hell out of here quick!" Did Zeo laugh too?

With all that booze, Al and Zeo threw some real "wingdings" at their home on Willamette, parties in which guests were told to throw the empty bottles under the dining room table. Arthur Wilkins once repeated a story he heard from a friend named John about a memorable fiesta given by the Marksheffels:

> The party went smoothly for a while. The drinks and food were excellent—the best money could buy. Suddenly Al and Doc got into what John thought was a mild argument. They wound up throwing things at one another and wrecking furniture. John told me, he said to Al, 'you're a good friend of mine, Al, but I'll never come into your house again.' He said he never did.

Since she had nothing better to do than supervise Al's every moment, Zeo also made a spectacle of herself down at his garage, where she threw fits fueled by the unfamiliar feeling of jealousy. One evening, he didn't answer the garage phone and didn't come home. "She made up her mind to find out why," Arthur said. "She hauled herself down to the garage, but Al had a hunch that this would happen so he was a no-show guy. Anyway she just hung around the garage until she got hungry. Then she sent out for food to be brought in. She was determined she was going to see Al so she slept in one of the Cads. That went on for days. Finally she gave up and went home. You could say that Al won that ball game."

She couldn't fence in her speed demon, and it drove her wild. In one of her tantrums, she made the wheels smoke on a brand new Cadillac. She destroyed the finish with a hatpin and blamed it on a pet dog she'd bought, a big white bulldog, Snip.

Throughout their marriage, Zeo took lovers. She hid them under the beds and in the closets. Al's lack of jealousy infuriated her. Sometime around the summer of 1919, Mrs. Marksheffel screamed for her unappreciative husband's attention. She demanded flowers. He ignored her. She spoke of suicide. He rolled his eyes. Zeo was so desperate for those flowers, for that modest token of his affection, she decided to shake him up with a lesson she first taught in a hog pen. The outlandish scene came complete with black crepe on the door and the smell of carbolic acid. As Arthur described it:

> One time she wanted to test Al's love, so she played like she died. Well anyway Laura and some other women dressed Doc all in white and stretched her out on the bed and put a bouquet in her hands. When they got everything done, one of them called Al and told him to hurry right home, that Doc had died. When he walked in the room and saw her stretched out he said, "I don't believe it. She's too goddamn ornery and mean to die." She jumped up and a helluva fight took place.

By all accounts, Albert was unamused. He didn't care that she cuckolded him, but the suicide scene went too far. He refused to forgive her for being such an emotional imbecile. Al said to Zeo whatever it is that wealthy, reckless, handsome businessmen say to their third wives by way of farewell in the closing moments of the departure scene. He left the house on Willamette and that was the end of pleasantries between Al and Zeo.

Or, as the *Kansas City Star* summed it up: THE MARKSHEFFELS FALL OUT.

Decades later, a municipal bureaucrat ordered the destruction of the old Marksheffel garage. Al's round-the-clock tiled motto about time and love was salvaged and turned into a raised flowerbed at the city's Monument Valley Park—a monument to a marriage that proved the theorem. The optimists could say she finally got her flowers.

Zeo would have laughed at such a sentimental thought. She was no piner. The instant Albert split the blanket with her, she became Zeo Zoe Wilkins all over again.

Wiles and Machinations

The hardened old two-fisted gold seeker of the Yukon who
made history and fortune as he penetrated the wilds of a
trackless wilderness a few decades ago probably would be
somewhat surprised should he meet the gold prospector of
today. . . . [She] begins her night's work by dabbing a bit of
powder on her nose, blackening her eyebrows, rouging her lips
and, perhaps, twisting a "spit curl" into shape. The mackinaw
has been replaced by a sable coat. The pick is replaced by
a vanity case. In the place of a grin of grim determination
has come a winsome smile, breathing the fragrance of fairy
perfume. The modern gold digger dines in luxury—she very
frequently wines, too, despite the Volstead law. And she goes
no farther than Chicago.

— *John D. Mueller, International News Service (1923)*

Chafed as it must have been, that ring finger itched. Zeo's renewed
manhunt had her motoring the Cadillac between Kansas City
and her home in Colorado Springs with her bulldog Snip. He was hardly
enough to keep her out of trouble in either town, for Zeo continued her
bootlegging.

The Colorado Springs police would describe the scene of one of her
midnight moonshine adventures as a "house run by Negroes," but it was
usually called a black and tan joint. "Black and tan" was an old saying
for anything that mixed the races. Zeo and many others were caught in a
booze raid in a house on South Weber Street near downtown Colorado
Springs that had customers of both races and sexes. It was right next to
the railroad tracks, and, if typical of its day, it featured liquor, drugs,

cards, dice, and vices of all other sorts aimed at the palate of the working man. One can only wonder what Dr. Wilkins was caught doing at a disorderly house when raiding officers illuminated her crime with police lamps. Maybe she was only bootlegging. As soon as the police charged into the house, a row erupted that the police chief would later call "one of the most sensational in police annals." Zeo didn't write of the incident in her diary. Alas, the sensational details are lost to posterity.

If a liquor sale were her only sin, easygoing Colorado Springs wasn't about to put her name in the paper or charge her with a serious crime. The local paper never published one line on the booze raid. The punishment for first-time liquor-selling was a fine, not a scandal. Maybe she didn't know that. Or maybe she was caught with something more taboo than booze. In need of a lawyer, she hired Ira Harris, the mayor himself, to represent her. One hefty fee later, any suggestion of charges was forgotten, but she was told to leave for good. Oh, she could visit, the city fathers said, spend a little money, but she wasn't living in Colorado Springs anymore if she wanted to keep it hushed. And that was the "finale to her career here," as one Colorado reporter put it. Though they got rid of her, the damage was done. "For years and years," local historians would observe, "reputations were tainted, tongues wagged."

That was Colorado Springs for you. In Kansas City, she could do what she pleased, though she couldn't always keep it out of the papers. In 1919, Zeo Marksheffel, her latest divorce far from final, took rooms at the Paseo Hotel in Kansas City. In her private quarters, she began practicing osteopathy again. Resuming her swashbuckling ways with men, she secured wealthy patients with her usual ease.

In August, Zeo met John T. McNamara at the Paseo. He appeared on referral for some "special treatments." His first words to her must have been endearing. Or maybe she saw through him at once and ached to vamp him.

John passed whatever physical tests Dr. Wilkins administered. The big question came up early. He had money, owned property, and didn't mind a woman who indulged in heavy drinking. They soon discovered a mutual love of speakeasies. In fact, he owned one. John McNamara was a saloon-keeper at 17th and Main streets in Kansas City. In the Prohibition era, which began on January 17, 1920, with the Volstead Act, he boarded up the business and took it underground, not that anything in Kansas City was all that far underground. Felonious liquor deals weren't his only game. His scam was to "play wealthy widows," as the public would eventually learn. "After he would get their money he would forget them and return to his wife." McNamara was married, and Mrs. Nellie McNamara intended to keep it that way.

Zeo mesmerized John. A lawyer who once opposed her said she dominated men like John with her "remarkable personality." John showed her his underworld, and she showed him hers. First they toured the liquor scene in Kansas City. By then she was drinking heavily and ingesting large doses of prescription drugs, or so said her brother Arthur.

Martin Quigley, a *Kansas City Times* reporter, would one day memorialize his first impression of a Prohibition-era Kansas City saloon:

> A blue and orange neon sign beckoned me to Music Dancing Mixed Drinks. . . . There was a photograph in the window of. . . the Read Headed Nightingale of Taney County, Orbalee Jones. Well, of course, that was nothing to miss. . . . I went in. I sensed its explosive energy. . . . The music had not yet started, the liquor had not yet lit its fires, the girls were not yet jouncing around, the boys were not yet making their moves, but there was already the tension of too much cock and not enough pussy in the smokey air. Which way a girl smiled could aim a fist. I figured this was a good place for a skinny stranger to mind the music, watch his step, and keep his hands in plain sight. . . . With my nose in my beer, I counted forty-two fellows and eighteen girls, few of whom seemed to be paired up. Every time the door opened more guys came in, and I guessed the ratio would go to eight to one by midnight, not counting me.

Zeo Zoe felt at ease in the thick of all the men. She enjoyed the odds. Though she began hosting after-hours parties at her home for his friends, it was John she wanted. She gave him presents of clothing, jewelry, and money. Zeo Marksheffel slowly nudged John McNamara west to Reno, Nevada, the mecca for the unhappily married.

Nevada had a monopoly on the quickie divorce business. Its laws, written when it was a mining state with a transient population, were the most lax in the nation. Several high-profile cases spread word of the short-term dissolutions. Divorcées-to-be flocked by the hundreds to Reno every year. Those who could afford it went for the six-month stay at Reno's posh hotels to meet the residency requirements for an easy decree. The governor of Nevada once said he was "ashamed of the reputation borne by Reno," but all those divorce tourists delighted the hotel men, not to mention the lawyers. What shindigs they must have had!

When Nellie McNamara caught wind of her errant husband's rumored trip to Reno, she invoked the full protections that the law then afforded her as his legal wife. In February 1920, she filed a lawsuit against Zeo Marksheffel for alienating John's affections. She sought fifty thousand dollars in damages and hired a premier law firm in Kansas City, Prince & Harris, to represent her. The firm formerly represented Tom Cunningham, so it probably took little effort to convince them of the merits of Nellie's claim. The attorneys wrote a complaint that publicly accused Zeo Wilkins of being a homewrecker. Said Nellie's lawyers:

> The Defendant through wiles and machinations and a wrongful and improper course of conduct, alienated the affections of said John T. McNamara and caused the said John T. McNamara to practically abandon the Plaintiff and to lose affection and regard for the Plaintiff; that the Defendant herein made love to the said John T. McNamara and has gone with him to various places of amusement both in the State of Missouri and outside the State of Missouri.

When Zeo lied and said she was a permanent resident of Colorado, the lawsuit was removed from the county courthouse to the United States District Court in Kansas City. Thus John McNamara's wife literally made a federal case out of his affair with his wanton osteopath.

It wasn't only for show, either. Mrs. McNamara's attorneys slapped subpoenas on Zeo's friends and favorite merchants, on the telephone company, Zeo's laundry man, City Hall, several janitors, an auto livery, and the woman who lived next door to Zeo and Al in Colorado Springs. Mrs. McNamara's lawyers also took the sworn testimony of Zeo at the courthouse, quizzing her at length about her affair with John McNamara.

Zeo's lawyers shot right back. She had much to fear and a good incentive to counterpunch. Unlike Tabitha Taylor, Nellie McNamara had a valid marriage and might actually get a money judgment against her. Zeo hired Judge James Orr in Colorado Springs to mastermind her defense. Orr worked up the file vigorously, interviewing a number of witnesses. Zeo also hired a famous Missouri lawyer named James Alyward, a partner in Frank Walsh's firm. Walsh had moved to New York. She had to pay Walsh & Alyward by the hour, and they did not work cheap. After only a few months of the feminine warfare entitled *McNamara vs. Marksheffel,* Zeo's lawyers billed dozens of hours and thousands of dollars for protecting her assets.

In March 1920, a Hollywood scandal wrecked Zeo's plans. The country's most popular actress, Mary Pickford, shocked the country with a Reno divorce and rapid remarriage to Douglas Fairbanks. It did not hurt their film careers in the least, but the State of Nevada was as embarrassed as a politician caught in a brothel. It temporarily suspended its quickie divorce law. In a fit of righteousness, the attorney general imposed a new requirement of a year's residency. This was far too long for Zeo.

In the meantime Nellie pursued her heart balm lawsuit. In 1921 she filed an amended complaint to add her latest intelligence on her foe's immoral conduct. Mrs. McNamara alleged that Zeo:

has represented on numerous occasions and to numerous parties that the said John T. McNamara was her husband, and to other parties that she and the said John T. McNamara were to become husband and wife if said John T. McNamara could obtain a divorce from the Plaintiff herein. . . . Defendant has entertained [him] by going for long and distant rides over the Boulevards of Jackson County, Missouri, and through the suburbs and summer resorts of the State of Colorado in her costly limousines and gave various parties . . . and further made [him] her confidential advisor with respect to financing large exploitations of oil development and on numerous occasions applied her art and profession as an osteopath and gave treatments and massages to the said John T. McNamara.

Zeo's conduct was "wanton, willful and malicious," Nellie's lawyers concluded as they renewed their demand for fifty thousand dollars in damages. John was becoming an expensive prize.

Zeo bid her lover farewell with a swift kick to his wallet. She tipped off John and several of his friends that a large quantity of bonded liquor was for sale at bargain prices at a house on the south side of Kansas City. McNamara closed the deal for twenty-five thousand dollars in cash. Surely some good old-fashioned Anglo-Saxon cuss words crossed his lips as he opened all those barrels and found nothing but tea. The man who liked to "play wealthy widows" had his comeuppance. Zeo kept nineteen thousand dollars from the deal. Nellie lost interest in her lawsuit in 1922 when John promised to "cease his attentions" to Dr. Wilkins. The reconciliation between the McNamaras was short-lived. Shortly after his affair with Zeo ended, John left his wife again. This time he moved to Chicago and opened a café. He would soon come to need an alibi that solidly placed him far from Kansas City.

12

Someone Will Be Admitting Light into Your Body

I have listened to divorce petitions so long that I am about disgusted with society. I don't know where it will end. Young folks get married with the understanding they can come to court and get divorces as easy as a meal. There seems to be a lack of affection—the basis of happiness.

— *Jackson County, Missouri, Circuit Court Judge Thomas B. Buckner, 1924*

In 1921, Zeo's divorce from Albert was final. She received ten thousand dollars in full settlement of any claims on him or his business. At the age of thirty-six, she was a woman of fading beauty and dissipated wealth. But she remained at heart a gold digger, and gold diggers don't pay their bills. Such tourists overstay their welcome, even in Colorado Springs.

She owed a thousand dollars to the estate of a man she pinched in a car sale. Her jeweler, Herman A. Hamilton, lent her twenty-three thousand dollars in cash and three thousand dollars' worth of diamonds to invest in the oil fields of Paola, Kansas, but the wells were no longer producing.

Zeo was apparently unsuccessful at seducing him into forgiving the debt. Either unable or unwilling to pay the note, she thought of a more straightforward way to deal with it. Zeo called up the jeweler and invited him to her home on Willamette. She told him to bring the mortgage on her oil wells, for she'd found a buyer. He believed her.

Hamilton entered her house. After he let his guard down, he

produced the documents. Zeo then snatched the mortgage out of his hand. As the startled jeweler began to protest, Zeo ran through the house and down the basement steps. She crawled out a basement window and fled. Knowing Hamilton would track her down, she took a train to Chicago and hid out for a while. Herman Hamilton filed a lawsuit against her and vowed to get a judgment.

Zeo's assets became entangled in the litigation. A judge ordered the seizure of the last of Grover Burcham's furniture and put it in storage. A lien was filed on her Cunningham bonds.

Zeo also owed about twelve thousand dollars to James A. Orr, one of her lawyers in the Cunningham, Marksheffel, and McNamara lawsuits. James Orr, by then a judge, took a security interest in her diamonds and then insisted on taking possession of them. Zeo sold the settings before she relinquished her rocks. Arthur Wilkins later said that she paid off that loan. Whether she did or not, it burned her to think about Orr keeping her diamonds.

She called in some muscle. "I marched myself up to his office with a fully loaded .38," Arthur said. "I told him I wanted Doc's jewelry or someone would be admitting light into his body. Judge Orr thanked me for calling and I came home with Doc's goodies." The next man would have to kill her for her box of diamonds.

In an effort to fight the plague of process servers and in obedience to the men who ordered her out of town after the black and tan raid, Zeo sold her home and ranch in 1921 and moved to Kansas City permanently. Her brother Arthur pleaded with her not to do it, but Doc broke her promise to let him live on the ranch for life. After all the petty jobs he'd done for her, "she turned around and kicked us off," Arthur said. "Me, her own blood brother, mind you . . . I was a damn fool." Arthur and Laura were brittle about it, and so was the real estate agent Zeo stiffed for seven thousand dollars.

Since she wanted to have a man around the house and Arthur was livid about the way she treated him, Zeo asked her brother Charlie to take rooms near hers at the Paseo Hotel in Kansas City. She rewarded him with a monthly allowance of three hundred dollars and rewrote her will to make him the primary beneficiary of her estate. But Charlie and Arthur were two different men. Charlie wasn't quite the liberal that Arthur was, and Charlie decided at this late date to try to parent his little sister. He objected to the parties, liquor, and men, men, men. Maybe he found some of the small packets of "white medicine" she stashed in her suite and wondered what they were. He eventually left because Zeo had "too much liquor and men company" around the place. "I returned many times since," he would later say, "but always found more of the same things than when I left."

Her brother Horace also begged her to change her way of life. "One time in 1922," Horace Wilkins said, "when I came [to Kansas City] from Ohio to plead with her, she angered me so I walked from her house disgusted. But when I returned home, I sent her money. I did so on several other occasions."

Horace blamed the liquor and drugs for her crazy lifestyle. What those drugs were exactly, nobody said. Prescription drugs, maybe. Opium, morphine, and cocaine were easy to come by in the circles she traveled; marijuana cigarettes were sold at three for five dollars in speakeasies of the era. Whatever they were, Horace decried her use of them. He loved his sister when she was sweet and kind, he said, but she had an uncontrollable temper. Coupled with her libido, her behavior suggested a cocaine habit.

In 1922, Zeo traveled back to Kirksville, Missouri, for an advanced course in a new osteopathic treatment regime called the Abrams method, which Horace was kind enough to finance in his ongoing effort to lead his sister to the straight and narrow path. She met quite a few men, but she was not the looker she once was, and it was not so easy to trap them. She returned to Kansas City alone.

Then she traveled to Texas for a long visit with her sister, Dr. Gertrude Wilkins-Clements, who was operating a sanitarium in Fort Worth.

Gertrude was a free woman herself by then. Her marriage to Dr. Kibby Clements had ended in divorce. Zeo stayed with Gertrude for eight months. She did not practice medicine while she stayed in Fort Worth. Instead she shocked Gertrude with wild parties and heavy use of liquor and drugs.

Zeo took up with a man by the name of Dr. O. M. McMurtrey, from whom she extracted several hundred dollars. The Fort Worth police became aware of her nocturnal activities, and so did her sister. Gertrude took action to try to save her little sister and made a patient of her, because Gertrude was certain Zeo's drug and alcohol abuse would kill her sooner or later.

Zeo would let no one order her to stay and get treatment. She flew into a terrible rage and swore she would leave the sanitarium at once, even if she had to throw herself out of a window to do it. So that is just what she did. She defenestrated herself.

Gertrude still refused to release her. So Zeo drank poison. On May 19, 1922, Zeo tried to hang herself in a closet with a trunk strap. Gertrude was stubborn, but she was no match for her little sister. Zeo tormented her with suicide attempts. Another time she tried cutting her throat with a broken milk bottle. Did she really want to die? She never inflicted any serious injuries on herself. Maybe she was only hell-bent on getting out of Gertrude's sanitarium.

After witnessing Zeo's many "suicide attempts," Gertrude couldn't take it anymore and called the authorities. The Fort Worth police took Dr. Zeo Wilkins into protective custody at the city jail on order of her older sister. Zeo flailed and screamed and made another "suicide attempt." But they could not hold her forever.

By then nothing could keep her out of a bottle or keep her from wrecking men. Nothing stopped her from practicing scams and seductions. She answered to no authority. Not religion, not the state, not her own conscience, and certainly not her family. No one could heal her neurotic personality. She'd had a good run of luck; her unusual beauty had translated into money and attention for two decades. She was no longer a young beauty. As Dr. Joyce Brothers once remarked, "Frequently, the girl who is certain that diamonds are truly her best friends is unusually attractive physically. The beautiful woman may be spoiled and she may expect more than the plainer girl; she may also be an emotional cripple who sells and lives by her looks. She may feel this is all she has with which to interest men and that she must make this pay well while she can. Exceptionally attractive women are usually very aware that their beauty won't last forever."

In her late thirties, Zeo Wilkins knew she could no longer live by looks and wits alone. She could not imagine growing old. She began to speak often of her demise and said it drew near. Still she refused all advice. Her siblings worried about her. She had set her course for an early death from booze, drugs, or suicide.

Not that Zeo was quite finished living it up. She still had her figure, and she would enjoy her final two years with more sex-maddened men than ever.

19

The Trysting Place

If you want to see some sin, forget about Paris
and go to Kansas City.
— *Omaha World Herald reporter Edward Morrow*

In 1922, Dr. Zeo Zoe Wilkins wobbled on her cloven hooves back to her spiritual home, Kansas City in the jazz age. She decided to rent a house. It had to be furnished, close to downtown, easy to find, near a streetcar line, grand enough to become her station—and it had to have several bedrooms. She found the perfect place for a hundred dollars a month on a corner lot in a quiet, immaculate neighborhood along Park Avenue. She transformed it into a medical clinic, by day anyway. When Zeo wasn't entertaining her own lovers, which left only narrow windows of time, she played the good fellow. During her wild parties, or between them as the case may be, Zeo let her friends commit adultery upstairs—for a fee. She called it her "trysting place."

As soon as she took the keys to 2425 Park, she hired the neighborhood odd-jobs man, a black man by the name of Dillard Davies. He lived a block over from Dr. Wilkins. She had no water service so she sent Dillard with a bucket to the neighbors' house. He returned with the water and a middle-aged couple excited to meet her. Ella Rohrs thought Zeo was "widely known" as the former wife of one of the richest men in the country. George Rohrs was a musician at the Gayety Theatre Orchestra next door to the Muehlebach. Of course he remembered Mrs. Cunningham and the fifty-dollar tips she once paid to hear selections from *The Tales of Hoffman*. Naturally, they were flabbergasted when Dr.

Zeo's trysting place. An arrow points to the window found open after Zeo's murder. (*True Detective Mysteries*)

Wilkins asked for a dollar to pay the water bill. The Rohrs learned that Dr. Wilkins was practicing osteopathy out of her home, but the doctor "didn't work on water," as they said of alcoholics back then. Zeo was intoxicated nearly every time Mrs. Rohrs tried to visit. Mrs. Rohrs often saw Zeo outside at midnight. Dressed in a kimono and house slippers, she walked her big white bulldog. Mrs. Rohrs didn't bother to strike up any late-night conversations.

Zeo became a patron of the neighborhood's tamale peddler. He would briskly push his cart up Park Avenue at the dinner hour until he reached her home. She was so slow in coming out that he took his pipe-smoking break every evening in front of 2425 Park. At one point Dr. Wilkins employed several servants, including two black housemen, a Japanese man, several nurses, and countless maids to keep the sheets changed. Despite appearances, no matter that the expensive cars and taxicabs were arriving at all hours, Dr. Wilkins "often seemed to be without funds," said Mrs. Rohrs. A black girl Zeo employed as a maid came knocking on Mrs. Rohrs's door one day to ask about "that money." The maid explained that Dr. Wilkins said that Mrs. Rohrs would pay her salary. Mrs. Rohrs refused, but Dr. Wilkins later talked the neighbor into paying the maid two dollars. Most of the servants quit in disgust. Several sought help from the city legal aid clinic. One filed a lawsuit against her for eight dollars. Only a woman named Sadie Shields was willing to come by to clean the place and answer the doorbell. Zeo paid her by deeding to her the little house on Tracy Avenue. Dillard Davies also agreed to tend her furnace and keep Dr. Wilkins in liquor for an IOU.

Zeo's supply of lovers, patients, and cash were not enough to feed her appetites, so she contacted some well-known osteopaths in Kansas City. She proposed a space-sharing agreement with John C. Klepinger, D.O., who had an office on 31st Street. Dr. Wilkins showed Dr. Klepinger, who was fifty-three, a new medical device called an Abrams machine, which she bought with a gift from her brother Horace. Dr. Klepinger was interested in the Abrams method and agreed to let her practice out of his office in exchange for training on its use.

Apparently he did not know much about Dr. Abrams's miracle cure for syphilis. That is the affliction Dr. Abrams focused upon in his literature. The ASO graduate called syphilis "the morbid soil" and blamed it for cancer and tuberculosis. With his electrical machine, though, Dr. Abrams promised to induce vibrations that could defeat the disease.

Even by 1923, medical science had debunked the elaborate electrical device called the "Oscilloclast of Abrams." It was coming into disfavor among osteopaths around the time Zeo bought her model and charged exorbitant rates for "electric treatments." A *New York Times* editorial in 1924 summed up the prevailing professional opinion of Zeo's new brand of medicine:

> Of all the charlatans that figure in medical history, not one, probably, tested so nearly to their limits the ignorance of human beings as did the late Dr. Albert Abrams. His grotesquely absurd system of

diagnosis and treatment received not a little serious consideration from people who passed for educated and not a few of them were persons of proved intelligence in other things. Men with a right to write "M.D." after their names have been found in several cities to exploit "electronic reactions Abrams." Whether they believe in them or not is a question to be settled with their own consciences. They are taking fees, and big ones not infrequently, for the application of a method the only possible benefit of which can come for a while from the suggestive power of crude but elaborate electric machinery and the glib use of words that have a scientific sound. The exploiters of his devices . . . all remain . . . quacks of the worst and most imprudent sort.

As he became acquainted with his new partner, Dr. Klepinger wasn't bothered by these questions, nor was he troubled by the amount of money she "borrowed" from him. "I managed to keep even," he said. Dr. Wilkins proved a valuable connection. He thrived on her leftovers. But Zeo talked often of her fear that harm would befall her. Dr. Klepinger thought she was hallucinating. Zeo's brother Charlie frequently stopped by. The siblings were very pleasant to each other in front of Dr. Klepinger. But when her friends came around, she took them into the back room and they got drunk. Dr. Klepinger decided at the end of the summer to terminate their arrangement. "Her habit of drinking was obnoxious to me," he later said. Besides, "her class of patients was widely different from mine. Hers were almost all wealthy. Mine were people of moderate means."

Zeo brought her Abrams machine and several patients to her Park Avenue home. Most were men, though not all. Anna Schultz was one of several regular patients. Mrs. Schultz liked Dr. Wilkins, remarking that the doctor had a "kindly nature," always talked cheerfully while giving treatments, and gave medical care to many who were unable to pay. Dr. Wilkins owned beautiful clothes and showed her finest dresses to Anna while lamenting changes in her fortunes. "I have no friends, and I don't wear these fine things." Anna sympathized with her troubled doctor.

Indeed a lot of women whose lives brought them in touch with Zeo seemed to truly like and admire her, despite a moral failure here or there. Eva Grundy, a middle-aged woman who lived alone in Kansas City and worked as a bookkeeper, was another of the doctor's female devotees. She considered Zeo a close friend. Dr. Wilkins had once tended Eva and saved her from "almost certain death." The larger-than-life osteopath awed the petite, slender Miss Grundy merely by asking her to come around once in a while. "She believed that I was good," Eva said. "She said she was leaving everybody in the old life and didn't want anybody around but new people." Eva believed everything Doc told her.

Zeo eventually made a friend of her neighbor, Ella Rohrs, when her husband was killed on Christmas Day 1923. George Rohrs, the Gayety Theatre musician, came up second in a street fight. He was slugged so hard his neck was broken. Dr. Wilkins paid sympathy calls, and Ella appreciated the gesture.

Zeo also enchanted her landlady, Mrs. Gertrude Palmer. She had to charm her to stave off eviction, for she never paid her rent. Dr. Wilkins insisted for months that she would soon make good on the debt—her considerable wealth was simply a bit tied up at present in Colorado. Zeo told her landlady that she had none other than the mayor of Colorado Springs himself in charge of her assets and affairs there. She claimed she owned forty thousand dollars in diamonds but they were held as security for a twelve thousand-dollar loan she owed to a lawyer in Colorado Springs. Zeo said she owned twelve thousand dollars' worth of furniture in storage at Wandell & Lowe in the same city, plus an interest in her last husband's business and a Cadillac motor car. She mentioned a sanitarium she owned in Texas that was operated by her sister. Mrs. Palmer was also informed that Dr. Wilkins had business connections with two prominent local doctors. One was Dr. Klepinger. The second was an osteopath named Dr. A. F. Blanchard, a classmate from the American School of Osteopathy.

Mrs. Palmer believed these tales of forthcoming funds. She liked Dr. Wilkins, even if she was "a trifle temperamental." She admired Zeo's high intelligence and apparent wealth. It was fun to know "the widow of a millionaire." The landlady was also impressed by her medical career, remarking that Dr. Wilkins "had her heart in her work and could lecture for hours about the Abrams electrical apparatus." She let Zeo slide on the rent. "Why, she once told me when her rent was unpaid, 'Mrs. Palmer, I shouldn't blame you if you would throw me into the street.'" It was enough to bring tears to the eyes.

Once Dr. Wilkins established herself on Park Avenue, she indulged in a number of overlapping love affairs. She ventured far beyond the all-too-common love triangle when, in 1923, she became entangled in a love octagon. Her lovers included Roy Hartman, Dr. Arthur Blanchard, B. F. Tarpley, Gus West, C. C. Selmer, Tom Swearingen, George Mahan, Charles Smith, and, there's reason to believe, Jesse E. James, and perhaps more, many more. They tripped over one another seeking her company and affection. Zeo handed out her sexual favors to acquaintances and patients like a senator handing out medals at a veterans' hospital.

The first lover she took at her trysting place was Roy Hartman, a single man of twenty-one. Roy stayed long enough in 1923 to be called her boarder. For some reason, Zeo called him "little Tommy." She may have been pushing forty, but she could still enthrall a man half her age for months on end. He remained the prince of her boudoir for almost two seasons.

But unattached Roy was the exception. Zeo preferred her lovers married, perhaps because she relished the role of mistress and the enthusiastic sex she gave to long-married older men who had grown bored in their marital beds. She was indiscriminate, collecting a menagerie of men of various talents. One was Tom Swearingen, a grocer. Another was Gus West, described in the press as an "Italian" and rumored to be connected to the Kansas City underworld liquor trade.

In the fall, Dr. Klepinger referred a patient to her to have his rheumatism treated. Benjamin Franklin Tarpley was an assistant yardmaster for the Kansas City terminal. He was forty-seven years old, not that Zeo paid attention to any number without zeroes in it. He was also a broad, blonde man with a handsome face, heavy-lidded blue eyes, and big hands. He liked to drink, attend parties, and have sex in the morning. In September 1923, Ben Tarpley undressed himself, lay down on Zeo's medical table, and was pleasantly surprised to receive more than an osteopathic treatment for his forty dollars.

Soon Ben Tarpley was parking his sedan in her alley six mornings a week and most afternoons. Zeo gave him a key to her house so he could slip into her bed at five to wake her with a quick bout of early morning lovemaking before the start of his six a.m. shift. He did this not occasionally but every morning for months. Zeo continued giving her inexhaustible lover genuine osteopathic treatments, but, after a time, they made arrangements by which Ben would drive her around the city on errands at two dollars per trip in exchange for medical care.

Or at least that's what he told Bessie Tarpley.

In the fall of 1923, Zeo's adventurous lifestyle caught up to her at last. She fell ill. She sought treatment from Dr. Klepinger. His diagnosis: "Too much booze." She sought a second opinion.

Dr. G. A. Droll received a call that a white woman was dying at 2425 Park. When he met her, he thought she was suffering from a high nervous tension. "She seemed dead to the world," he said. "However, her pulse was good, her respiration was normal and her flesh in good condition. No 'dope' indications were noticeable." Dr. Droll realized she was an alcoholic. "I told her she would have to quit drinking. . . . She broke down with emotion when I warned her about it."

"Charlie is a real man and loves me. He can help me," Zeo said.

"Who is Charlie?"

"My brother. He understands. I love him and he will not fail me."

"I suggest that you send for Charlie."

Her brother was then working as an agitator for the IWW in the labor camps near Seattle, where he was trying to recruit lumberjacks to the working man's cause. Charlie dropped everything and hurried back to Kansas City.

Charlie Wilkins found his sister so sick she didn't recognize him. He told Zeo's doctor how she got into such a condition. "Charlie told me the tragic story of the daily drinking, the boon companions at night and the revelry," said Dr. Droll. "'I just can't keep them out,' Charlie said, and he was almost overcome with emotion. 'She has been at it for several months.'"

Dr. Droll gave Dillard Davies a standing order to keep her friends away. But Zeo was not done drinking. She grew angry. She called the police to her home. When the officers arrived, they questioned Davies about crimes she was committing in the Prohibition Era. Davies was forced to answer "a lot of questions about drinking and whether she had been drinking."

As sick as she was, Zeo would not let any man dictate to her, not even her own doctor or her big brother. She tried to carry on as usual. While she was on the telephone with a patient, Charlie grabbed the phone and shouted, "You can't talk to her. She's a fake. She's the widow of a millionaire."

"She had been drinking heavily," Charlie later said. "Dr. G. A. Droll and myself finally prevailed on her to stop drinking. When I obtained her promise, I broke a large bottle of whisky that was in the house. My sister flew into a rage and said she would order more. Then I tore the telephone from the wall to prevent her from doing this. I knew that whisky was killing her."

Somewhere in his travels Charles Wilkins had learned to resort to his hands when dealing with women. When he thought it necessary, he was not above giving a woman a beating. He would slap a woman, choke her, and knock her down, to make a point. He was not above treating his sister that way. Vicious arguments followed as Zeo's health improved. Charlie "disapproved of the company she kept and because of her drinking. I suspected irregularities." He was referring to Ben Tarpley. Her numerous boyfriends highly perturbed her brother, who often behaved like a jealous lover himself. Did she, heavy cocaine user that she apparently was, cross that line as well?

Charlie didn't act like an older brother. He was so upset over her affairs with so many men—Tarpley in particular— that he grew violent. They grew more entangled. The fights continued. She would not stop taking lovers. They also fought over the number of her servants she had, each at a dollar a day. Money was always a touchy subject with Charles Wilkins. During one violent argument, Charlie knocked Zeo to the floor, forced her onto the front porch, and locked the door behind her. She was unable to reenter the house and was forced to sleep on the porch for an entire winter night.

In retaliation, she cut off his allowance. She called a lawyer and dictated a new will from her sickbed. Charlie entered the room as all this was unfolding and argued with her, pounding violently on the bed. At this Zeo's bulldog attacked him and sank his canine teeth into Charlie's leg. Dr. Droll warned Charlie that more of this commotion could kill his sister.

At the height of another protracted argument between brother and sister, Charlie struck and strangled Zeo. Once again she sicced her bulldog on him. Charlie took out his frustrations on the bulldog and later had it poisoned by a vet. Charlie told his sister that Ben Tarpley killed the dog. Zeo was livid about Snip. She told her brother, "If I find he had anything to do with killing my dog, I'll tell something on him."

Zeo confronted Ben Tarpley, who denied having anything to do with Snip's demise. The argument grew ugly. Ben took her key off his key ring, threw it on top of a bookcase, and walked out. Zeo called a cab and went to his home in Kansas City, Kansas. She waited in his driveway until Ben Tarpley came out to the car. There they had a conversation that must have turned the cabbie's ears red. Zeo threatened to tell Ben's wife of their affair at that very moment unless he submitted to her at once. Tarpley had no choice. He returned with Zeo to her home and couldn't leave until she was placated.

Their fight must have pleased her brother, but Charlie wasn't entirely satisfied. He also tried to get rid of Dillard Davies. Charlie grew to hate Zeo's odd-jobs man because Zeo told him that Dillard had "attempted an attack" on her. Perhaps Charlie believed her. He may even have suspected his sister of being capable of consenting to a sexual relationship which, in that time and place, would have raised more than an eyebrow; under certain circumstances it might have raised a posse. Charlie warned Davies never to return to the house and made it clear that if he did he'd be arrested. Zeo learned what her brother had done and flew into a rage, declaring that she would "run my own house," and recalled Davies to work for her, mystifying her brother.

Despite their strange and sometimes violent arguments, Zeo and Charlie remained curiously close. She wanted him nearby. She trusted him. She needed him for protection. He might have been the one who gave her a tabby cat to make up for the loss of Snip. "Wilkins thought the world of his sister," one friend said. Charlie frequently talked about her beauty. Charlie's friend said he once overheard Charlie tell Zeo she was "the only person in the world that he cared about, because she was the only person that seemed to care about him."

Around this time, Zeo's brother wrote a letter inviting a friend to visit Kansas City because he thought his friend's asthma would benefit from Zeo's Abrams treatments. The friend was Charles Smith, a prospector and a drifter, a bindle stiff who had worked in lumber and mining camps with Charlie Wilkins. He arrived on February 11, 1924. "When I got there," Smith said, "he said he did not know what was going on there or he would have stopped me from coming. He said that he had tried to stop me, but failed to reach me. He told me of the wild parties that were going on . . . how he had protested against them, but in vain. . . . One night after I got there, a gay party was in progress and Wilkins went in and chased all the guests out. He later told his sister he thought she was going too far and asked her to stop it."

Zeo charged Smith a hundred and fifty dollars for treatments. On the second day of her ministrations, Smith remained in the home all night for a particularly vigorous session. Zeo asked him to stay. After four days Charlie Wilkins expressed his disgust with both of them. He ordered his friend to leave. Zeo became angry and they had what Charlie called a "squabble." When Ben Tarpley showed up, she managed to separate her lovers before they hurt one another. There wasn't enough room in her bed for this many men. She made her brother and Charles Smith leave the house.

But later, they returned. Charles Smith declared that the Abrams method didn't help his asthma, and he'd had his fill of Zeo. He wanted to go back to Denver. In view of the fact he had spent considerable money making the trip to Kansas City, he went back to Zeo's home with her brother to ask for a refund. Zeo refused. The argument escalated. She tried to "rush" both Smith and her brother from the house. In response, Charlie "pushed" her, and "she fell," as Charlie Wilkins would later begrudgingly admit.

The incident scared Zeo. She called several of her friends and lovers and told them she was frightened of Charlie and Charles Smith. She complained about the loss of her bulldog Snip, her best friend. She knew by then that Charles had had the dog killed. She cried to her young lover Roy Hartman that her brother and his friend had threatened to kill her.

She called her friend Otis Green, an auto garage manager, on February 24 and told him that her degenerate brother and his ruffian friend took a hundred and fifty dollars from her the night before and both carried revolvers. She claimed to be terrified of her brother. She summoned Otis to her home again on Sunday, March 2.

Zeo unbuttoned her dress to show Otis the bruises her brother had inflicted on her. "He came to my house yesterday and beat me black and blue," she told him. "He almost killed me yesterday and I'm afraid he will. I don't know what I am going to do."

Green no doubt did what he could to make her feel better. He also offered to talk to a friend on the Kansas City police force. He reported back to Zeo that she ought to have her brother arrested. But she refused to do it.

She then called her occasional lover Tom Swearingen. "She was very excited and told of having trouble with her brother Charlie and a man named Smith," he said. The brutes had threatened her, and she was in fear for her life. "I have to make some changes here because I'm in trouble," she told him. By then she'd already cashed in the life insurance policy she bought for her adopted nephew. It was time now to cash in her diamonds and bonds and try to do something else with herself. She spoke of giving up her home and moving to a hotel.

She also called her friend Gus West on February 25. "What shall I do? I am going to get killed." She was crying. She asked him to refer her to a lawyer, saying her brother would not "let anyone come around the house." West told her about a man he knew and arranged an appointment for her. The lawyer was Jesse James Jr.

What on earth was Zeo thinking when she lifted her hand to knock on the office door of Jesse James, Attorney at Law? Had she known a thing about the only surviving son of the world's most famous bank robber, she might have found another lawyer—one not so well versed in outlawry.

But maybe that's what appealed to her.

Part II

THE SON OF
JESSE JAMES

14

Tim Howard's Real Name

I found one of those cheap novels about me and Jesse. There
is no truth in them, and they should not be sold to young boys
of today. We will not let our son Robbie read them. The one I
found was about us robbing a train. It is sickening to read how
Dingus [Jesse W. James] bragged about what he had done. I
never heard Jess ever brag about who he was or what he did.
— *Frank James*

Little Tim Howard thought that everyone's daddy kept a loaded
shotgun in the closet, disguised a Winchester rifle in his umbrella,
and carried on his person at all times a loaded Colt .45 revolver, a loaded
Schofield .45, and extra ammunition. "My father was always heavily
armed," Tim would later explain. "He told me that all men went armed
the same way. I thought that was true, because all the men I ever saw
at our home were as heavily armed as he." Tim also thought it normal
for a family to move often, under cover of darkness, from one home to
another, from one state to another, while Papa hid in the furniture-filled
wagon. He thought it normal for a father to be gone for weeks, even
months at a time. The absences meant tearful departures, but Daddy's
rare visits home were memorable occasions of surprise and joy. Tim was
thrilled by the hugs he received when his father returned from one of
his long rides.

On Christmas Eve 1881, following yet another move to a new home,
Tim's father disguised himself as Santa Claus and pounded on the door.
Tim and his sister were delighted to swear themselves good children
and dig into the bag of presents. As soon as Tim felt a Smith & Wesson

at the bottom of the bag, however, he knew Santa was really Daddy in disguise.

Tim's father was tall, rather heavily built, and "very kind," Tim said. "I remember best his good-humored pranks, his fun making and his playing with me." His father liked to strap his revolvers around his son's waist "and would say that I was Jesse James."

Tim's father took the boy on long horseback rides into the countryside with Tim clinging to the mane with both hands. "I recall very distinctly," Tim said, "that on one of these trips he sat me up on top of a rail fence, where I hung on by the stakes, and then he rode away and showed me how he used to charge the enemy when he was a soldier under Quantrell. With the bridle rein in his teeth, and an unloaded revolver in each hand snapping the triggers rapidly, he charged toward me on the gallop, and I thought it was great fun." Papa also read to Tim from newspaper articles about Missouri's famous bandits. "My father used to hold me on his lap and talk a great deal to me about his adventures in the war. He used to talk about the James boys, and would read to me the accounts of their adventures that were published in the newspapers . . . once he showed me a picture of one of the members of the guerilla band who was living then, and said laughingly, that he has a good long neck to hang by."

On April 3, 1882, the remains of breakfast sat on the family's kitchen table at their hilltop home on Lafayette Street in St. Joseph, Missouri. As his mother cleaned up the breakfast table, six-year-old Tim Howard played with a coffee grinder.

The gun blast must have been deafening in the small house.

The boy ran to the sound. In the parlor, Tim's father lay on the floor. Blood poured from his head. Tim's mother began screaming, and his little sister cried. Tim watched his father die in his mother's arms.

Then the policemen came, the news got out, and the crowds gathered dozens of people, hundreds of people, whispering and shouting. Little Tim kept hearing the same name: Jesse James, Jesse James.

That's how the little boy learned his real name was not Tim Howard. His father wasn't John Davis Howard or Thomas Howard. His dead father was in fact the hero of all the cheap blood-and-thunder paperbacks the man had relished reading to the boy for years. His father was Jesse James.

He was overcome with what he described as a "great anger." The child lugged his father's loaded shotgun from the closet and tried to aim it at the people standing outside the house. His mother wrested the shotgun away from him.

At six years old, Tim's world was shattered. With a single blast, he lost his father, his security, and his very identity. He would always recall it as vividly as if it just happened. For now and forever he would be known as the only surviving son of the world's most infamous outlaw.

Jesse Woodson James was raised in an antebellum Missouri household that included several slave children (bought one at a time, young and cheap; grown, like wheat, and sold). He was a teenager when the war broke out. As the proud son of slave owners, he joined a group of paramilitary guerillas known as bushwhackers. He followed his brother Frank into the service of a Southern guerilla leader named William Clarke Quantrill (which the James family always spelled as Quantrell). The terrorist led attacks on Union troops and pro-Union civilians as well as a murderous raid on the town of Lawrence, Kansas. Quantrill also led his irregulars against what Jesse James's son called "marauding bands" of abolitionists who committed "atrocities" against "people of Southern sympathies."

For that, Jesse James was more than a murderous thug to some. He was a symbol of political resistance, a point of pride, the "incarnation of the black spirit of revenge." To the lower Midwest in the late nineteenth century, a civilization that suffered indescribable cruelty during the Civil War, Jesse James was a Confederate hero both before and long

Jesse James Jr. plays his father in a 1921 movie about the elder Jame's life. (*Missouri Valley Special Collections, Kansas City Public Library, Kansas City, Missouri*)

after the South rang the knell for him. If you reduced his war career to its cultural essence, he was an icy salve for the burning heat of a humiliating defeat.

When the bloodshed finally ended in the Confederacy's disfavor, Jesse and his brother Frank embarked on a multiyear armed robbery spree, murdering and maiming those who dared to stand up to them, employing the tactics they'd learned in guerilla resistance. These violent crimes made Jesse James world-famous. After the Civil War, private corporations held strong sway over political and financial affairs. Class tensions ran high. Jesse James hit back at the corrupt federal government and unregulated railroads. In the words of sympathetic biographer Homer Croy, the railroad barons "could shake the contents of a farmer's pocketbook into their own private grain-sacks" and the unregulated banks "could charge any old rate of interest they wanted." Said the oft-quoted Harry S. Truman: "Jesse James was not actually a bad man at heart. I have studied his life carefully, and I come from his part of the country. Jesse James was a modern-day Robin Hood. He stole from the rich and gave to the poor, which, in general, is not a bad policy." To this day Jesse James represents every man who was ever knocked down or lied to, every man who ever felt the boot of the Man on his neck.

But Truman told a whitewashed version of the real man's criminal career, and everyone in Missouri knew that the James brothers had shed much innocent blood. Their war record included the murder of unarmed men and boys and the massacre of wounded soldiers. The name Jesse James alternately thrilled and terrified the Midwest for nearly two decades. Over those bloody years armed gangs pointed their pistols in the faces of dozens of train passengers embarking on new lives in the West and relieved them of their savings. Their victims stood abandoned of hope, shaking with sobs in train stations throughout the Midwest as they gave interviews to excited newspaper reporters. The banks the Jameses robbed were not insured. It was depositors, rich and poor alike, who were left to suffer. Even today it is impossible to say exactly how many people Jesse James maimed or killed during the war, how many victims he shot down during his robberies, how many women he widowed, how many children he orphaned, how many lives he laid waste; the numbers were considerable. Naturally enough, many quarters of Missouri harbored more than a bit of ill will toward the "romantic terrorist."

Even accounting for splitting the loot with other members of the gang, historians agree that Jesse James made off with tens of thousands of dollars over the course of his sixteen years of postbellum outlawry. The accumulated booty from an untold number of criminal adventures should have been enough to set his family up for life. But Jesse James never let any of the gold or paper money or bonds accumulate. An honest review of his life suggests that whatever money he didn't drink or spend on fast horses was pissed away at racetracks and card tables.

Several generations would suffer because of his crimes and the holes in his pockets. During the war the James family was targeted, beaten, arrested, and even deported from the state for a time. Later the manhunt for the infamous robber gang brought Pinkerton detectives to the James farm, where they lobbed an incendiary device into the kitchen, killing Jesse W. James's eight-year-old half brother Archie and shearing off the right hand of his mother Zerelda. Ultimately his crimes culminated in his murder, and he left a penniless young widow and two little children to muddle through the rest of their lives without a father. Jesse James made no provision whatsoever for his family in the event of his imprisonment, execution, lynching, or murder: no savings, no home, no farm, no land. The fabled generosity of Missouri's Robin Hood did not extend to his own wife and children. When the outlaw met his inevitable end, his wife, son, and daughter were left with nothing but his reputation and his guns.

The reaction of little Jesse's mother Zerelda only worsened an already terrible state of affairs. Jesse James Jr.'s mother and grandmother shared the same unusual first name because they were aunt and niece; Jesse Jr.'s parents were first cousins (it was not yet illegal in Missouri for first cousins to marry). The younger woman, called Zee James, moved to Kansas City shortly after she became a widow. Her husband's murder devastated her. She had no family to fall back on; her mother never spoke to her again after she married a notorious fugitive. Zee donned black and never changed out of it. She never remarried. She became a recluse, ultimately rendering herself bedridden with a grief that never healed.

Managing her eldest child was beyond Zee James's abilities. Months after his father's murder, when young Jesse was seven years old, a man who made the mistake of touching the outlaw's pistols in front of the boy saw a flash of what one newspaper would deem "the vicious temperament he has inherited." Zee James, fearing her late husband's pistols would be stolen, had decided to entrust them to her attorney. The man came to her home to take them. Within days the newspapers were telling his story:

> The pistols were lying on a table, and Col. Haire picked one of them up, whereupon young Jesse, in a rage, sprang forward and snatched up one of the pistols, at the same time exclaiming: "No, you won't take these pistols; they belong to my papa." Col. Haire paid no attention to the boy, but started to put the pistol he held in his pocket. The boy quickly cocked the one he held and snapped it directly at Col. Haire's head, so that had it been loaded his murder would have been certain. Discovering that it was not loaded, the boy ran to a bag containing cartridges, fully intent on shooting the Colonel. Interference prevented, but the will and determination of young Jesse were clearly demonstrated.

Jesse endured another test of character when he was seven years old. In Kansas City, in the spring of 1883, a year after his father's murder, he held the hand of his grandmother as they walked down Main Street. Jesse saw a familiar face approach. It was Charlie Ford.

After Robert Ford (with his brother Charlie's complicity) murdered Jesse James, the Ford boys were arrested and indicted for first-degree murder. They appeared in the Buchanan County courthouse in St. Joseph on April 17, 1882, which the *New York Times* noted was "thronged to suffocation." Wearing expressions of nonchalance, they pleaded guilty to the act of shooting an unarmed man from behind while his wife and tender-aged children were in the next room. Judge William H. Sherman sentenced the pair of them to hang by the neck until they were dead. Their executions were scheduled for the following month. But they cheated the hangman. The governor granted unconditional pardons to both men the next day. Robert Ford went west, where he was eventually murdered in Colorado. Charlie Ford had gone to Kansas City.

When Jesse Jr. saw Ford walking down the street, "I knew [him] the instant I saw him." He told his grandmother, "Here comes the man who killed my father."

The sight of Charlie Ford made Zerelda Samuel weak in the knees. She sat down in front of a shoe store. She remembered Ford; he visited the James farm ten days before the murder. Ford tried to walk by them, but Mrs. Samuel called out, "You don't know me, Charlie?" They had a conversation that Jesse Jr., watching in silence, would never forget.

"Yes, I know you. You are Mrs. Samuels [*sic*]."

"Yes, and you killed my brave boy; you murdered him for money. I ought to kill you."

"Mrs. Samuels, don't say that. If you only knew what I am suffering, you wouldn't talk to me that way."

"And what have you made me and mine suffer?"

"Mrs. Samuels, I have been in the blackest hell of remorse ever since it was done. But I didn't kill him. It was Bob [who] did it."

"Yes, and you knew Bob intended to do it when you brought him to my house. You ate bread under my roof with blackest murder in your heart, and murder for money, too. There will come a day of terrible reckoning for you."

Charlie Ford pleaded ignorance. He pleaded his never-ending agonies. Jesse noticed that "the perspiration streamed down his face and there were tears in his eyes. He begged my grandmother to forgive him and she said: 'If God can forgive you, I will.'" A conditional pardon was all she could muster.

Ford did not address any pleas for forgiveness to the boy. As Ford walked away from them, Jesse made a promise to his grandmother: "If I ever grow up to be a man I'm going to kill him."

This probably pleased Mrs. Samuel. She told her grandson that "God will never let an ornery man like that live until then." And indeed she was right. The following spring, Charlie Ford committed suicide.

After his father's death, Jesse Edwards James attended school for the first time. A classmate described him as a good boy and a good scholar. One would imagine that he loved school, that he found himself the son of a legend, the hero of a group of kids who, like the young Harry Truman, were punished for reading Jesse James dime novels at school. One imagines Jesse hunched in the school play yard in a tight circle telling stories of his father's skill with pistols, calling the hated detectives Pinks.

As a child, Jesse memorized all the stories he could lay hands on about train robbers. "He is said to know more about the train robberies of the past than anyone in the country," one account said. "He can tell the time and place of the principal 'hold ups,' and the names of the participants in them." He became "perfectly familiar with the exploits of his father, the places and dates of which he can rattle off as readily as his a, b, c's. His mind is stored with the history of the James and Younger brothers." He kept a huge scrapbook containing virtually everything ever written about his father. He was "not only familiar with every detail of his father's life, but he is also familiar with the history of every other outlaw that ever existed, and he can talk as glibly about the daring deeds of Robin Hood and other bandits of ye olden time as he can about the more recent exploits of the Younger boys and Jim Cummings. . . . To those who happen to know his identity the son of the famous outlaw is an object of great curiosity, and among the boys of the city he is regarded with awe, and wherever he goes young Jesse always commands their respectful homage."

But he was needed at home. His mother took in some sewing work, but it was not enough to meet their expenses. The extended James family could not or would not help the widow and her children. Jesse left school at age eleven or twelve to support his mother and sister. He took to the streets of Kansas City, where he started his working life as a bootblack and elevator boy. He was soon anxious for better work. One Sunday he saw an interesting classified:

> Wanted—An office boy. T. T. Crittenden, Jr.

It was a familiar name. The man who placed the ad was the son of former Missouri Governor Thomas T. Crittenden. Governor Crittenden was the man who worked out a closed-door deal with the Ford boys for the downfall of Missouri's worst criminal, the governor who proclaimed that the James Gang brought only disgrace and injury to the state of Missouri and deserved to die, the governor who counted as the largest achievement of his administration the ignominious death of Jesse James.

One can only picture the reaction of the son of Governor Crittenden when he learned the identity of the orphan who appeared in his place of business to apply for work. By one account Jesse offered to fistfight the other applicants. His name alone was enough to get him the job. The junior Crittenden said he could have the position if his mother and grandmother said yes.

To Crittenden's surprise, they did. Five years after Jesse James met a felon's end, the son of the governor hired the son of the outlaw to be his office boy. Crittenden even promised little Jesse's mother that he would "take the greatest personal interest in starting him right, and as long as I live he shall not want for a friend, if he conducts himself as he should."

About a month into his clerkship, Jesse got into an argument in the office with a boy who had followed him in from the street. Crittenden heard the commotion and asked Jesse to explain. Jesse said the boy wanted an orange he bought on the street corner. "I wouldn't care if he had asked me for it in the right way," Jesse said, "but he can't *make* me give him any orange."

"Well, you know what to do with him, don't you?" Crittenden said.

At that, Jesse decked the boy hard enough to knock him to the foot of the stairs.

Fortunately his employer was tolerant of such behavior. As further atonement, the junior Crittenden sold Mrs. James a tiny lot in Kansas City and fronted the money to build a small home. With his family clinging to a subsistence level, Jesse returned to school, but continued working at Crittenden's office on school breaks. Eventually, he left high school to support his family, all while keeping up payments on the house and studying in the evening under his mother's tutelage.

The public never lost interest in the outlaw's namesake. Many were curious to see where life would take him, whether he would reinforce and honor the legend. "With his inherited bent of mind," said the *Chicago Herald,* "and precocious interest in crime, he promises to rival his illustrious father, and it is not to be wondered at that he is regarded with great pride and hope by the latter's admirers."

Every so often, a newspaper reporter would call on Jesse. Occasionally he was asked to recite from memory his knowledge of train robbers. When a Missouri Pacific train was held up in 1890, Jesse told a reporter that the job was the "work of amateurs." Several journalists wrote profiles of the son of the desperado, like this widely circulated piece:

Jesse James, son of the famous outlaw of Missouri, is now a grown up young man who works for Armour Packing Company at Kansas City. He is now 20 years of age. He lives at 3402 Tracy Avenue, and the neighbors regard him as a model young man. He is honest, sober, and industrious.

Jesse James Jr. rides a bicycle to and from work. His friends call him Tim. He supports his mother and sister, and by his industry and frugality has just succeeded in paying for their modest little home, which is a story and a half frame building, with a porch running along one side. His employers have only good words for Jesse James Jr. and his fellow workmen all speak of him in the highest terms.

It was the *Boston Herald* that secured the interview of the year through young Jesse. In 1897, a correspondent convinced Jesse to take him on a tour of the James farm. The *Herald* probably paid the junior James to arrange a rare interview with Zerelda Samuel. In that day the *Herald* had a large budget for (and no qualms about) such expenses. It was a rare treat for the reporter. Zerelda Samuel charged visitors a quarter to look at her house, but she never talked to reporters for longer than one incendiary outburst. She boasted that she could tell a federal sympathizer on sight. A young lady from Kansas City who was touring the James farm once had the temerity to ask Zerelda Samuel for a drink of water. She replied, "There's a well full of it, back of the house. You freed my niggers and I've had to wait on myself since then. You can wait on yourself if you want a drink."

Perhaps James and the reporter were both nervous on the ride to Kearney. As they left the outskirts of Kansas City, they entered the Cracker Neck District, as eastern Jackson County was called, a place of sharply rolling hills and wavy horizons. Farm fields and scattered clumps of trees met the eye in each direction. The houses were far-flung and set far back from roads that seemed to meander down the section lines. Had he made the trek on his own, the reporter might have discovered that it was a challenge to find the place, as did some of the lawmen who had once hunted rebels across fields so bare of landmarks that they begin to seem after a time like green sand dunes in a vast, featureless landscape.

The James homestead, like the neighboring homes, was set far back from its frontage. For as many amazing events as took place in and around the house, it was an unimposing structure comprised of two small rooms. The house had long ago been stripped of antiques. Virtually every relic connected to the James family was sold at a premium.

Following his introduction by Jesse Jr., the man from the *Boston Herald* sat on the porch to interview Zerelda Samuel. For hours, he recorded the gut-wrenching stories she told: the death of her son Archie, the loss of her hand, the many times her home had been raided by federals, later by Pinkertons, and how her sons were driven to out-lawry. During her lamentations, the journalist looked over at Jesse Jr. and saw him brush away tears. Jesse knelt at her feet and said, "Tell us about that bomb-throwing again, Grandma."

The public couldn't help but sympathize with the young man and the rest of the family. He was, in many ways, another of his father's victims. The press had only kind and gentle things to say about him. They did not know what effect their fawning would have on him, but they would realize it soon enough.

The platitudes lasted until Jesse James Jr. decided to resurrect his father's role in a real armed robbery, a bold crime that sounded a polit-ical roar throughout the state and goaded the papers into two-inch head-lines such as UP TO HIS PA'S OLD TRICKS.

15

A Good Reputation Except in Police Circles

The fascination that a bold criminal exerts over some women is the same as that exercised by the soldier. Women love such men as a tribute to valor or the appearance of valor.
— The Ogden City Standard-Examiner

The county courthouse in Kansas City was the setting for extraordinary events in the city's history and in the lives of its residents. Like all county courthouses, it was the place where crimes were adjudged, business disputes settled, and marriages dissolved. Its visitors represented the extremes of the city's social strata: on the one end, judges and lawyers; on the other, private citizens whose appearances at the courthouse were strictly involuntary. Into their midst strode Jesse James Jr., a hard-working young man who succeeded in obtaining a cushy patronage job running a cigar stand inside the courthouse. Shortly after paying off the note on the family home, young Jesse (over his mother's objection) went into business as the exclusive distributor of the "Jesse James cigar." His father had been known to enjoy a good cigar. The robber's son made money from "many a sedate American [who] found thrills when he stepped to the counter for a 'Jesse James Five Cent Cigar.'" Yet the name meant so much in certain quarters that some critics thought it "almost a desecration that his name should be commercially perpetuated on a cheap cigar." Even so, Jesse sold tobacco in the courthouse to the curious of all stripes. Some men fawned over him and lauded his father. Even those who didn't smoke would buy a cigar from the outlaw's son just to say they did.

His father became a daily subject of conversation at the cigar stand, and Jesse was often drawn into the dialogue. His observations were studies in understatement. Jesse Edwards James had devoured every word of the highly romanticized version of his father's exploits heralded in *Noted Guerillas* by John Newman Edwards, the journalist for whom he was named. Jesse regurgitated Edwards's propaganda to anyone who asked. He often expressed his earnest opinion that the multiple murderer who fathered him had many "lovable and noble traits" and wasn't nearly the evil man some made him out to be. "No one has ever, to my knowledge, accused him of cowardice or of breaking his word," Jesse declared. "I defy the world to show that he ever slew a human being except in the protection of his own life, or as a soldier in honorable warfare." He also dickered with some of his father's biographers, saying that members of the James "band" were blamed for far more crimes and deaths than they could possibly have committed.

Perhaps that's one reason why Jesse took particular interest in the train robbery trials held just a few feet from his cigar stand. One of the most notorious bandits of the day was John F. Kennedy, a locomotive engineer from the Cracker Neck district who was repeatedly charged with train robbery. The region had been steadily plagued with the crime since the James Gang perfected the bloody art. Popular legends of train robber heroes like Jesse James spurred on many a young man to pirate the steel rivers. Some cross-country travelers were so terrified by the thought of entering Missouri that they went hundreds of miles out of their way to avoid it. State officials, infuriated by the violence, financial losses, and depressive effect on immigration and commerce, decided to get tough on train robbers.

Kansas City itched to hang Jack Kennedy, a known bandit. The authorities vowed to put him on trial until they got a prosecution verdict. Jesse James Jr. was a "strict attendant" at Kennedy's many trials.

He attended with a mutual friend named Bill Lowe. Lowe was from St. Louis. His brother had been christened James Jesse Lowe. Bill was happy to take up with the real namesake.

Jesse's friendships kept him inside the courtroom for a time. Two separate juries acquitted Kennedy of train robbery. He was also suspected of killing a woman during a grocery store stickup, but it seems the only witness to that particular robbery and murder was the victim.

During Kennedy's third train robbery trial, Jesse James Jr. decided to take the witness stand to testify for the defense. In a move that made front-page news from coast to coast, James provided a critical alibi for Kennedy. He called himself a friend of the accused woman-killer and armed robber. "I don't give a damn who knows it," he testified. "I don't care what the police suspect. I know where I was that night, and so do they. They can suspect all they damn please, for all I care."

When a third jury let Kennedy off, the newspapers vented the public's general frustration, quipping that he "was as free as the Kansas breezes that blow upon the hills." The press openly accused the defense of bribing the jury. Sharp-eyed reporters claimed to have seen a wink and a nod from jurors during the trial, though nothing was ever proven.

The Kennedy connection didn't seem to hurt the image of twenty-three-year-old Jesse James Jr. At his cigar stand, he made fast friends of many lawyers, judges, and political leaders. He enjoyed a good reputation "except in police circles." Through hard work, Jesse supported his mother and sister in the little house on Tracy Avenue, but the family was still mired in want. His mother was finally reduced to offering precious family mementoes for sale, remarking that "I am not in good circumstances and a little money would greatly assist me." Jesse was working so hard he couldn't sleep. As they put more water in the soup, he struggled under the pressure of running his business and being the head of the perennially impoverished James household.

Then on the night of September 23, 1898, shortly after another of Kennedy's acquittals, an explosion rocked Jesse. Literally. A few miles from his home, a gang of train robbers blew up the safe aboard Missouri Pacific Train No. 5 at a place called Belt Line Junction in Leeds, Missouri, just outside Kansas City. The blast was felt for miles. Six robbers had the audacity to board the train and man the engine themselves. They detached it from the rest of the cars, drove it a mile farther on the track, and blew up the safe. But they used too much dynamite and reduced the contents to atoms. The most generous report of their haul pegged it at thirty silver dollars.

The police department assigned twenty-six detectives to the case, but they weren't needed. According to some accounts, one of the half-dozen robbers had a soft spot, and he told his wife the details of the caper. She blabbed to a neighbor, and, in the natural progression of such things, William W. Lowe found himself in a police interrogation room.

Bill Lowe, who'd worked as a railroad man for years, insisted that he was "only joking" with his wife. But he had letters in his possession from Jack Kennedy and Jesse James Jr. detailing their plans to commit the robbery. The man had kept them as souvenirs, evincing a lack of judgment appalling in an accomplice.

He remained silent for days on end. He'd made a pact to stand or fall with his comrades no matter what happened during that robbery, but, after two weeks in detention, Bill Lowe finally grew tired of waiting for his friends to send a lawyer. He confessed to the crime and implicated Kennedy and James as the leaders in the heist. Lowe corroborated the story of a passenger on the train who had a confrontation with Jesse and could identify him, because Jesse's black kerchief kept slipping off his face during the robbery. Lowe also confirmed the rumors of jury bribery in Kennedy's earlier trials. With Lowe's confession echoing in their heads, the police came to Jesse's cigar stand in the courthouse and arrested him (or "kidnapped" him, per his supporters). James was described as "much surprised."

Police Chief John Hayes declared that they had enough evidence to convict Jesse James of train robbery. In his confession, Bill Lowe had stated that Jesse entered the express car and took a principal part in the robbery. Chief Hayes described a note signed "Jesse James" that appointed a place to rendezvous.

Almost every detail of Lowe's statement was corroborated. The police declared themselves ready to show that James's "respectable associations" were only one part of his life, and that he kept in touch with Kennedy, Bill Lowe, "the brothers Milton," and other characters "not above suspicion." The papers quoted Chief Hayes, who declared that James had committed several escapades "in a disreputable quarter of the city." This would be the quarter that featured an abundance of liquor and houses of ill fame.

James was defiant. "Let me tell you," he said, "I don't give a damn for Chief Hayes." He insisted that he was being persecuted in the way his father was. He branded the robbery charge a conspiracy "hatched in the brains of detectives . . . to pay off old scores that the detective fraternity had against the James family for years past." Within days of his "kidnapping," he found himself indicted by a grand jury along with Lowe, Kennedy, and three other men for the charge of train robbery, a hanging offense.

The newsmen went wild. SON OF THE FAMOUS BANDIT OF OTHER DAYS THOUGHT TO BE GUILTY OF TRAIN ROBBERY, said one paper. THOUGHT TO BE UP TO HIS PA'S OLD TRICKS, another headline read. CHIP OF [*sic*] THE OLD BLOCK, declared another.

One newspaper in Illinois opined that the arrest of the outlaw's son AFFORDS A STUDY IN HEREDITY. His trial for robbery "will decide the question whether from his desperado father or his vindictive hate-cherishing grandmother, Mrs. Samuels [*sic*], young James has inherited those traits which lead men to defy the laws and indulge in careers of crime and recklessness." Jesse was "following in his father's footsteps," said a Wisconsin journal, "and he is proud of it. He recently had a picture taken standing by his father's grave, with a large handkerchief in his hand."

The bad publicity devastated the James family. "What terrible lies have been told and written about me and mine," said Jesse's grandmother, Zerelda Samuel. "I don't suppose there was ever a family so lied about as mine has been." His mother Zee also took the accusation hard, and it damaged her already poor health. The Crittendens and other close friends of the family expressed a concern that Jesse's "vanity" had got the better of him. A letter to his Uncle Frank decried Jesse's decision to subject himself to "such malign influences . . . he seems to imagine that such notoriety and distinction as these little attentions give him magnify his importance; and he is not old nor reflective enough to understand that the beautiful and attractive fruit they are offering him is nothing but bitterness in the eating. . . . His mind, which is bright and his sprits which are abounding, ought to be directed into channels which would carry him as far as possible from all the sad memories of the past, with their mildew and canker."

But the past was unavoidable. Wherever he went, Jesse had a crowd at his heel. "Jesse smiles frequently when he talks," one reporter wryly observed. The local papers, curiously enough, did not share the sentiment. Said one dispirited editorial: "Much of the sympathy showered upon young James, in spite of the gravity of the crime with which he is charged and the evidence against him, is of that sort that fills the cells of wife murderers with tube-roses and sends jelly cake to a man that is going to be hanged. It is maudlin, and one need not expect to find reason in it."

In the meantime, out on bail, Jesse kept selling tobacco to the curious that surrounded him all day. As more newspapers circulated the story, the crowds grew. Many attorneys offered their services for free. Jesse employed several, including Frank P. Walsh, one of the best trial lawyers in Kansas City's history and a noted voice for civic reform. Walsh was happy to take on such a high-profile case against his arch-nemesis, a lawyer who was undefeated in the courtroom, whose name alone was "a terror to evil doers," Prosecutor James Alexander Reed.

At that point a curious thing occurred, and it could only have occurred in Missouri. Many farmers and citizens of Jackson County, once the stomping grounds of the daredevil Jesse James, had despised his lawlessness, but at the same time, as a newspaper in Chicago would try to explain to its readers, "they admired his daring and recklessness and believed that he had been almost as much sinned against as sinning." The public experienced a collective déjà vu. They rallied to the defense of their hero's son. People came to the cigar stand to pay "strange homage" to Jesse James, shaking his hand, touching his coat, and pressing flowers into his arms. He sold cigars "about as fast as he can hand them out." Girls showed up at closing time to flirt with him.

Even though public opinion surged in favor of the bandit's son, the prosecutor, James Reed, refused to drop the charges. But before the trial could start, the strange case against James took another Kansas City twist. The city of 160,000 was "fairly divided" on James's guilt. The trial was to begin a mere two weeks before an election. Several local politicians put licked fingers to the wind and took up Jesse's popular cause. Some of the most prominent lawyers, judges, and politicians in the county spoke in his defense, including the Crittenden family. They declared Jesse's warrantless arrest "a damnable outrage." Most happened to be Democrats. The Republican Party took exception. Kansas City was soon deep in political mud and about to undergo one of the strangest electoral battles in its already extraordinary political history. Jesse James Jr., and the old tensions his name conjured, was at the heart of it.

Fixed elections were familiar to a town notorious for corruption, furious public debate, and deep divisions between entrenched interests, particularly on issues of race. As observers accurately summed up the Kansas City model of democracy at the time:

> Politics in both the city and county was dominated by a criminal gang, assured of immunity from punishment. Public officers charged with the enforcement of the law were in visible alliance

with lawbreakers. Protected gambling was notorious. The fee system was in full force and was used for the wholesale blackmailing of members of the underworld. Elections were in charge of men who were absolute tools of the gang. False registrations were by [the] thousands, and the names of more than a thousand well-known citizens were stricken off the poll-books and they were refused the right to vote. Men were beaten and thrown out of poll-booths. Rowdies intimidated voters and kept them from the polls. It was often dangerous for a man to attempt to cast a vote in opposition to the nominees of the gang in control.

The gang in control was the Democratic Party. The political atmosphere leading up to Jesse's trial was boiling. The widely publicized case stirred up deep, old hatreds between those who had supported slavery and the Confederate cause and those who had been loyal Unionists and abolitionists during the war. The liberal Republicans mocked the conservative Democrats as "guerillas and train-robber sympathizers." "If you scratch a Democrat's back deep enough," said the *Kansas City Leader,* "you will find a guerilla, and if you scratch his back hard enough you will find a train robber." The Republican *Kansas City Journal* splashed a line of type in red ink across its front page:

IN ORDER TO VOTE AGAINST THE TRAIN ROBBER GANG
YOU MUST REGISTER TOMORROW.

"At first the Democrats were furious," the press reported. "Then it was found that the charges did not greatly injure the Democratic candidates here, while in the country districts the Democratic cause has boomed." Some of the Democratic candidates took to starting their political speeches with "Fellow train robbers . . ."

In the center ring, Jesse James Jr.'s trial was set to begin before Judge Dorsey Shackleford, himself a candidate for reelection. The judge was under tremendous pressure. The newspapers promised a spectacular trial, a "battle royal." But as the trial date approached, the judge avoided service of the notice that he was needed in court. He was ultimately a no-show. Jesse's trial had to be delayed because the *judge* failed to appear. It was, as one newspaper put it, a "serio-comic situation."

The election played out in the Democrats' favor. Shy Judge Shackleford was reelected and rescheduled the trial.

The national press went mad. The son of Jesse James—on trial for robbing a train. "In Missouri, the name 'Jesse James' was still magic," observed historian Richard Patterson. "No doubt many agreed with the region's die-hard Confederates who, rekindling the spirit of John Newman Edwards' editorials of two decades earlier, felt that young Jesse was getting the trial his guerrilla father never had."

Several newspapers in the country would enjoy sales on the story. The *Boston Daily Globe* was among those that put out a special edition when the trial finally began. Reporters and lawyers had to fight the crowds to enter the courthouse. Spectators took up "every square inch" inside. Jesse James was in the dock.

16

The Lost Cause

Pride makes most of us do many things we
wouldn't do otherwise.

— *Frank James*

In February 1899, the national press closely followed the armed robbery trial of Jesse James Jr. Its every development was imbued with special historical significance by sentimental journalists. Would the law finally claim victory against the James boys? Or was the case one of misguided retribution? Frank James caused a commotion by attending the proceedings. "The feelings of suspense seem to fill the very air of the crowded room," said one journalist. "The looks of deep attentive concern on every face are quite wonderful to see. There is no levity, no laughter, and there are no interruptions."

Prosecutor Reed's first witness was Bill Lowe. The confessed robber testified that he was silent for the first fourteen days after his arrest. He was waiting for his pals to offer help—a lawyer, for instance—but help never came. Assuming his friends had ditched him, he agreed to cooperate with the police.

For hours, Lowe testified about the planning and execution of the robbery. He was such a strong witness that the *Kansas City Journal* put it plainly: "It looks darker for Jesse James. . . . Every particle of evidence has been corroborated and corroborated again."

On cross-examination, James's famous defense lawyer, Frank P. Walsh, tried to shake his story. Lowe admitted that he was coached as a witness when he turned State's evidence, but Walsh could not trim a fraction of an inch from Lowe's testimony.

Then James took the stand himself. He was "calm, logical, and had the appearance of innocence," a reporter said. James was shown the letter and envelope that he'd allegedly sent to Bill Lowe concerning the rendezvous. He admitted the writing "looks very much like mine," but he denied that he was the author. Jesse swore he came home on the night of the robbery at eight p.m. and was sitting with his mother and sister when he heard the safe explode at twenty to ten. He and his family wondered what it was. He accounted for several trips to the scene of the robber gang's rendezvous by claiming he was bicycle riding and looking for a school where his sister Mary could teach for the winter. James's grandmother, mother, and sister took the stand and buttressed his alibi. The sight of one empty sleeve on the black dress of the elderly, renowned Zerelda James Samuel as she testified in an effort to save her grandson was a stark invocation of the profound losses the James women had endured over the years at the hands of blood-money men bent on cutting down the James menfolk.

A string of character witnesses vouched for Jesse. They were followed by a closing argument from Jesse's lawyer that reporters would remember for years. "For his concluding remarks," said historian Richard Patterson, "he saved his best punch, the fiery prose of an editorial of young Jesse's namesake, newspaperman John Newman Edwards, condemning the state of Missouri for the wrong done the Senior Jesse James. . . . Carefully molding Edwards's familiar phrases into the facts of the case at hand, Walsh left the jurors with these eloquent words to take with them to the jury room." Said Frank Walsh in his slow and soaring oratory for Junior, paraphrasing Edwards's defense of Senior:

> This trial means more than the mere fate of this boy. If you convict him we might as well tear the two bears from the flag of Missouri, and put thereon, in place of them, as more appropriate, the leering face of a detective and the crawling, snake-like shape of an informer!

After deliberating less than an hour, the jury acquitted Jesse James Jr. They gave the same reason another jury cited years earlier when acquitting his Uncle Frank despite the testimony of Dick Liddill: The jury disbelieved the coconspirator's confession.

The courtroom applauded the verdict. The newspapers were blasé about it and considered it a case of jury nullification—the willful refusal of jurors to convict in the face of compelling evidence. "It is hard to convict a train robber in Jackson County," one lamented. The prosecutor agreed. In a bold expression of his disgust with the jurors (or an admission that they were only after Jesse all along, depending on your point of view), James Reed dismissed the charges against the other five outlaws implicated in the Leeds heist. Few of those five stayed out of trouble. Kennedy wouldn't "blow upon the hills" for long. Within months he was charged in another train robbery in a case filed in Hartville, Missouri. He was found guilty and sentenced to seventeen years in prison.

Jesse would always attribute his arrest and trial to his family's political enemies, and he always had the last word on the subject. The following year he wrote a book he titled *Jesse James, My Father: The First and Only True Story of His Adventures Ever Written.* He called it "a good business venture for me. One of my objects, then, in writing this book, is in the hope that it will bring some money for the support of my mother." The cover of early editions featured a large portrait and florid signature—not of the father, but of the son. The second half of the biography was actually an autobiography devoted to Jesse's own train robbery trial.

The book was far from the "true story." Jesse quoted liberally from the writings of his father's great editorial champion, John Newman Edwards. He also devoted more space (three pages) to a tale of how his father saved a slave boy from being lynched than he did to his father's robberies (none). Indeed, Jesse Jr. seemed to deny—albeit in convoluted language—that his father committed *any robberies at all.* He would no sooner admit his father's misdeeds in writing than he would vote for a Republican. Jesse blamed the accusations against his father and uncle on the "gangs who were doing these robberies" and a "credulous public." James claimed he wrote the book without help, saying the publisher merely "looked it over and corrected the mistakes I made in grammar and punctuation. I am not a college graduate, so the public will pardon any mistakes in the book." In the final paragraph of Jesse James Jr.'s account of his own trial, he invoked the old partisan divide and remarked:

> I have had an uphill fight. I ask the public to give me the credit of having worthy motives, and of being desirous of succeeding in the world as a business man and a good citizen of the good old State of Missouri, on whose soil my father fought and bled and suffered as few men fought and as few men suffered for
>
> "THE LOST CAUSE."

The result of his trial played out perfectly to reinforce his father's legend of utter, reckless defiance ("I don't give a damn for Chief Hayes") and invincibility ("Not guilty!"). From that day forward, Jesse James Jr. was the darling of a particular faction of the Jackson County Democratic Party.

The trial and acquittal cemented intense public curiosity about the "only heir of the great land pirate." Indiana's *Fort Wayne Sunday Gazette* speculated:

> What will be his future? Will he find himself so hampered by the name of his father that he can not obtain a position? Will he find business doors closed to him and places of trust out of the question? Will he, now that the door of the prison is opened to him through no fault of his own, turn into a desperado and pursue the career which seems mapped out for him by nature and by fate? Few can blame Jesse James if he does so.

"My conduct in the future shall be as it has been in the past," he declared. The son of a gun would be accused of many other sins over the ensuing years, but Kansas City learned its lesson in 1899: Jesse Edwards James was immune from prosecution. As a celebrity whose tragic life story was known to all, he had public opinion at his command. No matter what he did, no matter how strong the proof, he was untouchable in this town. No twelve jurors could ever be expected to vote unanimously to convict him of anything. If the press and enraptured public had their say, "do what thou wilt" was the whole of the law applying to the son of Jesse James.

17

Jesse James Kidnaps Baby

The James family are nothing unless dramatic or tragic.
— The Kansas City Times, *1882*

Stella McGown was a sixteen-year-old farm girl from Oak Grove and new to Kansas City when she attended her first "big city" dance, a Valentine's Day party, in 1899. Jesse James Jr. watched her enter. She was probably the most beautiful girl he'd ever seen. She was extraordinarily attractive, with light brown hair and porcelain skin, and she looked tiny—almost childlike—while standing next to him. Jesse, twenty-three, was quite forward with her, but he was under tremendous strain. His armed robbery trial was set to begin in a week. He captured Stella's attention that night. She spent her seventeenth birthday watching him testify in his own defense. When the jury pronounced him not guilty, Stella staggered to her feet, hands clutched to her heart, and said, "Thank God. Thank God. Thank God." She'd always believed he was "completely innocent." Maybe she hadn't seen all the articles in the Kansas City papers or didn't hear the gossip that said Jesse hung out with rowdies, frequented the red-light district, and once kicked in a whorehouse door. Perhaps the reports were exaggerated, or she chose to believe so.

An intense and occasionally uncomfortable courtship followed. As Stella would recall:

> Now, when I invited my new beau, Jesse, to my home to have my parents meet him, the atmosphere was somewhat strained. My mother and father were too courteous and too kind, to show any

outright hostility to this fine looking, pleasant mannered young man who came courting their daughter. But certainly they were not able to feel any enthusiastic approval toward the son of the notorious "Bad Man".

The Sunday afternoon of Jesse's third visit to my home, I could not help noticing how stiffly everyone seemed to be perched on the edge of the uncomfortable parlor chairs, how the conversation seemed to sputter nervously and die, how my younger brothers and sisters sat around and stared in excited curiosity at our guest.

My father (Alfred M. McGown) asked, "You say you live with your mother here in town, Mr. James?"

"Yes, sir, Mr. McGown," Jesse replied. "With my mother and sister, Mary."

I was wishing that he'd go on to explain that he'd bought and paid for their cottage himself out of his own earnings, for he'd been working hard to support the three of them ever since earliest boyhood. I wanted Jesse to make my parents see what a fine person he was.

But then my mother, (Martha) just trying to keep the faltering conversation going, and certainly not intending to be unkind, began, "And your father?" breaking off in dismay after realizing the blunder too late.

"He was killed, ma'am, back in 1882," said Jesse. And a tense silence fell in the room, while my brothers and sisters exchanged thrilled glances, and waited to see where this tantalizing turn of conversation might lead.

It led nowhere, for Jesse rose at this point and said to my father, "It's such a fine day, sir, I wonder if I might have your permission to take Stella for a buggy ride?"

I jumped up in relief as my father nodded his assent.

They were wed on January 24, 1900, even though Stella was not quite eighteen years old and thus not legally eligible for marriage under

Missouri law. There seemed no reason to rush, but they could not wait another six weeks. The wedding of Jesse James Jr. was national news in January 1900. The young couple honeymooned on the old James farm near Kearney, fifteen miles northeast of Kansas City, where the outlaw Jesse and his bride Zee also had honeymooned in bygone days, the home loopholed for defense, raided by federals, bombed by the Pinkertons, and ruled by Zerelda Samuel, improbable a setting as it was for romance.

Immediately after the honeymoon, the newlyweds returned to Kansas City and the little cottage on Tracy Avenue to live with Jesse's mother and sister. Zee James made a point to speak to Stella about Jesse Jr.'s bizarre childhood, tendering the tales as excuses for his behavior. Zee described her son's early days as "a series of hasty moves under cover of night, one narrow escape after another," Stella said. Until his father's death, he was carefully kept away from strangers for fear he would let something slip, so he had no playmates. Once he was allowed to befriend a boy named Harry Hoffman, and they became friends for life. But Harry was the exception. For his first six years Jesse could only play with other children under strict supervision. When his mother was occupied he was forced to stand at the windows and stare out at other children.

"Zee wanted me to understand her son," Stella said. "He was temperamental and had been pampered and spoiled by his mother and sister, because he was the breadwinner." Stella would have figured it out on her own soon enough. On her first night in her new home, Stella said, "Jesse had mentioned several times that he thought he would take a bath. Finally his sister took me aside and told me it would be my duty to prepare the bath water, lay out his clothes, put the collar and cuff buttons on his shirt and brush his shoes. She said that it had been her job, and now it would be mine."

The teenager had no idea whom she'd married. She had only the vaguest notions of the crimes of the James Gang and their importance to the former Confederates of Missouri. She did not understand that her husband's father would be a third figure in their marriage, that they would forever live in the shadow of the prince of bandits. To educate herself about her husband's kin, Stella read dime novels about Jesse and Frank James behind her husband's back. She began to repeat the same sort of propaganda that her husband espoused, alternately justifying and denying Jesse Sr.'s criminality.

Jesse Jr.'s mother Zee James passed away on November 13, 1900, at the age of fifty-five. Had she lived a few weeks longer, she would have seen her first grandchild as, in December 1900, Jesse and Stella welcomed a baby girl. Jesse's sister Mary James was married a few months later. Left alone in the house with the baby much of the time, Stella now had more important things to worry about than the father-in-law she never met.

After Jesse Jr.'s very public brush with the law, he lost enthusiasm for working in the courthouse. A few weeks after his acquittal, he sold his cigar business at a nice profit and opened a cigar and candy shop at 121 West 9th Street, which intersected at that point with both Main and Delaware, in the Junction Building, a busy part of downtown Kansas City. One of his customers was a student by the name of Harry Truman. One day, Harry had a five-cent ice cream soda there. "When I'd finished it," Harry would later write, "I found I had no nickel, only a car ticket home." Jesse was kind to the lad, telling him to pay when he came in again. "I paid the nickel the next day!" Harry would later write, his exclamation point indicating one did not even consider stiffing Jesse James on a debt.

James did not stay in the sweets business for long; it wasn't particularly profitable. Upon surveying the commercial landscape in Kansas City and reflecting on his associations, Jesse decided to open a pawnshop in a tough part of town at 1215½ Grand Avenue. He called himself a diamond and loan broker. The company was called The Jesse James Collateral Loan Co. If he didn't already know a large number of people who needed the services of a pawnshop, he knew the name Jesse James on the door would do the rest.

The journalists of the time continued to keep him under public scrutiny. On one occasion, they interviewed a resident of Kearney, home of the James farm, and asked for a comment on Jesse Jr. "Here in Kearney," the man said, "the son of Jesse James is called 'little Jesse,' though he weighs 190 pounds, twenty-three more than his father did, and is big enough to conduct a Kansas City pawnshop." However his heft did not deter all thefts: in 1901, someone broke into his home and took cash and diamonds; in 1905, he was robbed of three hundred dollars. A newspaper editor gloated: "The young man now knows how people felt when his father transacted business with them."

Despite an occasional holdup, the pawnshop was successful and helped the young James embark on the long road to prosperity. But he did not enjoy his career selling guns and merchandise of questionable origins. "I always had a desire to be a lawyer," he would later say. "I make up my mind on the instant, as a rule, and one day while I was in the pawnshop I made up my mind to be a lawyer." He hired others to mind his loans and pledges while he attended the Kansas City School of Law. Years of intense late-night study paid off. He graduated as the valedictorian of his class in the summer of 1906. If only his mother and father had been alive to see it. "When I stood on the platform and received my diploma from the Kansas City School of Law," Jesse said, "I experienced the proudest moment of my life—excepting, of course, the day I was married." His law school graduation was a "triumphant achievement," Stella said, proof for anyone who needed it that the family was now free of any hint of lawlessness and the name Jesse James need no longer strike terror as it did in the seventies.

Of the thirty-seven men who took the bar exam in Jefferson City that year, Jesse's score of ninety-one was the highest. James was sworn into the bar at the age of thirty. Once again, the man with a bad name to live down—"not only a bad name, but in some ways the very worst he could have borne in his part of the world," as one journalist observed—made national news. The public relished the irony: the outlaw's son, now a lawyer. Said the *Washington Post:* "His father broke the law—under many extenuating circumstances, some still plead—but Jesse means to uphold the dignity of the law."

The newspapers went a step further to paint a pretty picture. "In all his life," one widely repeated remark went, "he never tasted whisky, beer or any other kind of intoxicating drink, and he does not use tobacco in any form." But it remained true in Missouri and much of the country that naughty little boys were still called "Jesse James Junior."

After his graduation from law school, James sold his pawnshop and declared, "I shall never specialize in criminal practice. There isn't enough money in that class of work. Few men who commit acts of violence have any money." He preferred corporate work because it paid better, but the criminal courts had other plans for him.

Jesse found work at a small firm in Kansas City, Hughes & Whitsett. He spent most of his time there learning to practice law. He eventually opened his own office in the Schutte Building on Grand Avenue between 12th and 13th Streets. To an Iowa reporter he remarked, "I suppose my father would say I am rather old to start in my life work. I am 31, you know."

Journalist Leigh Mitchell Hodges visited James in his new law office in 1907 to write a special feature that ran in the *Manitoba Morning Free Press.* Western Canadians were also interested in the legacy of Jesse James. Hodges shared the raw experience with his readers:

> You climb a flight of narrow, well-worn wooden stairs in an old-time office building on Grand avenue, Kansas City, and come to a door on which an inscription is painted in black letters. It is a professional man's sign, and it reads: Jesse E. James, Lawyer. Upon entering the room, which is lighted by one window, two objects at once claim your attention. One is a tremendous iron safe, such as are seen in jewelry shops; the other, a young man seated at a desk. He has a big head, topped generously with glossy hair, almost black, and his dark eyes sparkle with good nature and youthful enthusiasm as he turns to greet you.

The reporter couldn't help but ask James to comment on the crimes his father committed. It would have been a journalistic coup to hear the outlaw's confession from his son. He asked the question and later wrote:

> Now, at the man's estate, while he acknowledges that his sire acted 'unwisely' in some instances, he looks clean through you with his steady eyes when you mention the term 'train robber,' and says: "I don't know anything about that. I was never there to see, so I know nothing." There is something in his manner of speech that causes you to change the subject.

One of the first court appearances of Jesse James, Attorney at Law, was his own private prosecution. As the wire services explained in 1906:

NOT LIKE NOTED PA

Jesse James, Jr., Prosecutes Brother-in-Law, Who is Fined $100.

Kansas City, Nov. 30 – Attorney Jesse James, Jr., a son of the notorious outlaw of that name, was in police court to prosecute his brother-in-law, Luther McGowan [*sic*], for taking James' horse without permission and misusing it. McGowan pleaded guilty and said he had been drinking.

"You are his brother-in-law, what do you want me to do with him?" Judge Kyle inquired of James.

"He ought to be fined; I believe in law enforcement," said James.

One would assume that a lawyer *would* believe in law enforcement. As the son of a scofflaw, James felt it necessary to make that point clear to the judge. He "has taken to the active support of the law," noted journalist Hodges, "a thing his father riddled with dead-sure shots and knifed with such superb nerve as has few counterparts in history."

By fiat, criminal defense work became the first field Jesse entered. After years of listening to his family make excuses for every crime in the calendar, be it cold-blooded murder, terrorism, wartime atrocities, armed robbery, or conspiracy—what sin had his father and uncle not committed?—Jesse had a calling. He zealously defended some of the most callous murderers in a city full of armed bandits.

During his first murder trial in 1907 in Kansas City's criminal court at Oak Street and Missouri Avenue, James defended Albert Crone for his crime against his former sweetheart. Crone was a twenty-year-old jealous suitor who regularly roughed up his girlfriend, twenty-one-year-old Bertha Bowlin. He made a habit of hitting her with a brick. Once he knocked her to the ground before several horrified witnesses. He often threatened to kill her. On the night of July 19, 1906, he found Bertha sitting near her home with another man. Albert Crone savaged them both with a pipe.

Bertha and her new beau were found the next morning, unconscious and covered in blood. At the hospital, her heartbroken mother asked Bertha, whom she affectionately called "Dovie," how she felt.

"Awful bad," she said.

Bertha's mother asked her if she was going to die.

Through her facial fractures, Bertha was able to say, "Hu, Hu." Her mother understood Bertha to say she expected to die. Her dying declaration would be admissible in court.

"Who was it?" her mother asked.

"Bert."

"Bert who?"

"Bert Crone."

"Bert did this, Dovie?"

"Sure." She kept repeating the name Bert. Bertha died later that day.

The second victim, Frank Kern, awoke from a coma after two weeks and also identified Crone as his attacker. Three days after he left the hospital, Frank Kern received a visit from Jesse James and another attorney, who were representing Albert Crone. He would later say he was scared. He told the lawyers that it wasn't Albert Crone after all. Jesse James came to see him five or six more times. The victim also gave a statement to Jesse James at his law office in the Schutte Building. Again and again, he said Albert Crone was not the attacker.

But on the witness stand at Crone's trial for the murder of Bertha Bowlin, Kern pointed out that he was under oath for the first time, and he again identified Albert Crone as their attacker. Kern also testified that Albert Crone's lawyers harassed him. "They bothered me." They demanded repeated statements from him. Someone sent him threatening letters. He was too frightened to tell them the truth, he said. He told them what they wanted to hear.

The prosecutor offered several witnesses who also heard Frank Kern identify Albert Crone as the killer. Jesse James objected to this hearsay testimony every time, but he made a freshman error by claiming that such evidence was "incompetent, irrelevant and immaterial." It sounded fancy but legally it meant nothing. As the Supreme Court would later remark, "It has been many times held by this court that such an objection is too indefinite and uncertain, and counts for no objection at all."

In a peculiar move, Jesse took the witness stand himself to try to save his client. He testified that he visited Frank Kern in his home and at another attorney's office. He detailed all the times Frank Kern told him it wasn't Albert Crone. He denied threatening Frank Kern.

It was a desperate move in a hopeless cause, an impossible case to defend. The press reported that Jesse James's "maiden speech" was "argumentative, and he made no effort to be oratorical." The judge convicted Crone of second-degree murder, a merciful verdict given the evidence. Crone was sentenced to eighteen years. Once again, a bit of mercy.

James filed an appeal in Albert Crone's case, but the Supreme Court of Missouri was unsympathetic. The justices could tell even from a dry trial transcript that "the murder was a most brutal one, and the evidence proves beyond question that defendant committed it willfully, deliberately, and premeditatedly." The Supreme Court also found that "Kern was interviewed and harassed a good deal, after he left the hospital, by defendant's attorneys." It was the first of many cases James would over-zealously defend and the first of many losses.

As Jesse James Jr. continued building his law practice and defending high-profile cases, his family grew. He and Stella had four children, all girls. That Jesse's father, like his uncle Frank, had been a family man set the James brothers apart from their brethren in the fraternity of bandits. It was a critical part of the James legend. It put a human face on the ruthless serial killers.

A few years into Jesse and Stella's marriage, however, the marital passion ebbed. Jesse Jr.'s wife grew tired of wondering which side of midnight would see him home. She suspected him of carrying on numerous extramarital affairs, including trysts with a neighbor and the female clients of his law practice. The tumultuous relationship may have involved physical violence; in one family photograph, Stella appears to have a large bruise on her jawline.

Stella turned out to have a little more pluck than her age and diminutive figure would suggest. She left her wayward husband at least three times, sometimes for months at a stretch. A divorce suit was filed in 1909 but withdrawn. In 1910, a census-taker found the young mother and her children living with her parents. Later that year, it was Jesse who initiated another divorce action. The *Washington Post* and other newspapers across the country pointed out that the sons of both Frank and Jesse James were going through divorces at the same time.

Divorces at that time were quite infrequent, with only a few hundred cases brought each year. The overwhelming majority involved childless couples. The only grounds for divorce were desertion, vagrancy, cruelty, commission of a felony, bigamy, drunkenness, or the commission of "indignities." Most divorces were granted on the grounds of indignities, a legal term meaning conduct that renders the spouse's condition intolerable and life burdensome. The vague standard gave judges much leeway. Some routinely denied divorces on principle, particularly where young children were involved.

The national press gave prominent coverage to the James divorce suit. Jesse gave interviews. He said reconciliation was impossible. According to press accounts, Stella got into an argument with him and drew a revolver on him. On another occasion she allegedly searched his room at a local hotel. Jesse managed to catapult himself back into a flood of notoriety with a cruel divorce tactic in the fall of 1910. The startling headlines screamed JESSE JAMES KIDNAPS BABY. One day when his estranged wife went riding with their older girls, Jesse snatched their youngest child, secreted her in the home of a friend, and refused to disclose the toddler's whereabouts to a distraught Stella unless she signed a divorce judgment that he had prepared. Instead, she went to his hotel room and left behind what Jesse and avid students of the scandal interpreted as a threatening note:

> Jesse:
> The three children and i stayed all night here in your room last night. it is up to you to find out how we did it. There would have been a warm reception had you come home last night. Well, i missed you this time, but i mean to keep right on your trail until i land you. i could have done it last night while i was pretty close behind you, but it was not just the chance i wanted.
> Lovingly,
> STELLA

Eventually, the two-year-old was restored to her mother, and Stella countersued Jesse for divorce to prevent him from unilaterally withdrawing the case. The case came up for trial on January 10, 1911. After

Stella James and her four daughters. (*Missouri Valley Special Collections,
Kansas City Public Library, Kansas City, Missouri*)

listening to the evidence, the judge dismissed Jesse's case as groundless
and granted Stella's petition for a divorce, holding that Stella was "the
innocent party." Jesse was ordered to pay a hundred dollars a month in
alimony and another hundred dollars a month in child support. Stella
received custody of the children. Jesse was granted the right to weekend
visits with his daughters—but only with two at a time.

Two hundred dollars a month did not go very far. Stella had children to tend, and she had no education. She had few if any suitable

opportunities for employment in Kansas City. If she enjoyed a date, it's hard to imagine her ex-husband encouraged them. Within several months the newspapers announced "a motor car courtship and their four children reunited them." Jesse proposed again and Stella accepted. He gave up his rooms at the Victoria Hotel that night.

Perhaps he made extravagant promises. Perhaps he kept them, for a time.

With his marriage patched back together and spluttering along, Jesse concentrated on defending accused killers and building a personal injury practice. Among those he represented was Walter Majors, a known bank robber accused of a fatal shooting during the holdup of a Kansas City gambling hall. Majors was convicted and got a life term. But Jesse got his fee, so at least one of them made money from the crime. His father would have been proud of him.

On the civil side, Jesse obtained a judgment of five hundred dollars for a woman injured when her horse-drawn buggy was struck by a meat wagon, two hundred and five dollars for a man whose horse was killed and wagon damaged by a derailed streetcar, eight hundred dollars for an injured wagon driver, and his biggest civil judgment of all, a five-thousand-dollar verdict for the death of a railroad yard worker. Over the course of several years, James handled many lawsuits against the Missouri Pacific Railway Company, taking by operation of law what his father once took by operation of a Smith & Wesson.

Eventually he came to represent two wicked women. One was Dr. Zeo Zoe Wilkins. But before her there was Mattie Howard, Zeo's counterpart in the lowest depths of the Kansas City underworld. Mattie, known as Agate Eyes, was a desperate gun moll who would come to blame her lawyer for everything that happened to her.

18

Underworld Money

Lawyers wield an hypnotic influence over the average jury, and women are encouraged to take a chance on murder when they recall the long list of trials in which women were acquitted on the strength of their lawyers' impassioned pleas.
— *Minott Saunders, "What the Paris Criminologists Have Learned about Love Murders" (1931)*

In the 1910s and 1920s, Kansas City thrived both on crime and on law enforcement. Many made money from the vice-rich tourists and transients who passed through Kansas City, where the protection racket flourished. Federal investigator Rudolph Hartmann would one day describe Kansas City's peculiar civic code while under the leadership of "Boss Tom" Pendergast. "Gambling became a major industry," Hartmann observed, "and without any pretence of concealment gambling houses as numerous as drugstores advertised their existence. The underworld flocked to these establishments. . . . Kansas City is the widest open town in the U.S.A.—anything goes. Such conditions attracted the denizens of the underworld, from the petty sneak thief to the machine-gunning gangsters. Fences disposed of stolen property unmolested. It was impossible for the decent element among the population of Kansas City to do anything about these conditions." Voting in new leaders was no answer, Hartmann said: "The machine did the voting. . . . The city administration and even the police department was entirely dominated by Pendergast."

Through his thirties and early forties, Jesse James Jr. built his legal practice with a series of murder cases and bread-and-butter personal injury suits. Kansas City supplied dozens of the former and thousands of the latter every year, and he thrived within its system.

James's most well-known case as a lawyer in Kansas City was the murder trial of Mattie Howard. She was a debauched young woman with several aliases who made herself a fixture in the Kansas City underworld. The press called her a "bandit queen," a "gangster woman," and the "Golden Girl" with the "smile of death." She was also a pickpocket, shoplifter, bank robber, jewel thief, check kiter, lure for wealthy men, and one of Kansas City's "most noted women drunkards." The *Standard-Examiner* in Ogden City, Utah, found in Mattie Howard a woman who was physically lovely and "of medium size, brilliantly blonde, with a clear, fair skin and eyes which attracted attention wherever she went."

Mattie Howard had ample cause to need the services of Jesse James, attorney at law. He was also her bondsman. Mattie described Jesse as "a stubby-nosed man of medium height, with queer gray eyes and dark hair streaked with gray." Not that Mattie was much of a judge of men. She had a habit of outliving many of her male companions.

The first was Diamond Joe. On the night of May 22, 1918, Mattie went to a kitchenette hotel in Kansas City with Joe Morino, a pawnbroker with a shop on Grand Avenue in Kansas City. She happened to owe him money because she'd written him a bad check. She registered them at the Touraine Hotel at 1412 Central Avenue in Kansas City as "Mr. and Mrs. B. Stanley, City of Detroit" and paid in cash for a weeklong stay, the implication being that she needed a bed to work off the debt to Diamond Joe. There they stayed for a night.

But the next night, a taxicab was summoned to the hotel. Mattie, a second woman, and Mattie's boyfriend, Sam Taylor, dashed out of the hotel and into the cab. When the driver asked them where he was to drive, Sam Taylor cried, "Straight ahead!" and urged him to shut off the dome light.

Two days later, Morino's body was found inside the hotel room. His head had been battered in by a blackjack. The hand weapon that had delivered the fatal blows lay beside him. He'd been robbed of several valuable diamonds.

While on the lam, Mattie spoke to a police officer in St. Louis, telling him she needed to reach her attorney in Kansas City because of the dead man found in her room. Mattie and her boyfriend were eventually arrested in New Mexico. At the time they possessed an interesting assortment of criminal tools: jimmies, fuses, chisels, keys, a bottle of nitroglycerine, a .45 automatic, a sawed-off shotgun, and a blackjack.

Even though Mattie was caught, it took quite some time for her to be officially charged with the murder of Diamond Joe Morino. Meanwhile two more of her known devotees were killed. Rosco Conkling "Blackie" Lancaster died under a hail of police bullets on September 24, 1918. The police killed Tony Cruye on August 25, 1919. Still the Jackson County prosecutor waited until September 1919 to file second-degree murder charges against Mattie for Joe Morino's death.

Mattie pleaded not guilty to the murder. Despite the enormity of the charge she faced, Jesse James asked that Ms. Howard be released on bond. Jesse had pull with the judge on her case, the Honorable Ralph S. Latshaw. The judge's son, Ralph S. Latshaw Jr., and brother, Henry J. Latshaw, were both lawyers. Each had appeared in various cases as co-counsel with Jesse E. James in the past. The judge's other son, Ross, was an insurance man, real estate broker, and client of Jesse James's law practice who once convinced Jesse to file a discharge on a mortgage that had not actually been paid. Jesse easily succeeded in having Mattie's bond reduced, served as one of two bondsmen for a twenty-thousand-dollar bond, and sought delay after delay in her case. The newspapers reported that Mattie Howard had "fascinated" men who had "power and influence to get her trial constantly postponed and her bail extended."

While out on bail, Mattie was continually in trouble. She claimed that she was arrested nearly every day and even "had the unbelievable record of having been arrested eighteen times in one day." Mattie said she "became accustomed and hardened to [my] daily arrests, so that whenever [I] read or heard of a robbery of any kind, [I] would go to the telephone, call up police headquarters and say, 'Hello, Chief. I see where the paper relates _____. Do you want me?' This became very annoying to the Chief. He generally replied with gruff answers such as this: 'Naw, if we want ya we'll come and get ya', or else banged the receiver in [my] ear." The Kansas City press reported that Mattie also met with "Hollywood agents" who came to Kansas City to take her measurements in connection with "a try-out in motion pictures" following her anticipated acquittal.

Mattie Howard went on trial before a jury on October 21, 1919, in the criminal court in Kansas City. If she thought she'd walk out of there a free woman, she had cause for her confidence. Mattie was beautiful, only twenty-three years old, and American jurors generally did not convict women of murder, even on strong evidence, particularly when the lady was young and pretty. It was common knowledge then. This was the short-lived Golden Age of the Murderess.

Prosecutors across the United States had spoken out for years about the lax treatment of murderesses by the average jury, especially in the larger cities. The relations between the sexes at the time were such that men thought of women as little more than grown-up children. They usually weren't well educated, so perhaps there was some basis for the general masculine thinking that young women in particular had limited capacities. Nowhere was this thinking more clearly pronounced than in the jury room. The average man in America (and in Europe as well) would no sooner convict a woman of a handgun murder than he would a four-year-old.

In 1912, a prosecutor in Chicago bucked ridicule and called for women jurors to try women for murder, even though women were not even eligible to vote, let alone sit on juries. "It is next to impossible to secure a woman's conviction for murder in Chicago under the present jury system," the prosecutor explained. "Twelve men simply cannot be brought to believe, no matter how strong the evidence, that a woman is guilty of the gravest crime in the calendar. . . . It seems that men as jurors can never overlook the sex element and judge impartially and without emotion. The defendant need not be beautiful; if she merely appears feminine on the stand she is safe." From 1908 to 1919 in Chicago alone, twenty-five women in a row were acquitted of murder. "Some of them killed a man in the heat of passion," said Hearst reporter Winifred Black. "Some of them committed murder deliberately for revenge. And one or two of them took a human life for a chance at a little easy money, and not one of them was punished as the law directs that murder shall be punished."

As she sat through her own trial, Mattie was confident she would be acquitted. She knew as well as anybody that jurors didn't like convicting beautiful females. "Regardless of how wrong it may be to base a decision of that sort upon the physical attractiveness," she remarked, "this outward appeal to the eye has been the deciding factor in bringing about the acquittal of many beautiful women." Mattie's lawyer agreed. Jesse James encouraged her to believe the jury would not find her guilty. Mattie would later say her attorney supplied her with grapes and peanuts to chew during the trial so as to appear nonchalant.

If true, it was awful advice. Jurors needed a reason to want to acquit a woman, and only certain behavior on her part would suffice. "It is perfectly natural and normal for the masculine mind in a jury box to react tremendously to feminine tears and distress," explained Professor James E. Lough of New York University, writing in the *Washington Post* in May 1915 on the question of why juries wouldn't convict pretty women. "Try as the intellect may to steel the judgement against such an appeal, it usually fails to a marked degree. . . . Somewhere back in the neolithic period nature whispered to man that the first law of his impulse must be to guard the female." If she wouldn't shed some tears, Mattie Howard would have no sympathy from an all-male panel and prove herself exempted from the social premium on attractive young women.

Jesse James had every advantage as defense counsel in Mattie's case as he fought to save her future. The evidence was hardly overwhelming. Not one witness put that blackjack in Mattie's hand or even placed her in the room when Morino was beaten to death. There were no finger-prints found on the murder weapon—not that it was carefully examined. Like most of the United States, Kansas City hadn't quite grasped this particular breakthrough in forensic science. In the Howard case, the prosecutor was asking the jury to make quite a few inferences from scant evidence. Nobody offered any account of what truly happened to Joe Morino on the night of his death, though it hardly stopped the specula-tion. Mattie's lawyer could have reasonably argued that the proven facts made her no more than an accessory to murder.

James took a different tack entirely. He called Mattie Howard to the witness stand and asked her if she ever went to a motel with Joe Morino. She denied ever being there. She denied killing Joe. She said she wasn't even in Kansas City then. Jesse asked her few personal questions except to confirm that she had been married at seventeen but was separated from her husband. He asked her nothing about her background, life circumstances, her poor childhood, her unhappy marriage—all the mitigating factors that any halfway decent defense lawyer would have trumpeted. He did not trouble himself to introduce his client to the men sitting in judgment of her, to make them ache to comfort her. He elicited no tears. She couldn't have testified for more than ten minutes.

Because Mattie had taken the witness stand, the prosecution was allowed to explore her reputation. That it did. The prosecutor called her a "vampire" and referred to her mesmerizing "agate eyes." He referred to her habitual adultery and her collection of burglary tools. The prose-cutor declared her boyfriend Sam Taylor a known bootlegger and snidely remarked to Jesse James that Sam would be his next client. The jury also learned that Mattie had been heard bragging about how she had "put one over on the Kansas City bulls." Jesse (or Jess, as special prosecutor James Alyward called him) objected to this devastating evidence, but he was still objecting to offensive testimony as "incompetent, irrelevant"—fifteen years after the Supreme Court of Missouri had warned him in Albert Crone's murder case that it wasn't a recognizable objection. The judge let in much of the reputation testimony, which greatly damaged Mattie's defense.

A few days into Mattie's murder trial, another pawnshop proprietor in Kansas City, Adolph Gray of Gray's Shoppe, was shot in the chest and killed in a holdup. He died on the sidewalk outside his shop. The timing of this news wasn't particularly helpful to a woman on trial for killing a pawnshop owner. James asked for her trial to be suspended because he became involved in the Gray case on behalf of the seventeen-year-old boy who committed the murder.

After the brief interruption, Mattie's trial continued. On October 25, the Howard jury rendered its verdict. They convicted Mattie of second-degree murder. Back then jurors decided sentences, and they fixed her punishment at twelve years in prison.

Mattie was thunderstruck. But no one in the audience expressed any disagreement with the outcome. "The crowded court room slowly emptied," Mattie said. "No one in the crowd offered [me] a sympathetic glance. As an officer led [me] from the court room the Judge remarked, 'I have been Judge here for fifteen years; but she is the most beautiful woman I ever had to sentence.'"

She was not alone in expressing shock at the verdict. "The consensus opinion was that she would be discharged," remarked the *Kansas City Star.* "The saying, 'They won't convict her; she's a woman,' does not hold in Jackson County murder cases."

Her attorney managed to obtain her release on bond pending her appeal to the Missouri Supreme Court. Perhaps she clung to that last hope.

Even with a lengthy sentence hanging over her, perhaps because of it, Mattie could not remain out of the underworld. Maybe her pending imprisonment made her a particularly attractive companion to a certain class of men. Mattie consorted with the most desperate men in Kansas City. One by one, more of her companions bit the dust. While she was out on bond pending her appeal, another outlaw boyfriend, fresh from serving a prison stretch himself, met with Jesse James and threatened to blow the lawyer's brains out if Mattie wasn't saved from her prison sentence. Before he could make good on the threat, he was shot and killed in a Kansas City bank holdup. Many more deaths were connected to Mattie Howard, and Utah's *Standard-Examiner* was moved to describe her as "a siren of the social deeps, a criminal Helen."

"Spider" Kelly was killed in a Kansas City drugstore. Albert Pagil was shot by police and died of his infected wounds on March 12, 1920. Dale Jones, George Evans, and others followed Mattie's lovers to early graves. How many of them died trying to pay her legal bills?

"Not fewer than a dozen men have been killed because of their connection with Mattie Howard," the *Standard-Examiner* reported, "some of them ensnared by her and led to assassination, more of them criminals who were shot down by the police while engaged in crimes which Mattie Howard may have suggested or planned." During this time, Jesse E. James repeatedly obtained adjournments on her criminal case, thus dragging out the post-conviction proceedings at the trial court level and keeping his client on the streets of Kansas City.

Thankful for none of it, Mattie Howard blamed her conviction on Jesse James. She claimed that she was convicted of murder not because she was guilty but because Jesse James "arranged that [my] mother and other relatives would not be present" at her trial. She also accused her lawyer of purposely delaying her case to charge her more money. She accused him of having her repeatedly arrested so he could collect a bond premium each time from her associates. She claimed all of her defense fees came from the underworld and the payments went straight to her attorney. She was aware of one specific payment of one thousand five hundred dollars.

She said her demeanor at her trial was her lawyer's idea. He told her to "act cool and to display no emotion." She should have known better.

Any experienced manipulator knew that a voice filled with sorrow, a tear-stained face, and a wounded animal act plucked at the heartstrings of every man. Playing it cool was a terrible error, she realized later. The jury was given "the impression that [I] was a hard, cold-blood person. This was just what [my] deceiving attorney wished. He had planned that [I] should be convicted, and then, by appealing the case, he could draw it out for another long period and bleed [me] for more money."

She continued: "Many lawyers intentionally prolong cases of this kind in order to obtain every cent possible from a client who can furnish money. Then when the client's money is exhausted, his attorney lets him go to prison. [My] lawyer was of that type."

Mattie fled Missouri while her appeal was pending. Perhaps this irritated her bondsman, who was on the hook for twenty thousand dollars. James offered a reward of five hundred dollars for his client's capture.

The accusations Mattie made against her lawyer may well have been true. Though the State came up with several new witnesses on the eve of trial, James never bothered to object to the surprise testimony. He did not trouble himself to ask for a continuance so he could prepare to cross-examine them, though such a motion surely would have been granted. Though he filed an appeal, James committed legal malpractice at the appellate level as well; he never bothered to file a legal brief, despite ample time to write one. His failure to pursue an appeal in a murder case virtually assured that the appeals court would affirm the trial court's verdict. On May 26, 1921, the Supreme Court of Missouri indeed upheld Mattie's murder conviction and the twelve-year sentence.

The law finally caught up with Mattie in a Memphis pawnshop, and she went to prison on November 18, 1921. "It is said she laughed and sang when the prison gates were closed upon her," reported the *Standard-Examiner.* "Perhap[s] she had learned to scoff at disaster." Soon enough she would have occasion to scoff at the disaster about to befall her lawyer, and she would declare his ill treatment of her the cause of his misfortunes.

19

Under the Black Flag

*If we could always understand the burdens some people are
carrying, we could understand the wrong and mistaken
things they sometimes do.*

— *Mattie Howard*

The Progressive Era was a time of great economic growth in the middle part of the United States. Millionaires were made overnight, whether by oil, gold, silver, banking, land, or slots. Business boomed. Times were good. As a principal railroad junction, Kansas City was a way station for every man and woman in search of fortune or on the run. The city saw great wealth pass through it daily. As historian William Reddig remarked, Kansas City was always a get-rich-quick kind of a place: "Everybody but the Indians and the Negroes had a chance or labored under the illusion that tomorrow he would be able to retire in style."

Like other, lesser known residents of Kansas City, Jesse James Jr., thought that he had an easy windfall within his reach. He had only to finally cash in on his father's fame. In his case, he knew he had a sure bet. From the beginning, fortune hunters came calling. The offers started pouring in when Jesse Jr. was still a young man, shortly after his acquittal on the armed robbery charge. A "melodramatic company" offered him a starring role at a salary of fifteen hundred dollars per week for three months—eighteen thousand dollars, or more, if the show was successful. At the time, he lived in a house worth thirteen hundred dollars. A theatrical company in New York that was planning a "sensational melodrama" offered him a role as a robber or deputy sheriff at a handsome salary. Another company offered him a big salary to play a train robber in a play.

Any play he participated in would have been a smash. He was not the only child of a desperado to be offered such a role. A traveling show starring Eva Evans, oldest child of infamous nineties train robber Chris Evans, the Jesse James of California, reaped riches for all who took part, particularly Eva. Any stage production with a theme of "Robin Hoods versus the Evil Railroad Barons" was guaranteed to sell a lot of tickets, and an air of authenticity helped. So did a fabulous costume. Eva Evans wore tight pants and rode on horseback for her part in a heavily romanticized version of her outlaw daddy's exploits before his incarceration. She made a fortune, packing the theaters "until it seemed," said a reporter with interesting taste in metaphors, "as if the walls would bulge out and split at the seams."

But Jesse had to turn away from repeated offers of life-altering fortunes. The James family still had a few secrets. Jesse's grandmother hated publicity and lashed out at those who tried to tell stories of the James Gang. His mother was also widely known in the press to have "steadfastly refused all offers to write about her husband, keeping her feelings to herself except to say, 'They drove him to do it.'" Jesse's uncle Frank was acquitted in 1883 on a murder charge for his part in a fatal 1881 robbery in Winston, Missouri. He was acquitted in a second trial in Huntsville, Alabama. But he was suspected of many more murders. As he himself would half admit, he was the worst scoundrel unhung. Frank James was still a tantalizing target for a prosecutor with ambitions who might be willing to dust off an old indictment. If some state agent came up with proof, even at a late date, Frank James could find himself back in a courthouse and in the headlines. So nobody in the James family was talking, and they didn't want anyone else to talk either.

Jesse honored their wishes. As hard as it must have been, he refused each offer of easy money. To the press he would remark, "No amount of money could tempt me to go upon the stage or to make an exhibition of myself in any way. I am not a freak, and I am not an actor, so I will never be seen on any stage."

The public interest in Jesse James continued to grow in the early twentieth century. Perhaps the family's secrecy contributed to the furious interest in new disclosures. If anyone knew where the skeletons and treasure were buried, it was Jesse James Jr. The book Jesse wrote in 1899 only whetted the public appetite for more revelations, for he certainly did not spill any secrets in his little book. Even so, it went into multiple editions and stayed in print for many years, giving Jesse an occasional tidy sum for his effort. Reviewers, however, were harsh. Writing in 1936, Philip D. Jordan called the author a "not-too-brilliant son of the bandit"

Jesse E. James (lower right) and Harry Hoffman (lower left) sit in for Jesse James and Cole Younger during a September 1920 reunion of the Sons of Quantrill, a group of guerilla veterans who rode under the rebel leader's black flag and decades later still kept his portrait draped with ribbon. (*Jackson County (Mo.) Historical Society Archives*)

and remarked that "as a matter of fact, neither the account written by the phlegmatic son nor the scores of other romances of terror tell the true life of the criminal whom poets now immortalize. For the biography of Jesse James stands not clear-etched for all the world to read, but lies devious and hidden behind the powder smoke of rumor and romanticism. The facts are few; the rumors, many."

It was years of trial practice that helped James earn wealth. Over time and with some good cases, he built an estate that grew to impressive size. Then his grandmother died. The legendary Zerelda Elizabeth Cole James Simms Samuel passed away on February 10, 1911. Frank James died in February 1915. A newsman wanted to film the outlaw's funeral, but his nephew refused. "Frank wouldn't have liked it," Jesse said. The following year the last of the Northfield Raiders passed on to a higher judgment when Cole Younger died.

As his wife Stella would recall:

> It seemed to Jesse, Jr., that no one would be hurt by his participation in a portrayal of his father's life now. . . . He talked the matter over with me at length, before arriving at his decision. On the one hand, there was the fact that he was, at the time, a successful attorney with a good practice, a nice home, and four lovely daughters. On the other hand, with two of his daughters in high school and one already attending the University of Missouri, he had use for added income.

Jesse never doubted that he would profit considerably for the true story of his father's career. With so many girls to put through college, he bet everything on the venture. It would not be another book. James determined it had to be a movie, a big Hollywood-style action blockbuster that would put his father's wartime exploits on the silver screen. Jesse Jr. would be the star. He would wear his father's pistols and become his father reincarnated.

He decided to enlist the help of everyone he knew. Jesse and many of his closest friends mortgaged their homes and farms. He convinced his most respectable associates to share in the success of the film. He persuaded the king of Kansas City, Tom Pendergast, to invest in the picture. He convinced the Crittenden family to take shares. Curiously enough, they agreed to finance a movie that would abjectly glorify the most infamous criminal in U.S. history in order to reap some booty of their own from the legend. It was, in the words of film historian J.W. Williamson, "a weirdly ironic (and safe) scenario: the former capitalist enemies of Jesse James were investing their capital to help the bandit's now respectable son romanticize his father's legend in order to certify his own class acceptability."

The publicity for the project began before the movie was even written. JESSE JAMES WILL PERFORM, trumpeted the newspapers in summer 1920. Thomas T. Crittenden Jr., then a former mayor of Kansas City, announced the formation of a company to make the motion pictures starring Jesse James Jr. as his father. The head of the Mesco Pictures Corporation, formed for the project, was Thomas Pendergast. The vice president was Thomas Crittenden Jr. All stock was subscribed, they announced, and "local talent will be used largely in the cast." Creation of the film was a family affair with the extended James clan participating in the project. Investors collected working capital of two hundred fifty thousand dollars. Some accounts said it was as much as $1.4 million.

It was an extraordinary amount of money for any film project. At that time Hollywood's low-budget westerns cost as little as five thousand to seven thousand dollars. The big studio productions starring Tom Mix, the greatest western star of the day, cost around a hundred seventy-five thousand dollars. But James would spare no expense. His grand plans included renting the Dyer mansion in Kansas City, which he renamed Mesco City. Several city officials attended the ribbon-cutting ceremony.

Franklin B. Coates, a minor actor in Hollywood, agreed to direct the picture. "We are not making a 'dime novel' sort of story of the life of the outlaw," he told *Moving Picture World*. "We have taken care to make the picture accurate in every way." The part of Cole Younger would be played by Jesse's childhood friend, Harry Hoffman. When Cole Younger lay dying, it was Harry Hoffman and Jesse E. James who sat bedside to hear his confession.

The corporation quickly settled on the title: *Jesse James Under the Black Flag*. The phrase "black flag" was an expression for insurgent warfare. Whether or not the project's backers expected a movie about the famous outlaw's wartime exploits, what they got was Jesse James Jr.'s own version of family legends.

They filmed the movie in style, though not an authentic one. The interior scenes were shot not at the famous James farm in Kearney but on a studio set in Chicago. The outdoor action scenes were not filmed in Clay or Jackson counties or any of Jesse James's other stomping grounds

Jesse James Jr. (in the vest) plays his father in *Jesse James Under the Black Flag*. Harry Hoffman (right) plays Cole Younger. *(Missouri Valley Special Collections, Kansas City Public Library, Kansas City, Missouri)*

but rather in New Mexico. The extras weren't Midwestern farmers; they were Mexicans and Chief Red Fox and a small band of Sioux.

Jesse and Harry wore western cowboy hats. Jesse wore a vest embroidered with roses. The outlaws they portrayed wouldn't have been seen dead in such getups.

Jesse James Under the Black Flag premiered in Kansas City on March 21, 1921, along with a companion film, *Jesse James as the Outlaw.* The *Black Flag* film then went on an extended tour of the Midwest and South. Jesse Jr. and others traveled along with the show. In conjunction with the film, lobby displays were made of the guns, bridle, and spurs supposedly used by Jesse Woodson James and other members of his gang, including Cole and Bob Younger, Frank James, and Quantrill himself. One weapon, it was said, was picked up in the ruins of Quantrill's murder rampage through Lawrence, Kansas. "If it were possible for these old weapons to talk," said an Illinois newspaper, "people would shudder with the bloody tales that would be told."

On several stops, Jesse Jr. gave talks about his father to help promote the film. On one occasion, he tried to convince the gentlemen of the Advertising Club gathered at the Gunter Hotel in San Antonio, Texas, to view his father's legend in a kind light. A local newspaperman reported:

> Jesse James was driven to outlawry and was not the villain he was pictured in cheap novels and other lurid stories. . . . The story of how the late Jessie [*sic*] James joined an independent band of fighters in the sixties at the age of fifteen and fought for the cause of the Confederacy and how later he became a fugitive from justice, to meet death after twenty years in the saddle at the hands of an assassin, was recounted by the speaker.

The ads promised THRILLS GALORE. They promised the movie was "Historically Correct In Every Detail." "The most daring of all the Free

Lances was Jesse James," one display ad remarked. "Secrets of his life, which have never before been revealed, are now told for the first time."

The audiences found no family secrets. The thrills were few and far apart. What they got instead was a lot of silly propaganda about Jesse James. The film showed the most famous outlaw in U.S. history, the baddest of all bad men, spending most of his time on a sickbed or recuperating from gunshot wounds. The clear object was to elicit sympathy. The movie also told a preposterous story of how Jesse James risked his life to fetch a doll from a neighbor's house to comfort the sick little girl of a friend and then spent the night at her bedside to tend to her. Neighborly fella, the audience was told to think. The irony was not lost on anyone familiar with the fate of the real neighbors of Frank and Jesse James.

Though the title hinted at a "blood and thunder melodrama," one reviewer noted that "a beautiful love story runs throughout the picture." Reporter after reporter tried to put a good face on it. The film inspired one Missouri newspaper to remark that "no one can excuse lawlessness in any man, but at his worst Jesse James was a credit to his community, compared with many of our outlaws of today." The *Kansas City Post* said "it is a picture of which Kansas City (and the State of Missouri) may be proud." Though audiences were eager for this movie, the romantic tales it told were not the kind of pandering the public expected, not for thirty cents a head. Jesse, a paunchy, middle-aged lawyer, looked ridiculous trying to play his father as a teenage guerilla fighter. Viewers were openly disappointed not to find some "play up" of crime scenes. The movie showed the James Gang robbing the bank in Northfield, Minnesota, but the fat actor playing Cole Younger, Jesse's best friend Harry Hoffman, was so incompetent with pistols that it looks at one point as though his trigger fingers were in his armpits. The blunders and fact-bending made the film a peculiarity, obviously the product of someone working from a distorted picture of Jesse James, utterly unlike either the public perception or reality.

One theater reported a taxed-to-bursting crowd during the first showing, but empty seats thereafter. *Jesse James Under the Black Flag* was a complete failure, critically and financially. The director would never work in the picture business again. Though intended as a biographical epic, it became a tragedy—for the film's star.

The flop destroyed the outlaw's son. His wife would call it "the last great tragedy in the life of Jesse James Jr." He could not walk away from the losses suffered by his family and friends. The Crittendens alone lost considerable amounts and blamed Jesse and his poor acting.

"Jesse returned to his home in Kansas City, heartbroken and sick," Stella said. He sold everything to pay back what he could. He called his oldest daughter home from college, and she was informed that there was no money for her to continue. All of his daughters had to take jobs. He sold the beautiful home where they'd lived for many years at 4117 St. John Street and moved his family to the Gladstone apartments in 1923.

The troubled son of an outlaw, the boy who began his life with such a paltry legacy only to become a prosperous attorney, once again experienced the loss of all he had. He experienced the indignity of his girls having to work to support him. It was devastating, shameful. He struggled to resume his law practice, but he could not return to it for more than a year. As of November 1923, his family was politely describing him in the press as "retired."

At that low point in his life and career, he was approached about a very special role awaiting him in a political organization that was actively recruiting new members in Kansas City and desperately wanted his name on its rolls. Jesse James Jr. heard the call and took up the fiery cross of the Ku Klux Klan.

In 1922, the KKK came to Missouri. Within months, it had enough members to become a force in state and local politics, an extreme and powerful wing of the Democratic Party. The Klan boasted membership of five thousand men and women in the Kansas City area. Many were said to be professionals and clergymen. Klan recruiters aimed for the most respectable citizens first. One they sought and won was a Jackson

Jesse James Jr. stands alongside his father's headstone. (*Missouri Valley Special Collections, Kansas City Public Library, Kansas City, Missouri*)

County marshal, Harry Hoffman, Jesse's friend. He became the political organizer for the Klan. As hopelessly corrupt as it already was, Kansas City found itself split into new divisions based on religion. The Klan was exclusively Protestant and purported to stand for morality, patriotism, law enforcement, and separation of church and state. It also stood for tar buckets, whips, and vigilantism. It detested Jews, Catholics, immigrants, and blacks. And in the early 1920s it brought terrorism to Kansas City.

"In 1922," Harry Truman wrote in his memoirs, "the Klan revived terrorism." Truman was then a Jackson County commissioner (his official title was "judge"). One day he would be a senator and then president of the United States. Looking back on the sectarian violence much later, he bluntly described the times: "When the Klan was at its height, homes were invaded and people were tarred and feathered and run out of town." The Kluckers held two sorts of meetings, as Truman described them: the "political forum" and the "bed sheet variety." The former were held in Kansas City hotels such as the Baltimore Hotel, and the latter in torchlit fields, and as one joiner remarked, they were "curious, thrilling meetings."

Some politicians like Truman flirted with the idea of joining the Invisible Empire. But he balked at the oath not to hire Catholics. As the Klan grew more violent, sensible men began to fear it. Truman called 1924 the "high tide" for the KKK in Missouri. On April 14 of that year a Klansman fatally shot the mayor of Maysville, Missouri, on election day. Mayor Arthur F. Sisson had made remarks like he "sure wasn't voting for any damned Ku Kluxer."

In the Kansas City area, the bloodshed included midnight whippings and mysterious hit-and-run accidents that left dead black motorists on nearby Clay County roads. In 1925, the violence escalated to the lynching of a black man picked up between Kansas City and Excelsior Springs. He was accused of "attempting an attack" on a white woman. A crowd estimated at a thousand people, including a group that came by special train from Kansas City, saw Walter Mitchell lynched. Ironically, the same element of Missouri citizenry that supported the Klan and participated in the night violence defended it as insurance that the criminal would not escape the law on technicalities. The lynch mob cited as its grounds a "lack of confidence in the courts." The editor of the *Excelsior Springs Standard* wrote a front-page Sunday editorial defending the lynching because he felt murderers were so rarely punished. "The law's delay has been exasperating," he thundered.

In Kansas City, the Klan targeted the "Catholic machine" run by the Irish Catholic Boss of Kansas City, Tom Pendergast, and raised the flaming cross against Catholicism. Anyone who enjoyed a good relationship with Pendergast, such as Judge Truman, would fall into disfavor if he "klanned up." Truman ultimately decided not to join. The Klan decried him as "un-American." At his last Klan appearance, Truman defended the Catholics who served in the military under him and declared that if any of his Army brothers wanted a job, he was giving it to him, Catholic or not. Truman then told the shotgun-toting Kluckers they were "a bunch of cheap un-American fakers" and "cooly walked off the platform and through the crowd to his car."

Tom Pendergast was a violent man who took protection money from saloon owners and whorehouses. He was one of the most corrupt municipal officials of his era. But he was also a devout Catholic. He had every reason to despise the Klan. The press learned that the KKK had targeted Pendergast for "destruction." As one Klansman remarked, "thousands believed that this group would soon overthrow the throne" of the "entrenched political bosses."

One can only wonder what the president of Mesco Pictures thought when he learned that the star of the film he financed was riding shotgun for the Klan. Jesse James Jr. had turned on his old friend. Jesse knew his name had tremendous clout in certain quarters, and he decided to exercise his influence. He was taking a "fling in Democratic politics," as historian William Reddig would describe it. He positioned himself "as an insurgent agitating for the overthrow of 'King Tom' Pendergast."

It is not known if there was anything personal in Jesse's decision to betray his benefactor. Perhaps there were lingering questions about the finances of *Under the Black Flag*. Whatever his motives, the lure of the Klan proved irresistible for Jesse. His father was a bastard hero in the Confederate lexicon, the irregular who never surrendered. By joining the Klan, was Junior trying to make his papa proud of him? Or less abstractly, was he playing to the sentimentalists who regarded

Jesse Woodson James as the greatest of them all, the granddaddy of all avengers, the man who robbed his first train in 1873 near Adair, Iowa, masked in Klan regalia?

In the early part of 1924, James and his new associates prepared for municipal elections in Kansas City, scheduled for April 2. Between the leafletting, parading, meetings, and midnight rides, Jesse James was a busy man, too distracted to practice law. Judge Truman and a slew of other candidates were on the ballot. The question of the hour was the political strength of the Ku Klux Klan, Jesse's new zeal, his new society.

But in late February he could not pass up the chance to take on a wealthy new client. Five weeks before the election, James received a curious telephone call from a man named Gus West, a man who had connections in Kansas City's underworld liquor trade. West wanted to refer a woman to Jesse. She was having troubles with her brother and a man named Smith. Her name was Dr. Wilkins.

In late February a thirty-eight-year-old, much-married woman walked into Jesse's law office and asked for his help.

She had half a month left to live.

Part III

THERE COULD BE BUT ONE END

20

I Have Twenty-four Hours to Live

There appears to be a race of human beings who lay themselves
out to be murdered—they are, to coin a word, born murderees.
Palmer's victims feared and distrusted him, not vaguely, but very
definitely; his mother-in-law declared it would be the end of her if
she went to stay in his house; she went, and it was the end of
her. . . . What can possibly be the explanation for this curious
mental attribute in the victims of murderers? To the impartial
onlooker, it almost suggests a hypnotised attitude of a bird before a
snake; partly, no doubt, the explanation lies in that instinct which
forbids one to believe that anything terrible can happen to oneself
or to anyone in one's immediate circle; but that is not enough to
explain the phenomenon entirely. Perhaps, at some far future date,
when the laws of attraction and repulsion are more fully understood than they are at present, it will be discovered that murderers
and murderees send out wave-lengths that correspond as do the
wave-lengths of wireless between stations. Meanwhile, this curious
question must remain something of a mystery.
— *F. Tennyson Jesse,* Murder and Its Motives *(1924)*

On Thursday, February 28, 1924, Dr. Zeo Zoe Wilkins met Jesse
Edwards James at his law office in Kansas City. James knew
from their first meeting that Dr. Wilkins was "very much troubled."

"Someone wants to kill me," she told him. The statement surprised
him. "Two men have threatened to get me," Zeo continued. "I'm worried,
terribly afraid. They have made demands and said if I do not comply,
they will murder me."

She asked for physical protection. He took no action on that score.

Jesse did not believe her tales of death threats. He thought she was "possessed of hallucinations." Of course he didn't know then that Dr. Wilkins also possessed an uncanny ability to extract money from everyone of her acquaintance and perfect strangers on occasion by making up pitiful stories and fatal scenarios. She had been perfecting her art her entire life. Otherwise he might have suspected then that she was probing him for weaknesses, so that she might solicit him. He couldn't have lent her money in any great sum even if he so desired, as she may well have discovered. He didn't have funds to lend after his *Black Flag* debacle.

James learned Zeo Wilkins was "slow in paying her bills," he said, but she "persisted in earning money by giving osteopathic and electrical treatments despite her wealth." Dr. Wilkins discussed her "electrical treatments" at length. Zeo told Jesse she wanted to buy a sanitarium at Armour Boulevard and Main Street, a fresh piece of real estate that she would co-own with another doctor, perhaps to protect it from creditors. She wanted to collect money from her ex-husband, Albert Marksheffel, to establish the sanitarium.

Zeo asked Jesse to try to collect the money for her. She told the lawyer that Albert never repaid the seventy grand he borrowed to build his world-famous garage in Colorado. Dr. Wilkins "expressed a fear of losing the money lent in Colorado Springs," James said. She showed James two letters written by Al in which he begged for more time to return the money.

She did not show her new lawyer a more important document stored in one of her strongboxes at home: a copy of the letter she wrote authorizing her divorce attorney to accept ten thousand dollars from Al as full and final payment on that note for seventy thousand dollars. Al had paid the debt in full before their divorce was finalized.

Once she became better acquainted with him, Zeo made another request of Jesse James. She also wanted to sell her bonds and diamonds to finance her sanitarium. But they were not quite hers to sell. Six weeks before their first meeting, she received notice that a Colorado court had entered a judgment of twenty-six thousand dollars against her in favor of H. A. Hamilton, her jeweler. The lawyers in Colorado knew she had diamonds; the plaintiff had sold them to her. They already had her furniture and had sold her last Cadillac. She did not want to lose her diamonds and bonds as well. They were all she had left of her Cunningham fortune.

James agreed to represent her, and they began meeting frequently. The first five or six meetings took place at his law office. Then he began seeing her in her home. He would later say he was at her Park Avenue residence on several occasions—days, nights, weekends. Over the course of two weeks, Zeo and Jesse met at least nine times, possibly more, which was unnecessarily frequent given the straightforward nature of the tasks she'd asked of him. There was no discernible reason they couldn't have spoken on the telephone. Perhaps her finances weren't the only assets with which James became intimate.

If she behaved toward Jesse like she usually did toward men, much more than talk took place. Jesse was forty-eight years old, famous, did not wear a wedding ring, and possessed an imposing name and commanding presence. She must have presumed he was well-to-do. Everyone always did. Until recently, they had been correct, and Jesse could dress the part of a successful trial lawyer. Jesse always liked to keep himself impeccably dressed. His wife still brushed his shoes and starched his collars and cuffs.

He was also well known by then as a ladies' man. According to his own wife, Jesse habitually convinced his female clients to open their legs for him. Nine or more meetings, between this particular pair, were more than enough to justify this presumption: Their dealings quickly evolved from an attorney-client relationship to a sexual affair.

They were alone every time except one. On Sunday, March 9, Zeo's friend Eva Grundy was present for a meeting between Jesse and Zeo at her Park Avenue home. The occasion was the unveiling of her legal documents and valuables. Zeo presented everything to Jesse. While showing

Jesse her last will and testament she remarked, "I want you to look this over and tell me if my brother Charles can get a penny of my estate if he murders me."

She was serious, but at that point James felt sure she was delusional. He did not take her concern about her brother seriously. Jesse noted that her will had been prepared by a lawyer and signed in February. It named Zeo's nephew and adopted son, Horace Wilkins Ricketts, as her sole beneficiary. The will appeared to be proper and in order to Jesse.

At the same meeting, James looked at her Liberty bonds, corporate bonds, and her unset diamonds. Maybe he was a little surprised when he discovered that she was telling the truth about owning this fortune. He found the diamonds in his hands.

He closely examined them. He valued them at twenty-five thousand dollars, calling on the knowledge he gained during his pawnshop days. James must have been impressed by her wealth. It might have been the largest sum he'd ever seen since he started filming his movie. Now Jesse, still mired in debt, still living in an apartment, had twenty-five thousand dollars sitting in his palm. And the valuable diamonds were owned by a woman who had convinced herself that several people were out to kill her.

He immediately realized what a profound danger it posed to Zeo to have such treasure stashed in her house, particularly given the sort of men with whom she consorted. "I asked her why she did not put the money in a bank," James said, "but she said she was afraid of banks. She said, 'All bankers are crooks and ought to be put in jail.'"

Maybe she was thinking of some of the bankers she had known—B.B. Burnett or Amos Gipson. She was also thinking about Al Marksheffel. Why did Zeo ask Jesse to extract money from her ex-husband which she knew he did not owe? Perhaps she was delusional. Maybe it was some sort of post-divorce strategy, and she thought Jesse James could cow Al into paying twice. More likely it was a play for sympathy. Jesse could tell Al about all the threats made on her life. Or was she using an old document to impress her lawyer, intending to defraud him?

At some point during Zeo's last week on earth, James, by his account, made the necessary appointment with Albert Marksheffel. What did Al's face look like when he learned that Jesse James was calling from Missouri to collect on a debt? Al could have set Jesse straight. He could have convinced Jesse. Just as he'd once defended himself on manslaughter charges, he'd undoubtedly come across as perfectly calm and rational. He could have offered proof that he satisfied the note. What Al could have done he probably did do, and he might have shared some other interesting facts about his ex-wife as well. At some point that week James learned that his client was lying to him. Seventy thousand dollars, gone. A myth. A hefty percentage of nothing is nothing.

On the afternoon of Wednesday, March 12, Zeo was again in a state and made a phone call to her sister Gertrude.

"Someone is going to get me and put me out of the way. I'm going to lose my money and my life."

"Who is going to do all that?"

"It's some people you don't know. Please come by the next train. Please come by the next train. There is no way out. Only my relatives can save me."

"Her statements over the phone that day," her sister would later say, "that someone was going to get her, seemed to me at the time to be the result of hallucinations. I did not believe anyone was going to harm her. . . . She then spoke of her decision to undergo an operation, as she felt ill. . . . I did not take the telephone conversation seriously because my sister was believed unbalanced mentally, and I suspected her fears were imaginary."

On Thursday, March 13, Zeo showed up for a scheduled appointment with Jesse James Jr. at his law office. She waited for two hours. He never appeared.

Zeo pinned the pages of Thursday's newspaper to the bottom of her window shades to completely block any view of the inside of her home.

Later that Thursday, Zeo's landlady, Mrs. Gertrude Palmer, went to Park Avenue to dun Zeo for the rent. As of mid-March 1924, she was twenty-two weeks in arrears. Dr. Wilkins offered more stories of fatiguing business affairs. "She urged me to go [to] Colorado Springs to obtain money for her holdings there, which seemed to be tied up in litigation," Mrs. Palmer said. Zeo mentioned her attorney Jesse James Jr. with disfavor.

On Thursday night, Charles Wilkins visited his sister. When he arrived, a man in his fifties (who was never identified) was examining her Abrams machine. Zeo offered him an interest in the device for a hundred dollars. "I have to have the money in twenty-four hours," she said. The man left. Charles said he stayed alone with Zeo until midnight, left, and never saw his sister alive again.

On the morning of Friday, March 14, Zeo called her friend Eva Grundy and asked her to come over right away. "She asked me to get my trunk and stay with her at her house," Eva said. Zeo sent a taxicab to pick up Eva shortly before noon.

When Eva arrived she suggested they go out for lunch, but Zeo wanted to talk privately. While Eva went into the pantry to prepare a light meal, Zeo told her, "Be sure to examine the loaf of bread and be sure the paper covering is not broken." Zeo, in the full-blown throes of paranoia, was afraid someone was going to poison her.

At lunchtime on Friday, Dr. Wilkins had a second visitor, her morning man. B. F. Tarpley stopped by the house bearing two bags of fruit. Eva overheard their brief conversation.

"Now, if you want the $16 I owe you," Zeo said to Ben, "I can give it to you in cash, and if you don't you can take it out in treatments."

Tarpley was standing with his hat in his hand. "That's all right. I don't need the money now." He left the house.

Zeo resumed her conversation with Eva. "There are four persons trying to kill me. Mrs. Grundy, I have only twenty-four or possibly forty-eight hours to live. I have been threatened with death." She mentioned a doctor in Kansas City. Later, she mentioned her brother and how he mistreated her.

Eva remained in Dr. Wilkins's home until nearly midnight Friday. Zeo was "very excited and upset mentally." They talked for hours. "My life is threatened," Zeo insisted. "Four people are going to get me." Zeo paced the floor and said over and over, "I know they will get me. My one hope is to put over that sanitarium deal." It is not known how a sanitarium deal could possibly have saved her from a threat of death, and Eva couldn't explain it either. Perhaps in the back of her mind Eva suspected that Dr. Wilkins was indeed going to die soon. It would explain a few things.

"She was very nervous all of the time that I was there, and she was afraid of either being killed or poisoned," Eva said. "Every time she offered me some fruit I had to eat it first, and she would follow me. . . . She said she had only twenty-four or forty-eight hours to complete the deal by which she was going to open up a sanitarium on Armour Boulevard."

Zeo spoke at length of the proposal. "She offered me the position of financial secretary," Eva said. "She put some kind of a paper, a certificate, in my lap. I didn't touch it. She said, 'This is a thousand dollars. I have seven thousand more and about twenty thousand dollars' worth of diamonds. I'll pay you a thousand dollars and maybe fifteen hundred dollars a month.'" Then Zeo borrowed money from Eva as a "token" of Eva's "confidence" in the sanitarium proposal. Zeo promised to repay the loan when she received money for the sale of her securities. Eva gave her a check for fifty dollars.

Zeo begged Eva to stay, but Eva wanted to leave. Zeo asked Eva to return to Park Avenue at three p.m. the next day for an appointment Zeo had with someone. She wanted Eva to be present for the meeting. Eva promised to come.

They also spoke of her lawyer. "She said she did not have anything to do with him," Eva said. "Dr. Wilkins said she did not trust Jesse James."

The ides of March arrived.

On Saturday morning, Zeo took a livery car to Eva's bank and cashed the check. Eva met her there. Zeo told Eva she had to get back home. If her houseman Dillard left and closed the door, he would not be able to get back in. He did not have a key.

At eleven-thirty Saturday morning, Dr. Wilkins was visited by Mr. Holly G. Haworth, D.O., a thirty-year-old, 1917 graduate of Dr. Still's American School of Osteopathy who practiced medicine on Prospect Avenue. On the advice of one of his classmates, Dr. Haworth was interested in going into a partnership with Dr. Wilkins. He was particularly impressed by her Abrams machine and believed it was one of three original "oscilloclasts" operated by the late Dr. Abrams himself.

"She wanted me to go into business with her—to handle the osteopathic end of a practice or, perhaps, a sanitarium she intended to develop," Dr. Haworth said. "She mentioned Dr. Earl W. Smith's place at Main Street and Armour Boulevard as a likely place. She said she sought it before he got it and still would like to have it. If she couldn't get it, she said, she probably would establish a similar institution on the South Side."

They agreed to meet again on Sunday evening to form final plans.

"I never saw her before," Dr. Haworth said. "I never saw her again."

Around noon Saturday, Mrs. Palmer spoke to Zeo on the telephone about the rent. Dr. Wilkins advised that she was to "confer with some persons" on that day and then she would have it. "She was terribly disappointed because she could not pay the rent," said Mrs. Palmer. "She said, 'I'll pay you tonight or Sunday. I'm going to have a conference this afternoon and arrange for the money.'" The doctor promised to call Mrs. Palmer later. It was the last time they spoke.

Three p.m. came and went. Eva Grundy did not appear for the appointment and neither did anyone else. Eva never publicly disclosed who else was expected at the three p.m. meeting on Zeo's last day of life.

Ben Tarpley stopped at Zeo's house on his way home from work at three-thirty on Saturday afternoon. While Tarpley was there, Dillard Davies came to the home. He had a veterinary surgeon with him. Davies told Zeo that he owed the vet a dollar for performing surgery on his horse and asked her to pay it out of the back wages she owed him, which she did.

Ben stayed for a little over an hour probably doing what he usually did during his afternoons with Zeo. He left before five p.m.

What happened next would be told in headlines nationwide.

21

There's Someone Lying on the Floor

I have never seen a city that needed a religious revival more
than Kansas City does right now. I went from bad to worse
when I was in sin, and from worse to Chicago, and I thought
I had seen all there was to see. But I have changed my mind
since I came to Kansas City.
— *Alcoholic–turned–Presbyterian Evangelist*
Mel Trotter, April 6, 1924

Zeo was murdered on Saturday night. It happened around ten
p.m. She battled a man for her life and lost. Soon flames licked
the carpet. In only a few moments, maybe before the hasty killer even
left the house, the fire fizzled and died on the damp towel. Zeo remained
on the rug, cooling, stiffening, through the night. Her blood soaked
through the rug and floorboards and pooled in the basement.

Ben Tarpley knocked on the door early Sunday morning. When Zeo
didn't answer, he left his lunch on the porch. Later he phoned but could
not get through.

Eva Grundy came to the house repeatedly on Sunday. She called several
times. Mrs. Palmer also came knocking on Sunday to ask about the
rent again.

On Sunday evening, a man stopped by the house and pounded on
the door. He was Cyril Palmer, the adult son of Zeo's landlady. He had
a young woman with him who was not his wife, and he intended to take
her to the second floor of Zeo's home, remove all her clothes, and make a
racket. But nobody answered the door. Like the others, he turned away

in frustration. The windows were too high to see inside and the shades were drawn on the trysting place.

John Kincaid, the hot tamale vendor, shouted his wares outside 2425 Park on Sunday night but got no reply. He lit his pipe and waited. Dr. Holly Haworth arrived for his Sunday evening appointment to discuss final plans for the sanitarium, but no one answered his knock. He noticed the morning paper on the porch. As he retreated down the front steps, Dr. Haworth heard a strange noise coming from the alley. He walked to the corner and saw a man behind the house.

Dr. Haworth addressed the tamale peddler. "I heard a man kick some glass in at the back of that house just now."

The peddler tossed aside a match and said he hadn't heard anything. "Where?"

"Is there anybody in that house?" Dr. Haworth asked.

They both turned as a car approached. Eva Grundy emerged and walked up to the house.

"There she is now," Dr. Haworth said.

"No, that's not her. Not big enough. And this woman's too young."

"No," Dr. Haworth said, "that's not her."

Eva knocked, waited, and left. The peddler started pushing his cart down the street again. Behind him Dr. Haworth said, "There's the fellow who kicked in the window."

A man walked toward them and stopped Kincaid's tamale cart. "What were you fellows talking about?" he demanded.

"Tamales," Kincaid replied. He was terrified that this burglar might have a revolver. The stranger turned away and trudged through the snow, walking quickly south.

"If I were you I'd call the police, if I'd seen a man kick in a window," Kincaid said to Dr. Haworth, who agreed. The doctor scurried to a corner drugstore to find a telephone.

Two patrolmen responded in minutes. The peddler pointed out a set of footprints in the snow. The patrolmen overtook the man as he was about to enter an apartment building at 25th and Olive streets. The man was named Moore. Returning with him to 2425 Park, the patrolmen found a broken basement window. Moore said he had business in the area; he tended many furnaces in the neighborhood. He claimed to know nothing about any broken window. The revolver turned out to be a flashlight. The patrolmen pounded on the front door of 2425 Park. Failing to arouse anyone in the house, which seemed to be deserted, the officers let Moore go.

On Monday morning, the landlady tried calling again. She returned to the house Monday night. The Sunday morning papers were still folded on the porch. The mailbox held letters posted Wednesday, March 12. "After I had received no response at the place on four trips," Mrs. Palmer said, "I wrote Mrs. Wilkins a letter in which I said, 'Dr. Wilkins, in heaven's name, where have you gone? Let me know.'"

The landlady wondered whether her tenant had absconded with the furniture, so on Tuesday she returned to Park Avenue. She noticed a window on the side of the house was partly open. That was odd, given the chilly weather and late snow. Mrs. Palmer finagled a thirteen-year-old boy who lived next door into climbing a ladder for a peek inside. Isidor Cortez peered into the window. He scurried back down the ladder and cried out, "There's someone lying on the floor." Mrs. Palmer called the police.

Two patrolmen with the Kansas City Police Department, Dan Ahearn and William H. Pauling, answered the call late Tuesday. They knew as soon as they climbed the ladder that Dr. Wilkins was definitely dead. They crawled through the window to be greeted by the full smell of the corpse and the cries of a brown and white tabby cat. Coroner's investigator Samuel E. Edwards also had to crawl in the window to get to Dr. Wilkins's body, since both front and rear doors were locked and no one had thought to throw back the Yale bolts. Edwards had her corpse removed for examination. Zeo had been dead for nearly three full days.

The patrolmen found the hallmarks of violence everywhere they looked: blood splattered the walls in the living room, and books and letters were strewn across the floor. Cupboards, drawers, and shelves had been rifled through. Some of the chairs in the living room were broken. On the rug they found a bloody, rusty pocket knife. More bloodstains lined the washbowl in the bathroom. A small cellar window was smashed but a solid coat of dust appeared on the window ledge. The cellar floor was covered with blood. The stench of decay filled the house.

Zeo's body was removed to the undertaking parlor of the Eylar Brothers Funeral Home. A newsman by the name of Arthur DeGreve learned of her murder and followed her corpse. His piece for the front page of the *Atlanta Constitution* observed that she "lies alone in death, deserted by the score of fashionable friends and admirers who had fought for her favors in life . . . an occasional passerby stops momentarily in front of the establishment, looks inquiringly in and then proceeds on his way in slow and measured steps. No relatives have arrived and no funeral arrangements have been made. . . . Meanwhile police are hopelessly lost in a maze of new developments."

Zeo's only other visitors Tuesday night were Detective James Elder and Deputy Coroner H. E. Moss, M.D. Dr. Moss conducted an autopsy at the funeral home. He found Zeo Wilkins fully clothed, though he noted her underwear and dress were torn. Her bloody clothing was cut off and given to the detective. The coroner summed up the womanly figure known so intimately by so many with a few measurements and then delineated her injuries:

> Height 5 feet 8 inches
> Weight 130 pounds.
> Hair dark brown
> Eyes blue
> Complexion fair.
> Stabbed twice, right side middle line anterior part of the neck.
> Contusions middle forehead near hair line. Left eye black and

blue; eye protruding greatly. Multiple skin lacerations on the left
cheek and left side throat. Skin abrasions on the left chest wall.
Black and blue spots on the left chest wall.

Dr. Moss found no sign of rape. It was obvious to him that she had
fought ferociously with her murderer. Her shoulders and face bore many
scratches, her neck was branded with the marks of fingers, and her left
eye was destroyed. As he completed Zeo Wilkins's death certificate he
listed the cause of death as "homicide by knife stab wounds."

Dr. Moss's findings matched the condition of the ransacked house.
The police concluded that it was a "terrific fight." They also shared the
opinion of the deputy coroner that Zeo Z. Wilkins actually met her
demise on or about Saturday, the fifteenth of March.

The authorities considered and discarded a theory of suicide because
of the nature of the knife wounds in her neck. Either of the two neck
wounds would have been fatal, said deputy corner Sam Edwards. Presumably, she would not have fatally stabbed herself twice. He also
pointed out that the location of the wounds, if self-inflicted, necessi-
tated that they be done with the knife in the left hand. Edwards did
not believe they were self-inflicted because the knife was dull-bladed.
Much force would have been required to cause such injuries, not to
mention the fact that Dr. Wilkins was right-handed. By that time, more
was known of Dr. Wilkins and her "apparently high intellect." Such a
woman would have selected a less painful method of suicide, Edwards
surmised.

Charles Wilkins walked into police headquarters on Tuesday night
and announced that he had just learned of his sister's murder by reading
it in a newspaper. A *Kansas City Journal* reporter who was hanging
around the station noted that Charles "did not seem to be perturbed
over the death of his sister."

"The first I knew of it was from the early edition of the *Journal,*" he
said ("without emotion," the reporter noted). "It was a horrible ending.

I haven't seen my sister for several days. I telephoned her Saturday night and the telephone was busy. Sunday morning I telephoned her again, but central told me the line had been discontinued."

He was brought out back for a Kansas City–style police grilling. The big, tough man started on the wrong foot. When asked for biographical information, Wilkins declared that he was an "atheist, a radical, and an I.W.W." He guaranteed himself a stay in a cell at police headquarters with that line alone.

His interrogators asked Charles Wilkins about his sister for hours, and her stoic brother spoke at length. Charles said she was married many times, but he could only remember the names of three of her husbands. Her first marriage was to a fellow medical student named Richard Dryder, he said. And there were her marriages to Marksheffel and Cunningham. The policemen already knew those stories. Everyone in Kansas City who read the front page knew them. Charles said he'd recently had a falling out with his sister but decided to stay in Kansas City, though by one account he had a wife back in Seattle. Per press reports, he'd found work as a barber at 1036 East 5th Street. He told police that he was at work all night on Saturday night and had alibis to prove it. He also gave the police the names of some other men he thought capable of the crime. He was held pending further investigation.

The police brought Dillard Davies to the Flora Avenue station for questioning on the night Zeo's body was found. It may have been a familiar feeling for Davies. According to police, the thirty-five-year-old was an ex-convict who had served a stretch in the state penitentiary in Illinois for burglary. Even if he didn't kill Dr. Wilkins, he certainly knew that as a black man he might go up the river for it and could count himself lucky he wasn't in a country district where it wasn't a challenge to scrounge up a lynch mob and storm a jail.

Davies was asked if he ever sexually attacked Dr. Wilkins. He denied it. "She was drunk when she told that," he said. The doctor was a heavy drinker, downing on average three bottles of Jamaica Ginger every day, Davies said. She ordered it from the drugstore, and Dillard said he bought it for her sometimes.

As far as Dillard Davies was aware, Dr. Wilkins had no money. Davies said she owed him seventy-five dollars for work he'd done for her. She owed several merchants and grocers. She sold her motor car in Colorado Springs for fifteen hundred dollars recently to pay a debt there. Not long ago, she'd paid a four-hundred-dollar grocery bill with one of her fur coats. He told the police about Dr. Wilkins's vicious fights with her brother Charlie and what her brother had done to her bulldog.

Davies insisted the last time he saw Zeo was when he borrowed a dollar to get his horse treated. His horse fell sick, and he asked an old white blacksmith to treat her. "He doctored my horse and did not charge me anything for that," Davies said, "but he said I owed him a dollar for blacksmithing, and I asked him to go with me to 2425 Park to get his money, which is the home of Dr. Zoe Wilkins. We knocked on the door and Mr. Tarpley opened the door. We stepped inside and Tarpley rested his elbow on the mantel of the fireplace and rested his head in his hand. I went into the kitchen and got a drink of water, came back and Dr. Wilkins handed me a dollar which I gave to the blacksmith. We were only in the house a few minutes and left. This is the last time I had been there."

After that, he said, he sold a wagonload of junk for four dollars and bought two dollars' worth of horse feed. On Saturday night, he "itched to shoot dice." He lost his last two dollars playing dice, he said. The police questioned Dillard Davies for many hours, but he resisted their entreaties and traps meant to get him to confess to a murder he did not commit.

Both Charles Wilkins and Dillard Davies pointed the finger at another man: Ben Tarpley. Davies told them Tarpley was jealous. "When he came over he would go upstairs to see if any men were in the house and also make inquiries of me as to whether any men had been there during the night."

A reporter had the pleasure of shocking Mr. and Mrs. Tarpley at their home in Kansas City, Kansas, with the news of Zeo's murder. Ben Tarpley denied that he was Zeo's lover. He claimed he was only her chauffeur. He admitted arguing with her over a dog and confessed he kept early morning appointments, but denied he ever had a key.

Bessie Tarpley insisted that she was with her husband from late Saturday afternoon forward. She also denied any knowledge of an affair between her husband and this murdered doctor. "I refuse to believe my husband's relations with Dr. Wilkins were any more than a patient's," she said. "I know he's gone there as a patient, but until he tells me himself I'll not believe these stories about early morning calls."

Ben Tarpley was brought to police headquarters, where he repeated his denials. He told the police he last saw Dr. Wilkins on Saturday afternoon. He planned to drive her to an appointment, but after "some delay, Dr. Wilkins decided not to make the call." Tarpley was arrested. He was the third but far from the last man to be questioned on suspicion of Zeo's murder.

Late Tuesday night, hours after Zeo's body was found, a reporter in Colorado Springs knocked on Arthur and Laura Wilkins's door. The reporter carefully recorded the moment:

> Arthur Wilkins, a tall, sandy-haired man in working clothes, leaned heavily on the door as the reporter told him his sister had died, and then that she had been murdered. Had he heard about it? His breath escaped him in a long sigh and at the end of it came the almost inaudible word, "No."
>
> Mrs. Wilkins was in bed when her husband stepped to the door of her room and said, "Laura, Doc's dead." They were both stunned by the news; both trembling visibly when they entered the editorial rooms of the Gazette and Telegraph a scant half hour later to read the detailed accounts of the finding of the body.

Colorado Springs Police Chief Hugh D. Harper quizzed Art and Laura. He sent a telegraph to the Kansas City police, telling them to question Sadie Shields, Gus West, Dr. Arthur F. Blanchard, Tom Chase, and Dr. McMurtrey.

Arthur became "exercised" by the suggestion Charles Wilkins committed the murder. "But don't think I'd try to protect him if he did. I'd treat one man like another who did a thing like that." Laura told the police she last saw Zeo in Kansas City late in 1923 when Zeo was sick. "They told me when I got there that Dr. Blanchard had made threats," Laura said. "He had threatened to kill some other man because he was in love with Doc. I was worried about it all the time I was there."

Gus West, the "Italian" with underworld connections, had been infatuated with Doc for years, Laura reported. "When she married here, he threatened to come to Colorado Springs and kill himself on their doorstep."

Zeo's sister-in-law tempered her intriguing report with her next observation. "Laura Wilkins does not believe that any of the five persons named will prove the murderer," said the *Colorado Springs Gazette.* "'It was someone who had known Doc only a little while and had had an argument with her,' she insisted, with lips set in an obstinate line. 'Zoe would argue with anybody.'"

Dr. Holly Haworth spoke to the detectives about his involvement in Dr. Zeo Wilkins's tentative plans to open a sanitarium. He was an educated young man and a good witness, but he could not shed much light on matters. On the one hand, his involvement suggested the enterprise would be a legitimate medical endeavor. On the other, he sensed something amiss.

"Everything did not seem quite right," he told them. "I don't know what was wrong about the place, but all was not well. I don't know whether she was a habitual user of drugs. She might have used them occasionally. Anybody is likely to do that. She wasn't quite healthy, it seemed, and at times talked exaltedly of her Abrams apparatus. 'It is one of the three original Abrams machines,' she said. 'There is something inside of it that makes it exceptionally desirable to some people. There are at least three—perhaps four—who would give a lot to have it. What other machines will do in thirty minutes, this will do in eight or ten minutes. I have known it to cure persons considered incurable. I have had it only two years.'

"I was impressed because it all was strange," Dr. Haworth said. "I know nothing about the Abrams machine. I stayed on and talked about it for a while and left, agreeing to meet her at 8 o'clock Sunday night, when she was to introduce me to a woman who, she said, would act as a private secretary and business manager in the institution she planned to develop."

While he was there, he saw Davies come and go. "I noticed nothing extraordinary about him. He merely obeyed commonplace orders. Later Dr. Wilkins called a drugstore for prescriptions—I don't know what they were—and when the boy called with them, she took a roll of bills from her pocket and paid for the prescriptions . . .

"I went to the doctor's house in good faith. I thought I might entertain a proposition. She told me I didn't need to put up much cash and, once, when I arranged an appointment over [the] telephone, she said she was 'just worked to death' and needed assistance."

It was another confounding statement, difficult to reconcile against Zeo's remarks to others. She told Eva that certain men were after her for a large sum of money. She suggested they were involved in her sanitarium. If she were truly desperate for the funds to pay off some urgent debt, she should have been seeking more from Dr. Haworth. "She told me I didn't need to put up much cash," he said. Was that the behavior of a woman in dire need of an immediate infusion of a large amount of money on pain of death?

On Tuesday evening, a few hours after her body was found, Jesse James Jr. appeared at the police station to give a statement to the chief of detectives and to reporters. The *Kansas City Times*, morning sister paper of the *Kansas City Star*, printed one account of his public remarks. James said Dr. Wilkins hired him two weeks before in connection with financial affairs involving a person in Colorado. The Wednesday morning *Times* reported that James "made an appointment last week with Dr. Wilkins for today, when she was to entrust him notes and documents concerning the matter." James also said the woman appeared very much troubled and feared she would be killed.

Chief of Detectives Isaac B. Walston also gave a statement to reporters. Following up on James's hints, Walston said he sent telegrams to several cities to be on the lookout for a nurse employed by Dr. Wilkins, Albert Marksheffel, Charles Smith, and one other man who was not publicly named.

"Undoubtedly, the police believe, the murder motive hinged on financial affairs," the *Times* observed. Chief Walston was quoted in the *Kansas City Star* stating that Dr. Wilkins was being blackmailed and threatened. Walston said he thought her sanitarium never existed. It was a "myth" and a means of obtaining money demanded by some "high-jackers," he said. He thought Davies, Tarpley, and Charles Wilkins were "in on the deal." He did not elaborate. He did not explain why anyone might "highjack" Dr. Wilkins.

Chief Walston also announced that a team of six experienced detectives would conduct another search of the doctor's home the next day. Jesse James Jr. accepted an invitation to join the search.

Someone thought to ask Chief Walston how it was that the police held three men on suspicion of murder but had not obtained warrants for their arrest or had them arraigned. Chief Walston said they would wait until after a coroner's inquest to issue warrants. That was the way Kansas City investigated murder cases. Arrest first, ask questions later, and let circumstances dictate the terms of justice.

22

Throat of Adventuress Cut

Even paranoids have enemies.

— *Sigmund Freud*

Zeo's murder hit the newspapers in full force on Wednesday, March 19, 1924. The morning edition of the *Kansas City Times* favored her with the most prominent spot on page one, the upper left column: ZEO Z. WILKINS IS SLAIN. The article named the three men under arrest and delved into dozens of inches of detail about the case. The *Kansas City Times* and *Star* printed photos of Charles Wilkins and B.F. Tarpley taken the night before at the police station. They did not print a photo of Dillard Davies.

The Associated Press, United Press, International News Service, and other regional news wires carried the Wilkins story overnight. It played on front pages all over the country. Journalists everywhere took delight in rendering the perhaps not so surprising news of the death of one of the most well-known osteopaths in the country. The story received special attention in towns where she once practiced medicine and gold digging. "Nearly every city in Oklahoma has tried to claim Mrs. Zeo Zoe Wilkins, murdered osteopath of Kansas City, as a former citizen," wrote the editor of the *Ardmore Ardmoreite.* "Right now we speak up for Ardmore; she ain't never been in this here town." The headlines pulled no punches: THROAT OF 'ADVENTURESS' CUT led the *Nevada State Journal* in a headline that ran across five columns. The *Billings Gazette* in Montana went full-width across the top of its front page with SLAIN WOMAN AWAITED MURDER.

Zeo's murder was an occasion to rehash the most scandalous escapades of her public life. So there it was, for all to read, her entire career, everything and everyone from Dryden, or whatever her first husband's name was ("Particulars concerning these first matrimonial affairs have become clouded by the maze of those which followed," remarked the *St. Louis Post-Dispatch*), to the details of her shooting of Dr. Garring, the bank she helped wreck in Sapulpa, the suicide note left by Leonard Smith, and the Cunningham-Taylor affair ("a wallop that splashed ink all over the front pages of newspapers from one end of the country to the other"). There was a description of her marriage to her "chauffeur" and the "mysterious activities" of her last days. Many reporters undoubtedly remembered the most titillating chapters of her earlier "adventures." If they didn't, they visited the newspaper's morgue or clipping library to find a thick envelope with Zeo's name on it. Most misspelled it as "Zoe," sometimes even spelling it "Zee," the well-known nickname of Jesse James Jr.'s mother. They often repeated the impression that she was married to six men when actually, it was five; she married Cunningham twice.

The press came up with a variety of names to describe Zeo: romantic adventuress, national beauty, gold digger, breaker of hearts, beautiful child of fortune, siren of legend, toy of wealthy men, bride of six men, pet of Chicago hotels, pretty osteopath, pretty divorcée, ardent devotee of Cupid, woman of mystery, *la belle dame sans merci,* victim of her own intrigues, a woman of action, shrewd and daring. "She could not be forever the darling of fortune," one article remarked. "At last, Fate marked her." The *Osteopathic Physician Magazine* summed up her end with, "Death rang down the curtain on her hectic career."

The press always treated Zeo Wilkins light-heartedly, through all her crimes and foibles. Many found her "wild career" humorous even after she came face to face with a brutal killer. George Rothwell Brown of the *Washington Post* began his front-page eulogy with a rhyme:

What sums from these old spouses I could raise,
Procured young husbands in my riper days.

When Zeo Zoe Wilkins took a course in osteopathy she learned the knack of pulling a man's leg, and never lost it. Now three men are held in the investigation of her mysterious murder in Kansas City which has uncovered six amazing adventures in matrimony.

But the public chapters of her life hardly told the whole story of her Arabian nights, as six police detectives and her lawyer came to discover.

Jesse E. James, along with detectives Edward C. Kritser, William J. Doarn, H. E. Jury, T. J. Higgins, L. L. McFadden, and W. F. Jones entered Zeo Wilkins's home the day after her body was found and went through her belongings. They discovered more of her secrets. They read "a score of chapters" from Zeo's life. They read her diary. Several journalists prowled around the house taking down good quotes from her private papers, and two men from the *Kansas City Journal* found the stale lunch that Ben Tarpley left Sunday morning.

The scene inside was one of bloody chaos. The murderer was clearly after something, presumably valuables, but the police remarked that many things a robber would normally steal were left untouched. On the second floor the killer had ransacked her clothes, which could have dressed an entire harem: two wardrobe trunks, two suitcases, and a closet filled with expensive items. In the living room they found a pint of corn whisky, one-fourth full, sitting on a table. A house key for the front door, the only one they could find, lay on the mantel. The patrolmen also discovered more than a hundred paper packets containing a "white medicine." The coroner's office took possession of them for analysis. Unquestionably, narcotics agents would be interested in the substance.

James told the detectives that Dr. Wilkins kept valuables in a strongbox. In her dining room, he noticed that other documents he had seen in the same box were now scattered on the floor. The box itself was missing. The six detectives and the lawyer continued a thorough, hours-long search, but they did not find any diamonds or bonds. Her will was also missing. And the certificate for the Marksheffel loan, as well as the two letters from Marksheffel, were nowhere to be found.

They found dozens of love letters from "men of money and men who had nothing." Dr. Wilkins's address book held sixty-two entries; forty-five of them were men. The book contained mostly first names such as Ada, Anna, Bob, Little Tom, and Frank. The mailbox revealed that several men were receiving their mail at her home. One was C.C. Selmer; the other George Mahan, who was known to the police as a local pool hall proprietor.

A policy for ten thousand dollars from New York Life Insurance Company named as her beneficiary Horace W. Ricketts, her adopted son. A wadded-up roll of bills amounting to forty dollars was found tied up in a ball of cotton and stuffed beneath a mattress.

Other documents hinted at financial distress. A letter notified her that she was six hundred dollars overdrawn on a bank account: "The Exchange National were very nice indeed to cash your checks for you, and they should be taken care of. . . . I would suggest that you do not draw any more checks on them until you have a balance."

A letter dated March 6, 1923, was typed on the letterhead of a lawyer in Fort Worth, Texas, and addressed to an attorney for Dr. Wilkins. The letter demanded payment of $722.45 to Dr. O. M. McMurtrey of Fort Worth and went on to say:

> The idea that she does not owe this is simply absurd. Quite a host of witnesses saw this money loaned from time to time; some of them spent it for her for hooch and some other things, and, in general, I may say to you frankly that she has led a somewhat inglorious sort of life while down here. These facts are known by quite a number of people, including certain policemen. . . . If she expects to beat this debt she had better get busy because she is not going to do it without a run for her money.

Another letter contained a more personal plea. A woman in New York, who signed only as Cornelia, asked Dr. Wilkins to make good on an investment in an oil lease of seven thousand dollars. "Send me something," Cornelia begged. "You surely must be making money now. Two hundred dollars will be a big help. Zeo, please try and send me a couple of hundred by the first of the week so I can straighten out a few things. Every cent that comes in has to go to rent. . . . I've borrowed and so has Alice from every one we can get a cent from."

Police found "scores" of similar demands. The government had written her to pay up her taxes. Legal pleadings named her as a defendant in several lawsuits. Lawyers in Colorado were threatening garnishments. Several courts had issued judgments, including many divorces.

One discovery was "a strange note, written in an awkward hand":

Take something from me. Keep hands off all but Clark. This will be over in a minute. Obey it.

"Investigators believed it was written by someone who held the paper under a table to prevent other persons from seeing the message," reported one newsman. "Apparently, investigators say, it was written just before an impending physical clash." One wonders how they could have come to this conclusion. Anyway they could find no one named Clark with any connection to Dr. Wilkins.

A letter dated January 3, 1921, was addressed to James A. Orr and signed by Mrs. Zeo Z. Marksheffel. It stated: "I do hereby authorize you to settle all pending litigation and all matters pending between Mr. A. W. Marksheffel and myself and release him of all claims on account of being his wife, for $10,000 cash—and all jewelry given to him."

One newsman would write of the discovery of documents suggesting that Dr. Wilkins required her abortion clients to pay twice. The report stated that "her osteopathic skill provided an ample if sinister cloak for carrying out abortions on wealthy women anxious to avoid motherhood, who thus also became prey to her blackmailing wiles." Whether such a vague allegation should be given credence is unclear. No other reporter ever repeated anything along these lines. Providing abortions would have been outside her training as an osteopath, and blackmail was not known to have been in her repertoire. But nobody, by that point, would have put it past her.

When the police detectives examined the damaged rug on which the woman's corpse had lain, they found soot from burned paper and a half-burned, bloody towel. The fire had spread almost to Zeo's body before it petered out. On her osteopath's table in the middle of the room, a box stood open. It contained many newspaper clippings about Dr. Wilkins, most of them concerning divorce scandals, as well as calling cards engraved with the names "Mr. and Mrs. Albert W. Marksheffel" or "Mr. Albert W. Marksheffel." They found Dr. Wilkins's business card, which listed her Park Avenue home as a "temporary address." Another new set of business cards included her name as well as the name of Dr. A. F. Blanchard over her Park Avenue address.

Every hour of the investigation brought new names to their attention, "an ever increasing number of men—friends and patients of the slain woman—who had fallen victim to her charms," remarked that evening's edition of the *Kansas City Post.* "No enchantress of history ever seemed to have aroused the infatuation of more men admirers . . . men who had lived at her house, men who had received mail there, men who as friends had been contesting with each other in their efforts to protect her, men who had been jealous of her, and men who had been merely her patients, all are being brought into the whirl of the police investigation."

The woman's mess of a life overwhelmed them with theories on the motive of the killer. They considered three alternatives: a jealous lover, one of the enemies she feared, or a bandit after her treasure.

Jesse E. James gave a second statement to several reporters after the search of Zeo's home on Wednesday. It made the front pages of that evening's *Star* and *Post.* James said, "Dr. Wilkins told me four persons had threatened to kill her. She constantly seemed worried and possessed of fear." He did not name them. James revealed that Dr. Wilkins kept a hundred thousand dollars in unregistered Liberty bonds, securities, and diamonds in her home. Both the treasure and the strongbox in which it was kept were missing. He mentioned that his client kept valuables in the home because she "mistrusted banks." A reporter asked him if it were true that Dr. Wilkins was a drunkard. James disagreed with the description.

The *Post* added that James had an appointment to meet Dr. Wilkins "today," meaning Wednesday, March 19, at his office. James confirmed that Dr. Wilkins's new will did not name her brother Charlie as the beneficiary. James refused to name the new beneficiary. The *Star* and a second story written by the Associated Press both added that James was "to leave for Colorado Springs tonight." Added the *Star*: "The lawyer said he had an appointment today with Mrs. Wilkins to discuss the details of the Colorado litigation."

A *Kansas City Times* reporter was also present for James's second public statement about his client's murder. The next morning's edition of the *Times* quoted him at length:

> When Dr. Wilkins employed me, she confessed her fear of placing money in banks. She told me she believed all bankers were crooks and ought to be put in jail. Then she expressed a fear of losing the money lent in Colorado Springs, and opened the strong box to show me the agreement of trust.
>
> While the box was open she also showed me the other valuables, including a will, which I merely glanced at. She said her brother, Charles, was left out of the will.
>
> She told me she had given Marksheffel the $70,000 as a trust fund. The agreement was in pen and ink and was to the effect that Marksheffel had received the money as safe keeping to be returned to her upon demand.
>
> I was to have gone to Colorado Springs today to interview

Marksheffel in regard to the money. But now I suppose it is useless for me to go until the document of trust is found.

At another business meeting with Dr. Wilkins, she expressed a fear for her life. But I thought that she was unduly alarmed, and disregarded the matter. That was an error of judgment on my part. I shall never forgive myself for not reporting the matter to the police. I see now that she knew what she was talking about.

At another visit she gave me the names of two persons who had threatened her life.

If the documentary evidence of the $70,000 is gone, there is no way in the world to collect the money.

The *Kansas City Post* asked the police to divulge the names of the two men Zeo feared, since James wouldn't tell them. According to the *Post,* which was not always a slave to facts, they were Charles Wilkins and Dr. Blanchard.

Arthur F. Blanchard, D.O. was dragged into the investigation when police found his name on Zeo Wilkins's business cards. "Dr. Blanchard is a powerfully built, heavy set man with a physique and appearance not easily forgotten," commented the *Kansas City Post.* From the beginning Blanchard appears to have lied about his professional and personal involvement with Zeo. Even an all-night session at the city jail could not shake the whole truth out of him.

Dr. Blanchard said he was in the ASO Class of 1905 with Zeo and Gertrude Wilkins. "We were friends, of course, but no more than other members of the class," he said. "Being in the same line of endeavor, we naturally came in contact with each other at various times." He said that, if any business cards had his name over Dr. Wilkins's home address, they were printed without his knowledge.

Dr. Blanchard practiced both in Excelsior Springs and Kansas City.

He had three daughters by his first wife. He had remarried recently. He kept his family in a rental house in Excelsior Springs. For several years, he had maintained an office at 1110 East Armour Boulevard. He also kept an apartment in Kansas City. Coincidently, so he said, he closed up his office in Kansas City on the fifteenth of March, the very day Dr. Wilkins was killed. He was subletting his Kansas City apartment to his newlywed stepdaughter Gladys, he said. Some reporters went pounding on the apartment door and verified that a young couple lived there.

Dr. Blanchard insisted he was acquainted with Dr. Wilkins "only professionally. She called me to her home two months ago and wanted me to go into partnership with her. After talking things over, I told her I would not care to form a partnership. Several days later I learned she had had some cards printed, bearing her name and mine."

Three weeks before her death, Zeo had called him to her home to treat two patients, he said. She discussed her plans for a sanitarium. Dr. Blanchard said he wasn't interested, and they did not discuss the character or details of the management of the sanitarium. He denied knowing anything about any of Dr. Wilkins's other business dealings or habits.

The police found one of Zeo's many maids. Mary Battle told police that she worked for Dr. Wilkins from February 19 to February 27. She quit because the doctor never paid her. The doctor asked her to stay late on the night of February 23—or it could have been the 25th or maybe the 24th—to answer the door when Dr. Blanchard arrived at Zeo's home. He came in his motor car at seven-thirty in the evening. After Miss Battle admitted the doctor to the house, Dr. Wilkins said she could go. The maid declared that she knew nothing of the doctor's business affairs or finances. Dr. Wilkins was always very careful in what she said around her servants and often spoke in low tones or whispered when her servants were near.

Mary Battle's story was consistent with Dr. Blanchard's insistence that he hadn't been to Zeo's home for three weeks. But doctors don't normally make house calls at such an hour, and Mary never mentioned the presence of a patient that Dr. Blanchard was to treat that night.

In any event, Dr. Blanchard offered the police alibi witnesses. The next day's newspapers revealed that Arthur Blanchard was released after several hours of questioning because he "satisfactorily accounted for his movements the day the woman was murdered, authorities announced today." No details were given. Not every authority was done with Dr. Blanchard, though.

The detectives located Sadie Shields, Dr. Wilkins's long-time house-keeper in Kansas City. She told the detectives that Dr. Wilkins never paid regular wages, but she had deeded a house at 2226 Tracy Avenue to Ms. Shields in payment for services. It was worth about fifteen hundred dollars. Sadie last saw the doctor on March 12. Dr. Wilkins never spoke of her business affairs. Sadie could offer the police no information.

The police finally located Zeo's nurse, Clara M. Francis. Chief Walston himself took a statement from her on March 19. At first, Francis refused to give him her address, but eventually she said Dr. Wilkins first employed her in October 1923 when Zeo was sick with "walking typhoid fever." She was there five days and saw a "very friendly" Ben Tarpley every morning and nearly every afternoon. Ms. Francis also nursed Dr. Wilkins when she fell ill around the first of March until March 10. She had nothing else to tell them except to add, "I always found her very sociable, very agreeable, and of a good disposition."

Walston asked about the time Francis attended a meeting between Jesse James and Dr. Wilkins at which she handled a strongbox full of valuables. Francis told the police she knew nothing about any strongbox and denied any such occurrence.

As soon as she gave her statement to Chief Walston, Francis left for

Kansas. Reporters who tried to reach her were told she was called out of state to nurse a patient.

After the police questioned Francis, they found themselves confused about Jesse James's assertion that the doctor kept valuables in her home. James had said the nurse brought out the strongbox from its hiding place. James specifically told the police to question her. James was recalled to police headquarters on March 20 to verify his story of seeing the valuables. He held fast to his account of seeing the valuables in the strongbox. He must have erred in naming the woman he met at Dr. Wilkins's house.

The discovery of a stale lunch on Zeo's front porch made a liar out of B. F. Tarpley. The police shifted their probe to Zeo's last lover. He eventually admitted leaving it on her porch. "I frequently took her sandwiches from the lunch my wife prepared for me," he explained. First he told police that he took the last lunch to Dr. Wilkins on Wednesday. When the detectives pointed out that it was wrapped in Friday's newspaper, Tarpley repeated his story that he was last at her house on Saturday afternoon. But if he saw her that day, why leave the sandwiches outside? Finally he admitted the truth. "I left the lunch on the front railing Sunday morning."

He said he went there Sunday for an osteopathic treatment. After getting no response to his ring, he took part of his lunch from a basket and placed it near the door for her. He was not at the house Monday or Tuesday. "I just didn't go back," he declared, "but I intended to call her on the phone." Tarpley repeatedly insisted he had been taking treatments for rheumatism and "knew nothing about Mrs. Wilkins's personal affairs."

They suggested he was her "intimate," a "favorite at the house," a "devotee of the pretty adventuress," but Tarpley hotly denied any impropriety between himself and the doctor.

The Kansas City police saw through Tarpley's whoppers. The detectives had each man under arrest face the other two and repeat their stories. But Charles Wilkins, B. F. Tarpley, and Dillard Davies stuck to their guns.

Within a day of the discovery of the murder, the detective squad found itself with three viable suspects in custody. Charles Wilkins was an atheist with a violent streak. He killed his sister's bulldog—her protection. He was recently cut out of her will. Dillard Davies was what the police considered a natural suspect. He was a "Negro" with a known criminal history who knew the house and the victim well. A neighbor of the slain woman positively swore he saw Dillard at her house on Sunday morning. He was scrubbing her front porch, the neighbor said.

Seasoned detective Ed Kritser and his partner William Doarn searched the rooms of Charles Wilkins and the home of Dillard Davies on March 20. They found no diamonds, money, or papers. Kritser and Doarn then took the murder weapon, along with two other pocket-knives found in Davies's possession, to the 18th Street junkyard where Davies transacted business. Detective Kritser showed the three knives to junkyard employee Sam Russell and to the son of the junkyard's owner. Russell identified two of the three knives as Dillard's knives, including the murder weapon. "I've seen Davies use that to cut sacks," Russell declared. But the owner's son, Willie Seigel, wasn't so sure. He said the murder weapon resembled a knife he'd seen Davies use, but he wouldn't positively identify it as belonging to Dillard. The detectives brought Sam Russell to the police station to give a formal statement.

When police scrutinized the alibi offered by Dillard Davies, it fell apart. The detectives learned that he could not tell time, but this was not enough to account for the discrepancies in his story. Davies repeatedly said he spent all of Saturday night in a dice game that ended with breakfast the next day. The woman who hosted the game, Cornelia Allen, told police Davies did not appear at her home until half an hour before midnight. Another woman at the party, Helen Dilworth, said she left Cornelia's house at quarter after eleven Saturday night and never saw Davies there.

The Jackson County administrator's office launched an inquiry into the question of whether Dr. Wilkins had any assets, if for no other reason than to avoid forcing the county to pay for the woman's burial. "I understand there is considerable collateral and jewels missing from her home," said county administrator Floyd E. Jacobs. "If I can gather enough material facts to prove anyone owed Dr. Wilkins money, I shall file suit in an effort to retrieve the debt." Jacobs had an underling go through her belongings. He collected an entire trunk-full of papers from Zeo's home. After reviewing the documents, Jacobs's clerk, Charles Latchem, gave a statement. "As far as Jackson County is concerned," Latchem said, "Dr. Wilkins was poor. She left no record of property owned here, and she lived in a rented furnished house. The valuation of her personal effects would not pay for her funeral expenses."

The Colorado Springs police were drawn back into the investigation when their Kansas City counterparts asked them to track down and interview Albert W. Marksheffel. Zeo's last husband was brought to police headquarters in Colorado Springs to give a statement to Police Chief H. D. Harper. Marksheffel had little to say. He denied knowing a thing about the murder. He was in Colorado Springs Saturday night. He denied owing his ex-wife a cent. He had settled in full at the time of their divorce. A reporter in Colorado visited the El Paso County Courthouse, read the divorce file, and confirmed Al's story.

After Chief Harper quizzed Al Marksheffel about his recent

activities, the chief sent a telegram to the Kansas City police: "There was no possibility he had been in Kansas City in that time. He has been here for the last two weeks with the exception of two days spent at the motor show in Denver."

It was clear to observers that the killer either had a key or was admitted by the victim, a circumstance that would strongly suggest she knew him. There was no sign of breaking and entering and the half-open window was too high to reach without a ladder. Her killer obviously believed she had something of value to him. Money? Documents? A new will? Perhaps the doctor was correct when she expressed fears that Charles Smith would cause her harm? Chief Walston asked detectives in Denver to arrest and question Charles Smith.

They did. Smith denied that his behavior was ever threatening to the doctor. "While she took $150 from me on fake treatments," he said, "I never did more than protest against it." He figured that B. F. Tarpley was making up stories about him because Tarpley was "jealous of me when I was taking treatments." He added that Tarpley attended all the parties at Zeo's house.

Smith all but admitted the nature of his brief relationship with Zeo, though the tale was hard to believe. The detectives and reporters who talked to Charles Smith expressed wonder that Dr. Wilkins would associate with rough men and throw wild parties for "her pleasure mad companions," her "underworld" friends. "Police are amazed at the stories of her familiarity with these nocturnal figures," one reporter said, "who used her bathroom for shaving and slept on her floor." The public clamored for details. The *Denver Post* was there first, obtaining an exclusive interview with Charles Smith. It quoted him at great length about his relations with Dr. Wilkins:

> I have been suffering severely from asthma for some time and when I received [Charles] Wilkins' letter I determined to try his sister's treatments. When I arrived at Kansas City, Dr. Wilkins

insisted that I come and live at her home while she was carrying [*sic*; caring] for me. This idea did not appeal to me, but I did stay in the house four days.

During the time I stayed at the doctor's home and while around there receiving treatments I often heard Wilkins remonstrate with his sister regarding her actions and parties. In turn she upbraided him for some things he was supposed to have done.

I often saw Dillan Davis [*sic*; Dillard Davies], the Negro janitor, being held by police, while I was there. He told me that he had loaned Dr. Wilkins $15 and on one occasion he seemed angry when she refused to pay him back as he requested. There was also a Negro maid in the house that I understood had loaned the doctor some money.

The treatments of Dr. Wilkins failed to help my asthma and I left on Feb. 25. Her brother also had been taking some treatments for his back, which he claimed did not benefit him and he declared that he was disgusted with his sister's actions and wanted to leave. We had both spent considerable money going to Kansas City and while there and we asked her to reimburse us for this amount, but she refused.

After arriving in Denver I heard from Wilkins last on Feb. 29. In the letter, he mentioned that there was 'nothing doing' with regard to our collecting our expense money, and declared that he wanted to come west again and 'would be glad to get on a train and be shut of the whole mess.' He also said that his sister wanted me to write her a statement saying that I had received good treatment at her place and had been benefited by the treatments, but I refused.

Wednesday I received a wire from Wilkins saying 'Sister died. Will write details later.' I do not believe that Wilkins had anything to do with her death. He was a quiet man, a barber by trade, and when he saw how his sister was living he wanted to get clear of her and go west again. He was to have met me here.

The captain of detectives in Denver who quizzed Smith was satisfied that he returned to Denver on February 25 as he claimed. His landlord verified it. Charles Smith was cleared.

The Kansas City police continued to grapple with theories. But the men working the case were openly optimistic that the matter would be solved in short order. It was a matter of verifying all alibis but one. A newspaper in Fort Worth reported that "a close check is being made on the movements of those who are suspected of having been at the 'mystery house' about the time the crime was believed to have been committed." *Some* of those suspected, it should have said.

23

Now, a Mystery Woman

Whenever a crime is committed, the curtains open upon the
lives of men, but they do not always open all the way, nor do they
reveal everyone concerned; guilt remains offstage, and innocence
is paraded bare; you don't see what you want to see, but you get a
full view of what should have remained hidden.

— *Hans Habe,* The Countess

As more of Zeo Wilkins's secrets were revealed to the world, her
murder case remained on page one throughout much of the
country. Each statement released by the police created a fresh sensation as the press named husband after husband, lover after lover, suspect
after suspect.

The Kansas City detectives surely thought the investigation sufficiently complicated and scandalous, but there was more to come. A
made-for-headlines "mystery woman" entered the case. She had so much
to tell that she was afraid to come out of hiding. James Elder, a Kansas
City detective who worked out of the prosecutor's office, surprised Chief
of Detectives I. B. Walston by producing a statement from this new witness. Elder said he spoke to a woman who was with Dr. Wilkins Saturday
evening and could identify the last man seen with the victim. Detective
Elder refused to name the witness, however. He wouldn't even share her
name with Chief Walston. He was asked whether he could actually produce this lady, and Elder said she'd left town. This anonymous woman,
said Elder, was with Dr. Wilkins until nine-thirty on the night she was
killed. The man she saw with Zeo was Dillard Davies. The witness also
said Dillard was surly and impatient Saturday night. At one point he

said to Dr. Wilkins, "Get this woman out of the house. I won't wait any longer."

Detective Elder produced the notes he took during his interview of the mystery woman. Quoting her:

> When I left the Wilkins home at 9:30 o'clock . . . Doc and Dillard were the only ones in the room. Dillard came into the room and motioned me with his hand to leave the house and told Doc to get me out of there before it is too late. Just before I left Doc asked me to call her up as soon as I got home. I reached my home about 10:05 p.m. and called her number. At last I called the telephone supervisor and was informed the receiver must be off the telephone. I went out to the house several times Sunday and tried the door, but found it locked. Sunday night I drove out with a friend and tried the door and found it locked, so I left.

The mystery woman remained in hiding for another day. She was afraid for her life. Curiously, the man she fingered was already behind bars. Dillard wouldn't be leaving his cell anytime soon. Why did she flee? Why did she try to avoid being identified, even to the chief of detectives? It was enough to give the man from the *Kansas City Journal* a late night. He excitedly reported that "the needle of guilt trembles on the compass of mystery, ready to point to the slayer."

On Thursday, March 20, two days after Zeo's body was found, the mystery woman agreed to speak to the police if they withheld her name from the press. Eva Grundy appeared at the police station. She told the detectives that she last went to Dr. Wilkins's home at seven-thirty Saturday night. She was more than four hours late for their three p.m. appointment. When Zeo admitted her and Eva took a seat, the doctor was angry. Standing over Eva, bending over to get in her face, Zeo exclaimed, "Why didn't you come out at 3 o'clock? Are you double-crossing me too?"

It was a curious choice of words. Who double-crossed her at three o'clock? The phrase has always signified treachery, a swindle, the betrayal of a bargain, the behavior of one who wins the race after promising to lose it.

Zeo went on. "You've got to account to me for every minute of your time from 3 o'clock to 7:30."

Eva laughed and said she meant no harm. She had a "dinner engagement."

Dr. Wilkins strode away from her and then, in a dramatic voice, said: "Mrs. Grundy, I'm afraid you're too late—too late! And I'm so sorry— oh, so sorry! You are too late!" Eva wasn't quite sure what she meant by that.

Eva stayed for two hours. Dr. Wilkins was "nervously excited" the entire time. She paced the floor. "I know they will get me," she repeated. Eva tried to soothe her by encouraging her to remove her hat and not to leave the house as she had planned. Eva also promised Zeo she would remain all night, but Eva was afraid to sleep upstairs for some reason. She asked for quilts to sleep on the lounge.

At nine-thirty p.m. Zeo's brother called. Eva overheard Zeo say, "Yes, yes, Charlie. That's all right, Charlie. Yes, yes, good night Charlie." After getting off the telephone, Zeo seemed in brighter spirits. "That was my brother Charlie." Then she returned to thoughts of her impending death. Zeo started her Abrams machine, declaring that she was going to teach Eva to use it and give it to her. "I desire someone to have it who will do some good with it." But Eva said she didn't want it.

Eva repeated to the police her story of Dillard Davies's rude remarks. Though Eva was supposed to stay the night, the plan was changed—at Dr. Wilkins's insistence, Eva said. "But she admonished me to be sure and call her when I reached [my] hotel." Eva left around nine-thirty, taking a streetcar. She would later say she thought about calling the police when she transferred from one car to another at 31st Street and Brooklyn Avenue. "Everything seemed strange at the house," she said. But not strange enough to make the call.

At five minutes after ten, Eva arrived at her home at the Green Gables Hotel, 3329 Troost Avenue, and dialed Zeo's number. The telephone was out of order. It remained out of order.

And that's as much as they ever really got out of Eva Grundy.

The police brought Dillard Davies out of his cell and forced him to face Eva. She repeated her story as policemen and reporters looked on. Davies became angry and rose from his seat. Mrs. Grundy exclaimed, "That's just the way you looked when you came in the room the last time and told me to go. That's the way you talked, too."

The mystery woman's story, reported the press, "forged the chain of circumstantial evidence so tightly around Dillard Davies, Dr. Wilkins' Negro janitor, that a murder charge was predicted within the next two days by I. B. Walston, chief of detectives."

Eva's identity did not remain a secret for long. Although the police had asked journalists to withhold her name, the *Kansas City Journal* published Eva's name and address on its front page on Friday, March 21, six days after the murder. Reporters for the *Journal* found her in her home. The police made her name public to all the city's reporters late Friday night, but by then Mrs. Grundy had left her hotel again.

On March 20, Arthur Wilkins appeared at Kansas City police headquarters to help the police with their murder investigation. He did what he could, but he could not tell all he knew without implicating himself. He was asked to verify Jesse James Jr.'s story about a treasure in her home. The police were inclined to believe the tale, but perhaps they had their own reasons to doubt things that Jesse James told them.

Arthur told the police that Zeo had no Liberty bonds or any other bonds. He said his sister was broke. Arthur said she once had diamonds, but she had given them as collateral to Judge James Orr of Colorado Springs. "I have heard her speak of a trust fund," he added, but Marksheffel paid back the business loan. "It's true my sister gave him a good start in business, but he repaid whatever he might have borrowed."

Chief Walston asked if he wanted to see his brother. A jailer led Charles into the chief's office. A reporter from the *Kansas City Times* memorialized the moment:

> There was no light of affection in Arthur Wilkins's eyes. With his wife he stood apart from his brother and looked at him. The prisoner advanced and extended his hand timidly and his brother received it without a sign of emotion. The greeting was a cold one. For half an hour the brothers conversed generally. Neither made an effort to prolong the meeting when the chief asked whether they had said all they wished.

Arthur gave a statement to the press that night. "The police are investigating from the wrong angle," he said. "They are relying on things Dr. Wilkins told people who visited her. She was hardly responsible for what she said." He also insisted that Zeo was "broke for about a year." His sister had owned diamonds worth thirty-five to forty thousand dollars. These she gave as collateral for a loan of twelve thousand dollars made by Judge James Orr of Colorado Springs. Her Cadillac was stored in Colorado Springs but it was sold last week to satisfy a judgment. She did not have any Liberty bonds, Arthur declared.

Dr. Gertrude Wilkins-Clements came from Fort Worth on March 20. Blanche Wilson came from Cleveland. When Gertrude walked into the police station, she was barraged with questions from waiting reporters, but she declined to discuss the case with them. She was too grief-stricken to make any sort of statement except to confirm that Dr. Zeo Wilkins was her sister. The reporters watched as Gertrude gave Charles "an affectionate greeting."

Arthur, Horace, and Blanche joined Gertrude at police headquarters. Together they spoke for four hours with Charles in a private room on the night of March 21. Then they spoke to the crowd of waiting reporters. Desperate to free their brother Charles from jail, they laid bare the truth about Zeo for public inspection. "For his sake, they desperately tore away the veil from the slain sister's past life," one reporter observed. "They told with merciless frankness of the murdered sister's incorrigible willfulness and of the insane determination with which she resisted their efforts to curb her erring steps."

Her family said they believed she had been insane for some time and that Charles was innocent. Zeo suffered from hallucinations and had leveled similar wild charges against her family. "The accusations she made against [his] morality she had made against all the rest of us," Gertrude said. "Our brother Charlie never killed our sister."

Her family declared as false the statement Jesse James made about the Marksheffel trust and about diamonds and bonds. They declared that Zeo was broke; her diamonds were entrusted to her attorney in Colorado Springs; she did not owe Al Marksheffel anything. Arthur Wilkins never shared the fact that he had retrieved the diamonds from James Orr and brought Doc's "goodies" back to her. He did not admit the truth until the end of his life, long after the police would have found that fact relevant to the murder inquiry, long after it corroborated Jesse James's story of seeing the diamonds in Zeo's home days before she was killed.

Arthur's wife Laura insisted Zeo had spent her entire Cunningham fortune. She described Zeo's wild spending, the Cadillacs, the diamonds, the honeymoon that cost five thousand dollars. "One month her phone bill was six hundred dollars," Laura said. "And those were only a few of the extravagances. No one knows what she spent for clothing, tips and gifts."

Many of the Wilkins siblings' anecdotes had nothing to do with the inquiry into their sister's murder. They were eulogies of sorts, the remembrances of a shocked and wounded family that had grappled for years with the enigma that was Zeo Zoe Wilkins. "We tried to save our sister from her suicidal course," Gertrude said through sobs, "but the only effect was to send her into a terrible rage. She had fought like that with all of us."

Zeo's siblings also went through her small brown diary page by page, "interpreting obscure passages and supplementing information the notebook gives only sketchily." They mentioned the time she threw herself into hog manure to have her way. Horace talked about the way in which Zeo fooled with old Andy the caretaker. He also mentioned that he lent her eight thousand dollars recently to buy an Abrams machine. As further proof that she was "mentally unbalanced," Horace revealed that she thought the machine would foretell her death.

Her brothers and sisters divulged more of her secrets to the eager reporters as they discussed her husbands and her wild career. But even as they exposed Zeo's true nature to save Charles, her siblings still expressed deep affection for their wayward little sister. "We loved her," Horace Wilkins said:

> She was our youngest sister, and she had more mental ability than any of us. Both Arthur and myself have pleaded with her to quit the life she was living and be someone in the world. We believed in her and the woman she could be if we could draw her away from the life she was leading. But our attempts only resulted in terrible misunderstandings. Our sister was insane. Liquor and drugs had undermined her character—had made of her a person of two characters, one gentle and sweet and lovable; the other, insane and uncontrollable.

He had apparently forgotten all about Helen the Better and Zeo the Evil, the dichotomy that developed not when she became involved in liquor and drugs but when she was still a girl growing up in Ohio.

The intimate disclosures and confirmation of her amazing number of marital adventures catapulted the case to national prominence again. For days Zeo's murder led the news nationally. The shocking revelations from her diary made for the biggest news story of them all, even making the front page of the editorial section of the Sunday *New York Times* on March 30, 1924, under the headline DIARY BARES TALE OF LOVE AND FRAUD.

Perhaps the disclosures did help authorities look more skeptically

on the case against Charles Wilkins, but they helped the other potential defendants as well. As her diary disclosed to the world, there were
literally dozens of men and women who had cause to want her dead.
The trail went back decades, for the revelations about her past, said the
Atlanta Constitution, showed her "to be a cold, calculating woman who
sought always to feed the spirit of adventure she had nurtured since
childhood."

The funeral services for Zeo Zoe Wilkins were a stark contrast to her
life. There was no music. No "*belle nuit.*" None of her lovers were there,
not even any of the recent ones. Not Roy, George, Arthur, C.C., Ben,
Tom, or Gus. The morticians did what they could to make her look
alive. They performed ten dollars' worth of "surgery work" to repair the
gashes in her face. They applied heavy makeup. They gave her an open
casket funeral even though the body was in such a poor state. The smell
of embalming fluid could not have masked the faintest trace of sulphur.

Horace gave her a burial that cost nearly three hundred dollars,
including a coffin lined with silver and green crepe. The rites were simple.
There was no eulogy. The pallbearers were hired men. Zeo was buried in
a white dress and stockings on March 25, 1924, in the Forest Hill Cem-
etery in Kansas City. Those relatives who saw Zeo out of this life were
Horace, Arthur, Gertrude, Blanche, her nephew Horace Ricketts, and
her brother Charles. Horace Wilkins provided a thousand-dollar cash
bond for the temporary release of Charles with the consent of the police,
which allowed him to attend the funeral with them despite the fact that
he had been arrested and held on suspicion of murdering her.

Perhaps Mrs. Palmer was one of the three friends who reportedly
attended. The landlady always liked Dr. Wilkins. "She was not crooked,"
said Mrs. Palmer after the death of her tenant. "I always found her most
honorable. If there were any wild parties at the house, I do not know
of them. Mrs. Wilkins dealt in big money and wore good clothes. She

always had persons doing things for her. If she wanted anything, she would have it brought to her. Last summer, when she was ill for two months in Colorado Springs, everybody said 'you'll never get your rent.' But I'm sure, if she had lived, she would have paid me."

One is tempted to try to pinpoint the moment that sealed Zeo's fate. Was it the moment she told the wrong man about the diamonds she kept in a lockbox in her home? Or was it much earlier than that? At the sanitarium in Texas perhaps? In the hog pen, one could argue. If only the woman blessed by God, luck, or genetic variation with sharp intelligence, great beauty, and tremendous strength of will, the woman who managed to pull herself up unaided from the muck of Ohio, could have been steered early on toward higher aims, higher hopes, what could she have accomplished with her gifts? As soon as the question is posed, some detail of her career comes to mind, and the thought dies.

24

James Refuses to Answer

Why, the whole State to-day reeks with a double orgy—that of
lust and that of murder. What the men failed to do, the women
accomplished. Tear the two bears from the flag of Missouri.
Put thereon, in place of them, as more appropriate, a thief
blowing out the brains of an unarmed victim, and a brazen
harlot, naked to the waist and splashed to the brows in blood.
— *The closing words of "The Killing of Jesse James" by
John Newman Edwards,* Sedalia Democrat, *April 13, 1882*

On Friday, March 21, three days after the body of Dr. Wilkins
was found, Kansas City Coroner Dr. Chett McDonald opened
an inquest into her murder. The inquiry began at nine-thirty that
morning before a coroner's jury of six professional white men amid
a crowd too large to fit inside the county courthouse. Dozens of witnesses were expected. Lawyers and journalists joined relatives, friends,
and lovers of the murder victim. The room was packed. Officials
present included H. P. Ragland, assistant prosecutor appearing for
county prosecutor Clarence A. Burney. Ben Tarpley and Dillard Davies
were brought from jail. The crowd witnessed Charles Wilkins sharing
a hug and kiss with his sister Blanche. "All seats were occupied an hour
before the hearing began," one newsman noted, "and all standing room
was gone as the first witness was called."

The questioning fell to Samuel Edwards, the coroner's investigator
who had crawled into the dead doctor's window and taken possession
of her body at the murder scene. As his first witness, he called Jesse E.
James.

Perhaps the coroner and his assistants expected one of Kansas City's most famous residents to tear the veil of mystery from the case. Nobody was better positioned to explain the state of Dr. Wilkins's finances or to contextualize the mysterious remarks other witnesses attributed to her. Moreover, he was an attorney at law. As a member of the bar, he was an officer of the court, an advocate for justice. They undoubtedly expected his remarks to greatly aid if not guide the inquiry into his client's bloody murder. It was apparently this same sort of logic that had led the chief of detectives to make the curious decision to allow James to participate in the search of her home. Thus, he "testified to a hushed room," as one journalist observed.

James said under oath that Dr. Wilkins had recently appealed to him for help because she feared for her life but he dismissed her fears as irrational. "I made a mistake in judgment," James said. "I should have provided physical protection for Dr. Wilkins, because in her death everything developed as she had predicted to me. . . . I realize now that everything she told me was true."

James said Zeo Wilkins foretold her murder. "Dr. Wilkins lived in fear of two men whom she named. They had made demands on her, she told me, and said if she did not comply, they would murder her."

Edwards asked James to name them.

James said one was Charles Wilkins. He refused to identify the other man. He said he gave the name to Chief Walston but would not repeat it at the inquest because "he is not under arrest."

The audience might have been taken aback at that. The purpose of the inquest was to determine who should be arrested. The laymen on the coroner's jury were expected to listen to all the available evidence and issue a written recommendation at the conclusion of the inquest describing how she died, and if possible to assign blame or at least direct the inquiry. A coroner could not issue arrest warrants, but he had a duty to pursue the issuance of a warrant if the evidence required it. James's refusal to repeat Zeo's fears of harm in their entirety because the man "was not under arrest" thwarted the purpose of the inquest.

Unfortunately, Mr. Edwards was a negligent cross-examiner. He did not push for an answer. The journalists in the audience had their own suspicions about the identity of this second man. "In this connection observers recalled that police had asked Denver authorities to arrest Charles Smith," noted the reporter for the *St. Louis Post-Dispatch.* "Other witnesses have told detectives that Miss Wilkins feared a man named Smith."

Edwards asked why Dr. Wilkins feared these two men. James said that Dr. Wilkins would not comply with certain requests of theirs. Edwards asked what those requests were, what motive these two men would have for killing her. James declined to answer.

Edwards pressed this issue. James agreed to tell the jurors exactly what had been demanded of Dr. Wilkins, but only "privately." It seems the six men on the coroner's jury left the jury box and gathered around the lawyer. "He is said to have whispered to them that demands had been made on Dr. Wilkins for $50,000," the *Kansas City Star* reported. "James, it is understood, did not tell who had made the demands."

James was called on to explain his dealings with Dr. Wilkins. He testified she hired him on February 28 to collect the debt from Albert Marksheffel. Edwards asked James to describe their contacts. James said that Dr. Wilkins had visited his office five or six times and that he had been to her home on several occasions. James said Dr. Wilkins was last at his office on Thursday, March 13, to see him. She waited for him two hours, he said, but he did not return. He said he understood she was nervous and agitated and paced the floor. James said he called her Saturday and made an appointment to see her at three p.m. on Sunday.

But he had an "unexpected call to Topeka" Sunday and did not keep the appointment. He said he telephoned her house Monday but got no answer. He called again on Tuesday, he said, but again "no one answered" his call.

As Jesse James Jr. testified under oath, one of the most burning questions in the minds of onlookers concerned Zeo's fortune in diamonds and bonds. Jesse James was the only person so far who said she had this wealth stored in her home. Her family was insisting that she was broke, essentially calling James a liar. James had claimed that her nurse was present for that meeting and even brought the strongbox from its hiding place. But the police had questioned nurse Clara Francis, who denied the tale. James had since learned the woman's true identity.

James may have surprised a few people when he testified that Dr. Wilkins "opened the strong box to show me the agreement of trust. While showing me her will, she asked her nurse, Eva, to leave the room. While the box was open, she also showed me the other valuables, including a will, which I merely glanced at. She said her brother, Charles, was left out of the will. She told me she had given Marksheffel the $70,000 as a trust fund. The agreement was in pen and ink and was to the effect that Marksheffel had received the money as safe keeping to be returned to her upon demand. In looking over her letters and papers, later found on the floor of the ransacked house, I found several papers which I recalled seeing in the same box with the certificate of trust. Apparently whoever took the strong box tossed some of the contents aside."

"Did you see anything else?"

"There was a quantity of unregistered Liberty bonds. Dr. Wilkins said the amount was in excess of $40,000. I did not check the bonds, but from the number and the fact that they were in denominations of $500 and $1,000, I judged there must have been $40,000 or more in bonds. I also saw gold bonds in industrial corporations. I did not examine them. I judged their face value at about $30,000."

James added that she was going to sell them to establish a sanitarium. She kept them at home because she didn't trust bankers. Dr. Wilkins had consulted famous attorney Clarence Darrow several years before in Chicago, James said, and Darrow advised her not to trust bankers.

"Why did Dr. Wilkins show you these valuables?"

"She wanted me to handle them for her. But I refused to do what she asked me to do."

"What was her request that you refused?"

"I consider that a privileged communication and cannot answer." Then he added that he had already told Chief Walston and would tell Prosecutor Burney "if desired."

Privileged? The murder victim's attorney chose a strange occasion to dwell on ethical niceties intended to protect his client's privacy. If he honestly believed that the remarks Dr. Wilkins made to him were protected from disclosure by the attorney-client privilege, then his ethical obligation was to keep those statements privileged, even after her death. And yet he had already repeated some of her "privileged" remarks to him in public and in private, all in violation of any privilege. He certainly took no steps to protect his client's privacy during the search of her home so carefully recorded by the journalists allowed inside.

Edwards returned to the subject of her treasure. Did the strongbox contain other valuables besides the Marksheffel trust and these bonds?

James described several unset diamonds that he believed were worth $25,000. He was again asked if he saw anything else of value, and he described reading a will written by an attorney in February 1924. He could not remember the name of the lawyer who wrote it or any witnesses who cosigned it.

"What did the will contain?"

"I will tell part of the contents," James said, "but cannot tell all without the consent of Lieutenant Commander Hull and relatives of Dr. Wilkins." Attorney-client privilege again, in other words. Hull was the Navy recruiter in Kansas City, and James meant to imply that only Zeo's adopted son could waive the privilege and allow him to speak freely. Lieutenant Commander Hull presumably was not in the room at the time. "Dr. Wilkins told me," James added, "while I was reading the will, that if she was murdered her brother, Charles Wilkins, was not to receive one penny of her estate."

Edwards returned to the subject of the two men Dr. Wilkins feared and asked James about them again. She described them as moral degenerates, James said. "Her brother was one of the men," James added, "and

I'll say this much about the other man: he is a graduate in medicine." He added that he had already told Chief Walston the name of the threatening mystery doctor and would tell county prosecutor Clarence A. Burney "if desired." At one point James referred to him as "Dr. Smith." He repeatedly refused to elaborate or to offer any hint why he chose to withhold his evidence against this "Smith."

Did she ever mention Dillard Davies or B. F. Tarpley?

James said she didn't. He never saw either at her home. "She never expressed to me any fear of Davies or Tarpley," James said. "The names she mentioned were her brother, Charles, and another man." She told James her brother often beat and choked her.

She did not fear Marksheffel. "All she wanted from Marksheffel was the return of the $70,000 he was keeping for her. I was to leave last Wednesday for Colorado Springs to represent Dr. Wilkins in an attempt to get Marksheffel to return her money."

Edwards asked James how he became acquainted with Dr. Wilkins.

"I have told Chief Walston. I will tell no other person except C. A. Burney, the county prosecutor."

James was not asked to provide an alibi. He was not asked to reconcile his conflicting statements concerning his last appointment with Dr. Wilkins.

To the Kansas City journalists present for his testimony, James's story sounded watery. The *Star* ran the subhead:

JAMES REFUSES TO ANSWER.

Jesse James Jr. left the witness stand and never again made another public remark about the murder of his client. A silence fell over that courtroom, and the silence has remained unbroken ever since.

25

Forge Chain around Negro

A society is at the mercy of a murderer who is remorseless,
who takes no accomplices, and who keeps his head.
— *Edmund L. Pearson*

The testimony of Jesse E. James underscored the importance of the testimony of Eva Grundy. James had named her as the woman present for a meeting on Sunday, March 9, at Zeo's home. Eva could place James in the house and could verify his story of the treasure. But Detective Elder brought disappointing news. Elder said the "mystery woman" had left the city and would not appear at the inquest.

Samuel Edwards performed poorly while questioning Jesse James. H. P. Ragland, assistant prosecutor, handled some of the questioning as the inquest continued. Ragland called Gertrude Palmer to the witness stand.

Mrs. Palmer described Zeo's fears of her brother Charles in great detail—the arguments, the new will, his furious response, how he had her beloved bulldog put down. Mrs. Palmer also said that Zeo's telephone was out of order from Sunday onward to her knowledge. She said she last spoke to her tenant on Saturday around noon. Dr. Wilkins said she was expecting funds that afternoon and would call Mrs. Palmer afterward. She never did.

"Did the doctor ever express to you any fear of Jesse James, her attorney?" she was asked.

"Well, I don't know."

"Did she say she tried to get rid of James?"

"Well, I was led to believe she wanted him to cease handling her affairs."

Attorney Charles W. Prince took the stand to share the stories of Dr. Wilkins that he had collected as an attorney in the Cunningham litigation. Mr. Prince also represented Nellie McNamara in her lawsuit against Zeo Wilkins and spoke to a number of witnesses under oath. No privilege hampered the testimony of this member of Kansas City's legal fraternity.

Prince testified about the time Zeo pinched John McNamara in a liquor deal. "She just beat John to a trimming," he said. "John's game was to play wealthy widows. After he would get their money he would forget them and return to his wife. He tried to trim Dr. Wilkins, but she outsmarted him." That deal cost John nineteen thousand dollars, Prince said. He confirmed that John McNamara was operating a café in Chicago at the time of the murder.

"Dr. Wilkins was an intellectual genius," Prince added. "She was a mental monstrosity. She was surrounded by underworld characters, dominating them with her remarkable personality. I represented her former husband, Thomas Cunningham. At that time I uncovered evidence where she was experimenting with a slow poison, intending to give it to the aged millionaire.

"The homes of Dr. Wilkins were often used as trysting places for sweethearts. Dr. Wilkins was a 'good fellow' to her friends, I have learned from various sources."

Zeo's neighbor Ella Rohrs testified that Dr. Wilkins had recently given her several furs, including an ermine cape and muff, for safekeeping. "Dr. Wilkins sent them to my house by a Negro maid," she testified. "Later I saw the doctor and she wanted me to keep them for my own. She said she was afraid someone would steal them from her. I told her I wouldn't accept them as a gift. She appeared to be intoxicated.

She was that way most of the time since I became acquainted with her a year ago."

After the testimony of Ella Rohrs, the coroner received good news. Someone had succeeded in serving a subpoena on Kansas City's "mystery woman."

Eva Grundy walked into the coroner's inquest like a character from a Hollywood nail-biter. Her ensemble included a veil, heavy coat, gloves, and large floppy hat. She ducked as a photographer from the *Kansas City Journal* snapped a picture of her outside the courthouse. Detective Elder led her into the courtroom. "She is a small woman," noted the *Kansas City Post,* "a brunet [*sic*] with dark eyes. She was attired fashionably in a plush coat with fur collar. A heavy black veil hung over her face."

Eva took the witness stand—none of the reporters mentioned if she removed her veil—and began her story with the events of Friday, the day before Zeo was murdered. Eva said she had not otherwise seen Dr. Wilkins in "quite some time."

But she *had* been seen at Dr. Wilkins's home a few days before then. Jesse James saw her there. The questioner, Samuel Edwards, apparently didn't think to ask about it.

Eva Grundy testified that Dr. Wilkins lived in "mortal fear" of four men. Eva only knew the names of two: Charles Wilkins and "Dr. Smith of Kansas City."

Eva testified that she learned the details of the sanitarium deal on Friday when Doc offered her a position there. "Dr. Wilkins said she would dispose of bonds and securities to be applied on establishment of the sanitarium," Eva said. Doc wanted Eva to meet Dr. Holly Haworth and serve as the financial secretary. But Eva said she decided not to take the position.

"What caused you to change your mind about entering Dr. Wilkins' employ?" Sam Edwards asked.

"It developed that the sanitarium she was going to open wasn't very nice. She told me it was a beautiful place with three stories. She told me that I was to stay on the first floor; that I was never to go to the second or third floors. I asked her why, and what was to be on the second and third floors, and got the impression from Dr. Wilkins' reply that the place was not to be right. 'Well, you just won't go up there,' she replied. She said she wanted me to stay on the first floor and meet the patients because I had a good education and a good appearance and nobody would 'suspect' me. She said she would pay me a thousand dollars a month as secretary and financial manager of the place."

Zeo put a certificate for a thousand dollars on Eva's lap. Eva said she did not want the position. Zeo pleaded and said, "I'm having a room set in order at my house and you are to move there and live with me."

"I told her I wouldn't be connected with it for ten thousand dollars a month," Eva said.

Dr. Wilkins offered her more and spoke of furniture, furs, and a trust fund. "During the time I was there she talked of a good many things, such as Liberty bonds, $40,000 worth of diamonds and about $30,000 worth of furs," Eva testified. "All the above stuff was in the house except the furs."

Despite her misgivings, Eva agreed to meet Dr. Wilkins again the next afternoon. But she was several hours late. Asked to explain why she did not see Dr. Wilkins at three p.m. Saturday, Eva said she "didn't care to go." She again described Zeo's angry reaction when she finally appeared that night. "Doc had her hat and coat on and was very much excited and very nervous. She said she had only a few hours left and that if the deal didn't go something was going to happen to her. Doc said they were trying to get her." Eva saw a large brindle junkyard bulldog in Zeo's home Saturday night. "Dr. Wilkins told me that Dillard had brought her the dog."

As Eva spoke to Zeo in her living room, Dillard approached them three or four times. "At about nine o'clock Dillard came into the room and said, 'I must go, Dr. Wilkins.'"

"'Dillard, you go to the kitchen,' Zeo said.

"He then went back to the kitchen, and in a few minutes, he returned and motioned to me with his hand to leave the house. Doc told Dillard to go back in the kitchen; he did so. In a few minutes he came back and told Doc to get me out of there before it would be too late, because he wasn't going to wait any longer.

"Doc then told me to go and go quick. I did not go right away, but waited until about 9:30 p.m. When I left, Doc and Dillard were the only ones in the house. Just before I left, Doc asked me to call her up as soon as I got home.

"I reached my home about 10:05 p.m. and called her number. . . . At last I called the supervisor and was informed the receiver must be off the telephone."

She was asked to elaborate. "I received a busy signal. I waited a few minutes and then called her again. I repeated this four times, and received a busy signal each time. At last I called the supervisor and was informed by her the receiver must be off the telephone, as there was no one talking on the line."

Under further prompting, Eva provided specific times: "They gave me the busy signal repeatedly until 10:30 o'clock and then the supervisor told me the receiver was off the hook. However, I continued to try to call Dr. Wilkins until 11:30 o'clock that night."

Edwards's final question to Eva Grundy was, "Is there anything else you would care to tell in connection with this case?"

Eva came up with, "Friday I asked Dr. Wilkins what was the matter with her face, and she told me that two months ago her brother, Charles, broke her jaw on the right side and splintered it on the left side. She had to have all of her teeth extracted as a result, she told me."

After she finished testifying at the inquest, Eva Grundy consented to have her photograph taken for publication in the *Kansas City Journal.* She is free of hat and veil and wears instead a broad smile.

When Charles Wilkins was called to testify for the first time, he was asked whether he was an atheist. Wilkins was reticent.

'MYSTERY WOMAN'

MYSTERY WOMAN

Left: Eva Grundy wears a heavy disguise on her way to testify at the inquest into Doc's murder. Right: Eva Grundy consents to have her photo taken afterward. (*Kansas City Journal*)

"Do you believe in God?" Samuel Edwards asked.

"I believe in no ruling power."

"Well, will you abide by an oath?"

"Yes, sir."

Wilkins said he'd come from Seattle last December because his sister was ill. In fact, she was so sick that she had not even recognized him until the day after his arrival.

The questioning soon focused on the darker side of the siblings' relationship. Charles was asked about the quarrels with his sister, the fights that had turned violent, and the argument that drove him from her home. Charles admitted that Zeo once tried to "rush" him from the house in the presence of Charles Smith. His friend Smith was shaving at the time Zeo demanded that they leave, and Charles told his sister they would leave shortly. Zeo attempted to force him out of the house. In response, Charles "pushed" her, and "she fell." He helped her up off the floor, he added. He blamed it all on liquor and men.

He also said she showed signs of illness. She believed her Abrams machine could tell the date of her death. "My sister said that there was something 'wonderful' on the inside of her machine and that it possessed the same magic qualities as did the machine owned by Dr. Abrams himself. She pointed out that Dr. Abrams had predicted his own death to the hour by means of his machine. She believed she could do the same with her machine."

The next witness was called.

"What is your name?"

"Dillard Davies."

"How do you spell it?"

"D-i-v-i-e-s."

"How? Do you call that 'Davies'?"

"Yes, sir; Davies. D-i-v-i-e-s."

"Don't you mean D-a-v-i-e-s?"

"Yes, Davies."

It took more than one attempt to explain to Davies that he could refuse to answer questions on grounds of his Fifth Amendment privilege against self-incrimination. He answered freely and denied the testimony of Eva Grundy that made him the last person to see Dr. Wilkins alive. "I can't help what that woman says," Davies said. "I wasn't there Saturday night. I was in a dice game and hadn't been in the house since three o'clock Saturday afternoon." Davies denied any wrongdoing. He denied being at the house Saturday night, Sunday, Monday, or Tuesday. He denied owning the knife used to kill the doctor. "Anybody with two bits can buy them."

Davies said he spent the rest of Saturday selling a wagonful of junk and papers. He spent half of the four dollars in proceeds on a sack of horse feed and a bale of hay for his team of horses and blew the other half gambling. Davies again said he went to a dice game. He got there at eight-thirty that night and didn't leave until well into Sunday. Everyone in the courtroom knew his alibi witnesses did not support his version of his Saturday evening. Davies remained on the stand until the inquest was adjourned to the following morning.

On Saturday, March 22, the proceeding continued with a larger crowd. Many women were at the courthouse more than an hour beforehand to snag front-row seats.

Samuel Edwards began the session by quizzing Davies again. Reporters present for both sessions noticed more confidence in Davies. "He answered questions quickly," a reporter observed, "and frequently volunteered explanations not asked for."

From the witness stand, Davies said Dr. Wilkins was intoxicated most of the time. He admitted keeping her in liquor—Jamaica Ginger in particular. Davies repeated his claim that Charles and Zeo Wilkins fought. "Charlie choked her, cursed her, kicked her and knocked her down on the bed," he said.

Edwards asked what they argued about.

"I don't know. It was something about her being a millionaire's wife and not having to work."

Twice Charles had choked her when they quarreled, Davies said. Once Dr. Wilkins set her bulldog on Charles, which is why he had the dog poisoned. "And last night in jail," Davies offered, "Wilkins tried to get me to go on the stand today and admit that I had choked his sister."

The questioner did not ask Davies to elaborate.

"Did you kill Dr. Wilkins?" Edwards asked.

"No, sir."

"Do you know who killed her?"

"I don't know."

The inquest continued for hours. Several of Zeo's lovers would take the witness stand to share what they knew and would admit, including

Gus West and Tom Swearingen. Gus and Tom both swore that Dr. Wilkins feared Charles Wilkins and Charles Smith.

Dr. John Klepinger described his brief business association with Dr. Wilkins and the back-room drinking that caused him to terminate the arrangement.

"Did some of her patients look like they might be underworld characters?" Samuel Edwards asked him.

"A few of them might have been," Dr. Klepinger said, adding, "I saw two persons here a moment ago whom I had seen go to that room with Dr. Wilkins."

Cyril Palmer and his mistress, who were sitting in the courtroom, quietly stood and hastily made for the door.

Samuel Edwards asked Dr. Klepinger to point out the people to whom he referred.

Dr. Klepinger stood up and surveyed the crowd. "They're gone now. The man was small, and wore a moustache. The woman was young and well dressed."

Some Kansas City detectives left the room to search for them, but the couple had made good their escape before they could be identified.

After a day and a half of testimony, the coroner's inquest adjourned until Monday. The police would keep busy during the entire weekend building the case against Dillard Davies.

On Sunday, Eva Grundy was summoned and closeted with Chief Walston and Davies. At least one newspaper reporter held his ear to the door and reported that "at first the negro's voice was loud in protest against Mrs. Grundy's accusation. Mrs. Grundy held firmly to her statement at the inquest."

Davies was again questioned for hours. The police requested that he take scopalamin or "truth serum," said to have the power to force confessions. The press learned that Davies had agreed to take the serum if the "white folks he trusts" told him it was all right. The police called his former employers, Mr. and Mrs. Perry, to obtain their permission.

The Perrys promised to visit Dillard in jail to talk to him about it. Scopalamin was said to have been discovered by a Texas physician and "experimented with, in police connections, on three Alabama Negroes," reported the *Kansas City Sun*. Mrs. Perry spoke to Chief Walston. She said she'd approve the administration of the truth serum on Davies provided that she be present when he was questioned and that the serum be administered to Charles Wilkins and Ben Tarpley as well. The police refused her conditions, and the serum was never administered to anyone in connection with the case.

At the same time, police performed another search of Davies's home. Detective Kritser, accompanied by Detective W. F. Jones, found a pair of bloody boots under his bed. They took the boots to one of the police department's forensics experts, Dr. Watson Campbell. Dr. Campbell said the stains came from blood, but he needed a week to tell if it was human blood.

On the same day, the police revealed another critical discovery. It was "the only material clew" besides the knife. It was an envelope that apparently had been gripped by blood-covered fingers. It held three business letters about Dr. Wilkins's Abrams machine. The bloody envelope was found in the dining room on Sunday and given to Lieutenant William L. Gordon, the forensics (then, the "Bertillon") expert at police headquarters. Missouri had passed a law in 1919 requiring felons to submit to all the things allowed by the Bertillon system for identifying convicted criminals, including thumbprints. The lieutenant was expected to make a report to Chief Walston on the print, presumably to say whether it was clear enough for comparison purposes. The results of Lieutenant Gordon's examination were never made public. Missouri wasn't quite yet on the cusp of accepting fingerprints as evidence and training experts to explain them to jurors. It would be another nine years before an appeals court case made mention of fingerprints. The Kansas City police had to fall back on time-tested crime solutions.

THINK NEGRO SLEW BEAUTY, the headlines read. "Physicians have determined that she was assaulted before being murdered," the newsmen now insinuated.

The *Kansas City Journal* managed to get an interview with Dillard Davies. He "came clean," proclaimed the *Journal,* which quoted Dillard at great length.

"They always are harpin' on my blood-stained coat and boots," Davies said jocosely. "If you want another bloody clew, look in my barn in the old crokes sack behind the barrel—and you'll find a blood-stained halter rope I used March 15, 1924. I operated on my horse. That's about all the clews I can give in this case. If I could help solve the mystery of Dr. Wilkins' death, I certainly would do it. But during my stay in the house so many persons came and went, I cannot remember their names or their actions."

Reporters bearing lit matches found the bloody rope in Dillard's barn later that night. They proclaimed it "by far the bloodiest bit of evidence yet unearthed. The rope, ironically, perhaps, is a strong hempen one with a noose at the end of it."

The coroner's inquest resumed on Monday. This time, several prominent black residents of Kansas City attended, along with a large group assembled by the black women's club movement. The ladies had taken an interest in the case and wanted to make sure Dillard Davies was not "railroaded."

They must have been disheartened to hear the announcement of coroner's attorney Horace Guffin. He was a new figure in the case. He returned from a trip to Washington and agreed to take over the questioning of witnesses at the inquest. He said he had closely examined the murder weapon and found oat shells and bits of hay in its grooves—after Dillard Davies admitted using a knife on the day of the murder to cut open sacks of horse feed.

The announcement did not temper his cross-examination of the other suspects, though. As the inquest resumed more suspects took the witness stand and none took the Fifth. Horace Guffin called Ben Tarpley to the witness stand. He warned him that he could refuse to answer on Fifth Amendment grounds. Tarpley waved the warnings aside and agreed to tell all he knew.

Guffin focused on the fact that Tarpley, once a daily visitor, suddenly discontinued his regular visits. Tarpley claimed that he tried calling Sunday "but the line was busy." Guffin did not believe Tarpley when he said he never tried reaching her after Sunday.

Guffin asked, "Do you mean to tell this jury that despite your habit of calling at the Wilkins home twice daily that after a call on Sunday you ceased calling, not even attempting to telephone her again?"

"I certainly do," Tarpley said.

Tarpley was again invited to explain his luncheon offerings. "Dr. Wilkins was broke, and often was without food," he said. "She was in about as bad shape financially as I was."

Guffin asked him about his last afternoon with Zeo. "What were you doing all of that time?"

"We were talking," Tarpley said. "I believe we talked about the doctor's finances and her troubles." Tarpley mentioned that Zeo asked to borrow two hundred dollars, which she intended to give to Dr. Blanchard so he could buy a bargain lot of bonded whisky.

Guffin pressed him to admit to an affair. Tarpley grew agitated. Guffin wanted to know if he ever had a key. Tarpley replied in a loud voice: "I never did have a key to that house."

"Did you ever see any diamonds or bonds, or a great amount of cash in Dr. Wilkins' house?"

"I never saw any valuables, but Dr. Wilkins told me several times about diamonds she owned which she said were worth $40,000. I asked her why she didn't sell some of them and get something to eat."

"What did Dr. Wilkins say to that proposal?"

"I don't know that she made any answer."

Guffin re-called Dr. Arthur Blanchard, who repeated his earlier denial of any personal or professional relationship with Zeo. He said he went to her house to treat patients "and on one occasion she called me in to treat her brother Charles. . . . She called me to her home two months ago and wanted me to go into partnership with her. I didn't accept her offer."

Guffin then pulled the business card from his pocket.

"Do you know these business cards had been printed?"

"I do now, but the cards were not printed with my knowledge."

"Who advised you of these cards?"

"A patient showed me one of the cards on an interurban car recently."

Charles Wilkins took the stand. Under Guffin's questioning he remarked, "I cannot understand why he [Dr. Blanchard] should deny having had a partnership with my sister. There never was any question about it. I was in the house at various times when the affair was discussed between my sister and Dr. Blanchard." The practice would eventually expand to larger quarters and then a sanitarium, Charles said. But Blanchard quit the partnership in anger because Dr. Wilkins refused to let him have fifty dollars which he needed, Charles said.

Guffin changed the subject to Charles's arguments with Zeo. Charles admitted pulling the telephone from the wall during their fights. "It was after she had promised to quit drinking. There was a gallon jug of whiskey in a closet. When she promised to quit, I took the jug and poured its contents into the sink. 'You've poured out twelve dollars' worth of liquor,' said my sister. 'I am going to run my own house. I'll call up and get some more.'

"Then I told her she should not telephone for more and I tore the telephone from the wall so she could not." His differences with his sister were all about the kind of life she was leading, he insisted. He suspected Tarpley of "intimacies" with his sister. "When Tarpley came to the house, my sister always got rid of me right away."

"How often did he come to your sister's house?"

"He did not miss coming twice daily the three or four weeks I lived in the house." Tarpley had a key, and he'd seen him use it.

One of the last witnesses was Earl W. Smith, D.O., whose name came up for the first time during the inquest when Eva Grundy and Jesse James both mentioned Zeo's fear of "Dr. Smith." He was an Abrams practitioner at his Physico-Clinical Laboratories at 3500 Main Street in Kansas City. His name was in Dr. Wilkins's private telephone book.

Dr. Smith said he first treated Dr. Wilkins three or four years ago when she was living on Tracy Avenue. She had a case of ptomaine poisoning. He was called again to treat her at various times after that. Dr. Smith said he never had any quarrel with Dr. Wilkins. She told him of plans to build a sanitarium.

The newspapers reported little of his testimony. "The chief point of interest," one remarked, was Dr. Smith's testimony that Zeo once showed him some diamonds she kept in a jewel case under her pillow. That was two or three years ago, Dr. Smith said.

Some were still suspicious of Dr. Blanchard. Among other reasons, they wondered why Charles Wilkins and B. F. Tarpley both insisted that Dr. Blanchard associated himself professionally with Zeo from late December until late February and that he terminated the arrangement because Zeo did not pay him. Dr. G. A. Droll also testified that Zeo was planning to enter into partnership with an Excelsior Springs osteopath. Charles Wilkins said he had the cards printed up. Both Charles and Ben said they received treatments by Dr. Blanchard many times. At the inquest Blanchard was not asked to give his alibi. Coroner's attorney Horace Guffin declared that there were discrepancies in Blanchard's testimony. "Many of Dr. Blanchard's replies were evasive and unsatisfactory," Guffin said. "I wish to question him further."

The osteopath was "arrested for questioning" and brought to police headquarters. The *Kansas City Star* snapped his photo as he entered the police station. Chief Walston also summoned Detective James Elder, who had taken charge of the Wilkins case for Detectives Kritser and Doarn. Dr. Blanchard was quizzed by Chief Walston, Horace Guffin, and James Elder for about an hour. He brought his attorney Loyd Martz with him, though it was reported that Martz waited in the hallway. They did not forget to ask Dr. Blanchard if he had an alibi.

Blanchard stuck to his story. He hadn't seen Zeo since February 28. He was never interested in her sanitarium, chiefly because of his health and age. He was nearly sixty and had a bad case of diabetes and could not exert himself.

After their session, Chief Walston again reiterated to the press his belief that Dr. Blanchard had accounted for his movements on the day of the murder. Chief Walston was personally convinced Dr. Blanchard knew nothing of the crime. The chief added that Mrs. Walston had been receiving treatments by Dr. Blanchard at his Excelsior Springs office and thought he was a reputable osteopath.

At the conclusion of the coroner's inquest, the coroner's jury found that Zeo Wilkins met her death as the result of knife wounds made with murderous intent. "We are unable to determine the person or persons upon whom criminal liability shall be placed," they stated, "but circumstantial evidence warrants the recommendation that the prosecuting attorney's office investigate further the actions of Charles Wilkins, Dillard Davies and B. F. Tarpley." They made a truism of the old line from Dashiell Hammett: "The current practice in most places in the United States is to make the coroner's inquest an empty formality in which nothing much is brought out except that somebody has died."

The county prosecutor, Clarence A. Burney, every inch a Pendergast man, heard some of this testimony, as did his assistant James Anderson. After discussing the case they decided to jointly charge Wilkins, Davies, and Tarpley with first-degree murder. All three men were arraigned on March 24 and held for preliminary hearing. Anderson wrote the complaint against them, and Detective Kritser signed it. Tarpley was held, Anderson said, because of his "failure to make certain explanations"; Davies, because of "discrepancies" concerning "his movements the night of the murder"; and Charles Wilkins, because of the many people who spoke of the victim's fear of her brother, coupled with the fact that he killed her dog. All three men were transferred to the county jail.

Their preliminary hearing was conducted March 29. Although three men stood in the dock, the prosecutor's office knew it could not defend the case against at least two of them. Assistant Prosecutor James Anderson consented to a bond for the release of Tarpley and Wilkins. Judge James J. Shepard set bond at ten thousand dollars each. No bond was set for Dillard Davies.

At another proceeding April 12, Anderson asked the court to dismiss the charges against Tarpley and Wilkins on the grounds of insufficient evidence. He had no case against them. The judge did so. Anderson argued that Davies should still be held because of the bloodstains found on his clothes and boots and because he had no alibi. Davies was not provided a lawyer for the hearing. The judge ordered Davies to remain in custody.

When the judge dismissed the murder charge against him, Charles Wilkins vowed to search for Zeo's murderer. "The man who killed my sister is at large," he told the press. "I shall continue working on this case. I have some evidence in my possession which I hope will assist in bringing the murderer to justice."

B. F. Tarpley also gave a statement to the reporters when he was finally cleared. He was bitter about his arrest and confinement and "persecution." Bessie Tarpley stood by his side.

The black women's clubs in Kansas City followed the unfolding mystery of Dr. Wilkins's murder and grew concerned about Dillard Davies's continued imprisonment. They became convinced that authorities intended to nail the black man for the murder of Dr. Wilkins despite the lack of any direct or compelling evidence that he killed her. On March 28 a reporter for one of the city's black newspapers, the *Kansas City Sun,* interviewed Dillard Davies in the county jail. The *Sun* had taken an interest in the case and wanted "to determine the extent of Davies' implication, if any."

Davies told the reporter he was born in Gainesville, Texas, but had lived in Kansas City for years. He said his wife died in November. He said he did odd jobs and sold junk for a living. "His talk," the *Sun* reporter observed, "revealed him as being of low mentality." Davies once again insisted that he had not seen the doctor since the afternoon of her murder.

The city's black newspapers, including the *Call* and the *Sun*, ran front-page stories announcing the formation of a group calling itself the Negro Civil Protection Association. Most of its members were women; many were social workers and school officials. Twelve of the ladies volunteered to visit all the black churches and walk door-to-door throughout Kansas City's black neighborhoods to collect spare change for the Dillard Davies Justice Fund so they could hire a lawyer to defend him. A mass meeting was held at a community center. Within a few days, the fund rose to a hundred and fifty dollars.

The *Sun* explained to its readers that the police were trying to drag a confession from Davies. It reported that Mrs. Perry, a white woman who once employed Davies, had been approached by the police. The detectives asked her to convince Dillard to admit to the crime. She refused.

The case of *People v. Davies* continued in the justice court. At the next hearing Davies was represented by black attorney James B. Gibbs, who filed a motion to free him for lack of evidence. Assistant Prosecutor James Anderson opposed the motion, stating that the blood on Davies's boots was human blood after all. He called a detective to the witness stand to state the case against Davies. James Gibbs cross-examined the detective, asking if the police tested the rope in Dillard's barn, the one he said had horse blood on it, as did his boots.

Detective Edward Kritser denied finding a rope in his barn.

Dillard's lawyer produced a photograph of the bloody rope. It had appeared in the *Kansas City Journal-Post.*

The detective said the reporters must have taken the rope with them.

The judge denied the motion but Dillard's attorney won a request to allow him out on a ten-thousand dollar bond. Members of the Negro Civil Protection Association furnished the bond premium. Dillard was immediately removed to the Old City Hospital. "His nerves had been shattered under the continual investigation," reported the *Kansas City Call.* He had spent dozens of hours in interrogation and a month in jail and still faced a charge of murder in the first degree.

Wrote the editor of the *Kansas City Sun* in an April 19 editorial:

WHY IS DAVIES HELD?

It is ridiculous to try to bring one's self to believe that the authorities think Davies guilty. Just try to imagine white men who believe a Negro guilty of, or connected with, the murder of a white woman releasing that Negro on bond and you can readily see just how ridiculous a thing it is.

Nobody in authority believes Davies guilty. If they did he would be in jail, without bond, awaiting trial for murder . . .

Davies is poor, unfortunate and practically friendless. Whatever defense he is getting is due to the kind-heartedness of Kansas City's Negro Club Women who have been working since his arrest to secure him a fair trial. They are collecting quarters and dimes and a few dollars to give him attorneys for his defense. Their effort is commendable.

But why should they be put to further trouble?

Six months after Dr. Wilkins was killed, Judge James Shepherd finally dismissed the first-degree murder charge against Dillard Davies. Detective James Elder then arrested Dillard again and had him arraigned before Judge James H. Austin on a charge of second-degree murder. Months later all charges against Dillard Davies were finally dismissed. He was released for the last time on November 11. No other official action ever took place in the investigation of the murder of Zeo Zoe Wilkins until decades later, when the old police files were thrown onto a bonfire.

26

Stalked to the Grave by the Ghosts of Her Wild Career

Some things you can't find out; but you will never know you
can't by guessing and supposing: no, you have to be patient
and go on experimenting until you find out that you can't find
out. And it is delightful to have it that way, it makes the world
so interesting. If there wasn't anything to find out, it would
be dull. Even trying to find out and not finding out is just as
interesting as trying to find out and finding out, and I don't
know but more so.

— *Mark Twain,* The Diaries of Adam and Eve

n March 1924, the murder of Dr. Wilkins was the talk of the Midwest. Thousands of people were so engrossed in the unfolding
tale of her life and death that they wanted to see her trysting place. On
Sunday, March 23, nearly four thousand curious people passed 2425
Park Avenue, Kansas City. "It was a come-and-go crowd," a reporter
observed. "Few of them paused for more than a minute or two, and none
attempted to peer into the windows. In one hour in the afternoon eight
hundred motor cars were counted—endless streams past the house—
and scores of persons walked by, gathering for a few moments in groups
on the sidewalks and in the yard." Despite this furious public interest in
the case, the mystery ended in speculation.

Which man finally got the best of Zeo Zoe Wilkins?

Did the beneficiary of her estate kill her? The police tried to track
down her adopted nephew, Horace Ricketts. His alibi was irrefutable. At

the time of the murder he was in the Navy on active duty in the Pacific aboard the U.S.S. *Ramapo*.

Did someone kill her for revenge? An enterprising reporter spoke to one of Zeo's old enemies, Tabitha Taylor, who called herself the true widow of Thomas Cunningham. He had finally passed away of natural causes two years earlier. Tabitha gave him a single quip. "Poor old Tom is out of their clutches."

Was the mystery burglar, the man who broke her basement window, the real killer? "Authorities now believe," reported the *Denver Post* on March 21, "the police allowed the murderer to slip thru [*sic*] their grasp by letting this man go."

Another possibility is that her murder was a *crime passionel,* and the list of eligible suspects in that scenario was quite long. In early May, nearly two months after the murder, the police finally found Zeo's young man, Roy Hartman. He was questioned both by the police and by prosecutors. He admitted leaving Kansas City when he learned of the murder but denied knowing a thing about it. The police announced they would put Roy in a lineup to be viewed by recent holdup victims. The police also questioned her lover George Mahan, who told police he stayed with Zeo a year ago but left the home because there was so much "coming and going and irregularity." He insisted he had not seen her in a long while. That is all that is known of either young Roy or George, so their stories end here.

Another theory floated by detectives was that a jealous woman killed Dr. Wilkins. "The fact that Dr. Wilkins had numerous men patients," remarked the *Kansas City Post,* "many of whom were reported to have become infatuated with her and to have continued their visits to her as friends, may have prompted some jealous woman to revenge, police believe. The police also are giving equal credence to the theory that a jealous man murdered Dr. Wilkins. Only a strong love or a strong hate, the police pointed out, could have prompted the vicious mutilation and scratching of the face of the victim." Of course, a fight to the death with anyone may well have left the same sorts of wounds. What sort of man would gouge out a woman's eye? What sort of man would choose a small, dull blade and kill so slowly and clumsily?

For a time, Dr. O. M. McMurtrey, the osteopath from Fort Worth, came under scrutiny. Zeo owed him money, and Arthur and Laura Wilkins told the Kansas City police to speak to him. Whether the police followed up is not known, but a United Press reporter was able to reach him for one brief comment. "Dr. Wilkins showed signs of mental derangement when she lived here" in Fort Worth, Dr. McMurtrey remarked. "Her relatives were aware of her condition, but she was not considered sufficiently unbalanced to warrant placing her in an insane asylum." That is all he had to say for print.

Charles Wilkins provided an alibi the police could not shake, though the details and actual names of his alibi witnesses were not disclosed. A search of his rooms did not turn up any pertinent evidence. And yet Zeo feared him. He beat her many times. He believed she was rich, and he was jealous. He was so angry about her trysts with his friend Charles Smith that he knocked her to the floor, and it wasn't the first time. Arthur Wilkins granted an interview in the 1950s shortly before he died. He was asked who he thought was responsible for Zeo's murder. "There was a lot of people that think my brother killed my sister Zeo Zoe," he said. "Maybe he did, maybe he didn't. I think he did. That's the way my family operated."

But his wife Laura thought it was someone whom Doc met shortly before her death—someone with whom she argued about money. That couldn't refer to Dr. Blanchard, whom Zeo had known since medical school. The only men she was known to have met shortly before her death were her new lawyer, Jesse James, and Dr. Holly Haworth.

Zeo's brother Horace Wilkins disagreed with Arthur as well. Horace told the press early in the inquiry that he did not believe his brother Charles murdered his sister. "My brother was fond of his sister. It would have been impossible for him to have killed her. The man I suspect is higher up in the world than any of those heretofore connected with the case. He wished to get my sister out of his way. I believe the investigations so far have been along the wrong line." Davies was also innocent, Horace believed. If he had anything to do with it, then he acted at the behest of someone "higher up," Horace said. "There is more behind this than has come out." A reporter asked him whether Zeo did indeed keep a fortune in her home. "He intimated," the *Kansas City Post* reported, "that he believed she had money."

Ben Tarpley seemed to overcome suspicion. He would not have come Sunday and left his lunch had he killed Dr. Wilkins the night before, the prevailing logic went. And, yet, if he came over daily, as others insisted he did, he ought to have noticed that something was amiss—the open window, if nothing else. Tarpley should have discovered and reported her murder. He may have had a spare key. He was a liar and a perjurer. He refused to admit that he committed adultery with Dr. Wilkins even when other witnesses well established the fact. Tarpley had a steadfast alibi in his wife Bessie, though it couldn't count for much given the fact that Mrs. Tarpley was oblivious to her husband's months-long affair.

Was it Dillard Davies after all? He insisted that he wasn't at Zeo's house the night of her death, but he did not truthfully disclose his whereabouts. His testimony could not be reconciled with Eva Grundy's equally adamant statements under oath. One of them was lying. If Eva was telling the truth, perhaps it took only moments for Dillard to beg for a few dollars and leave. On the other hand, he might have resorted to desperate measures in order to collect his back wages.

If theft was the killer's motive, Davies was not a good suspect. He was completely illiterate. He could not tell time. He could not spell his own name. It is impossible to picture him rifling through documents he could not understand. He was unemployed, had no family, and had problems with booze and dice. He was someone who had to plead for a dollar. If he murdered Dr. Wilkins, it is hard to believe he'd leave behind easily pawned valuables.

The *Kansas City Post* was among several publications that speculated against the evidence that her murder may have involved a rape. "Probably an attempt had been made to attack her," the *Post* surmised. "Her body, the clothing torn and disarranged, was lying with the arms and legs spread wide apart after the manner of victims who were tortured in medieval times on wheels." But the medical examiner ruled it out.

Was it Dr. Blanchard? Did the spurned doctor turn violent on her? The detectives and newspapers speculated about it. The United Press reported on March 25:

> Authorities today said indications were that Dr. Wilkins had been slain by someone with a knowledge of anatomy. Instead of her throat being slashed as it would have been had she been killed by an unskilled person, two deft incisions had been made with a knife which were certain to have caused death. They believe that Dr. Wilkins possibly had been injured in a quarrel and after attempts to revive her failed, her throat was cut. Her body showed signs of having been recently subjected to strenuous treatment, possibly osteopathic, which officials now believe might have resulted from attempts to revive her.

The statement was among several unattributed speculations printed in the press. Numerous murders have been laid at the feet of medical professionals by journalists certain that a victim's wounds could only have been made by someone "with knowledge of anatomy," and in many instances, the assertions are later proven false. Moreover, Arthur Blanchard was not the only doctor who had dealings with Zeo. And to her sister Gertrude, Zeo had made the remark, three days before her murder, that she was about to lose her money and her life. When Gertrude asked her to explain, Zeo said "it's some people you don't know." Gertrude knew Arthur Blanchard—they'd all attended medical school together.

Then again, Dr. Blanchard was, like B. F. Tarpley, a liar. He contradicted other witnesses as well as himself on the most mundane points, such as his financial transactions with Zeo and the question of the business cards.

And then there were the bizarre statements of Jesse James to consider.

James repeatedly said two men had threatened his client. "She gave me the names of two persons who had threatened her life," he said at one point. "Dr. Wilkins lived in fear of two men," he said at another. Since he was hired within days of the violent incident involving Charles Wilkins and Charles Smith, it is logical to conclude, as did observers, that in her conversations with her lawyer, Zeo specifically named these two men.

But James seemed to be confused by the time he testified. Initially he refused to identify any suspects except Charles Wilkins. Indeed, he repeatedly pointed the finger at Charles Wilkins while declining to name any other. Rather than relay all he knew, he shut out the press and the public, not to mention the coroner's jury. Apparently he didn't care if his murdered client's case was properly investigated or not.

And yet later, contradicting himself—and not for the first time—he apparently referred to Charles Smith as "Dr. Smith." Perhaps he was actually confused. If so, he should have made that plain. An alternative explanation is that James deliberately promoted confusion.

Another curious aspect of his testimony concerned the date of his next appointment with Dr. Wilkins. Early on in the investigation, he'd said he had an appointment with her on Wednesday, March 19, and he repeated that remark on the witness stand. He then added that he had an appointment with her at three p.m. on Sunday, March 16, but he missed it. It was a curious day for an appointment, if its purpose was to discuss legal affairs. The woman was already dead anyway, as it would turn out. So if he missed an appointment on *Sunday,* when, exactly, did he reschedule for Wednesday?

Why was a Sunday appointment even necessary? Zeo could have given him the documents concerning the Marksheffel trust in one of their many, many earlier meetings, or in their Wednesday appointment.

Why hadn't he mentioned earlier in the investigation that he was to see Dr. Wilkins on Sunday afternoon? One possible explanation for this new detail is that he knew Eva Grundy might testify. If Jesse was the man Zeo and Eva expected to see at three p.m. on *Saturday,* then his testimony that the meeting was set for Sunday was, perhaps, preemptive. That is, if Eva testified that Jesse had an appointment with Zeo Saturday afternoon, Jesse, by citing Sunday, could shrug and say he must have been confused as to the date.

As it turned out, Eva did not disclose the name of the man who stood up Zeo hours before her murder, the man Zeo feared was double-crossing her.

Another contradiction: he denied planning to fence her diamonds. Yet James examined them. *Why?* If he refused to do with them whatever it was that she asked him to do, what reason would he have for forming an opinion on the value of the diamonds and the bonds six days before their owner was murdered?

The list of items missing from Zeo's home after her murder was another damning fact. The six items known to be missing were her will, the Marksheffel loan, the pair of letters from Al asking for more time to pay the debt, the bonds, and diamonds. He was asked to review her will; he was asked to enforce her Marksheffel loan; he was asked to sell her bonds and diamonds. Who else would have an interest in destroying or stealing these specific, disparate things? Charles Wilkins cared about her will. But he would have no reason to care about matters concerning Al Marksheffel—and vice versa. If James had nothing to do with his client's murder, then it was a clumsy coincidence for him that the killer took or burned several different documents and valuables that, by his own testimony, Zeo intended to entrust to him. Everything missing from her home was connected to one man and one man alone: Jesse Edwards James.

Another statement he made at the inquest would have seemed suspicious only to any attorneys who were in the room at the time. James repeatedly insisted that the Marksheffel trust was no longer enforceable because it was missing. He said specifically that "there is no way in the world to collect the money." His testimony on that point was legally indefensible, and it is impossible to accept that he himself might have believed it. As a law school honors graduate and experienced attorney, he was without a doubt at least vaguely familiar with the common-law "parol evidence rule." It is an ancient legal maxim universally recognized under American law and specifically recognized in Missouri at that time and now. If a contract, last will and testament, or similar document went missing, it was of course still legally enforceable. Its contents could be established in court using "parol" or oral evidence. Anyone who was involved in its preparation or knew what it said could testify to a missing document's terms. Any other rule would make an ass of the law by inspiring dishonest destruction of contracts as a means to avoid them. Why did Jesse James say the missing trust was uncollectable? It was a flat-out lie.

He also chose not to report any conversation he had with Al Marksheffel when he made his appointment to go to Colorado Springs, if it was true that he had such an appointment. The county administrator told the newspapers that if anyone owed Dr. Wilkins money, the county would open an estate and pursue the claim. If James feared what might come out during a civil inquiry and wanted to head it off, the lie served that purpose.

After testifying that he missed an appointment at Zeo's home on Sunday, James said he tried calling her Monday but nobody answered the telephone. He waited a day and then tried reaching her again on Tuesday but again no one answered. How could it be that "nobody answered" his calls if the telephone wasn't ringing in the first place? Many people tried to reach the doctor during the time her body lay undiscovered. Others had said the line wasn't working, and observers had long ago come to the conclusion that the telephone came off the hook at the time Zeo was murdered. The testimony of four other witnesses—Eva Grundy, Gertrude Palmer, Charles Wilkins, and B. F. Tarpley—would well establish the fact that the phone was out of order when others, including an operator, tried to reach Zeo. Her telephone wasn't ringing for anyone else. James could not have made these calls, at least not as he described them. If he did not call her (after missing their Thursday appointment, perhaps after missing two appointments in a row), maybe it was because he knew she was dead—before her body was discovered.

He certainly had a motive. His *Black Flag* ruination was ample cause for committing a murder for great gain.

It seemed a crime of which he was capable. Jesse first leveled a loaded gun at other human beings when he was six. He first put a gun to a man's head and pulled the trigger with murder in his heart at *seven*—the same year he vowed to kill a man, Charlie Ford. Before he reached adolescence, he knocked a boy to the foot of a staircase for having the audacity to demand a bite of his orange. As a young man, he hung out with notorious characters such as suspected murderer Jack Kennedy. Jamesiana scholars believe he likely was guilty of armed robbery at twenty-three, despite the verdict in his favor. Jesse was also a pawnbroker, a habitual adulterer, an underworld lawyer who followed a dubious ethical code, a zealous Klucker, and a lousy husband. For his whole life, the press and public expressed the idea that he had inherited a criminal bent from his infamous father, the common avenger. He'd spent his entire career defending not only his sire but other despicable criminals like Albert Crone and Mattie Howard. He had no moral compass. He made decisions "on the instant, as a rule." As to Dr. Wilkins, he learned most of her secrets.

Instead of piercing the veil of mystery surrounding the case, his testimony only made him a suspect. Was it conceivable . . . was Jesse up to his Pa's old tricks again?

Did his lies and evasions under oath reveal the truth?

Did Jesse James Jr. agree to help Dr. Zeo Wilkins defraud her creditors of the last of her Cunningham fortune and then dry-gulch her?

When Jesse's own testimony put him under suspicion, Kansas City authorities demonstrated their willingness to look aside. After James testified in detail at the inquest about the fortune in Dr. Wilkins's house, the press asked the police to comment on it. Unnamed police officials "discarded as fiction the story of the fortune" that James told them, reported the *Kansas City Star*. Although the police at first believed that Zeo "could hardly have disposed of all the money" she received from Tom Cunningham, the *Star* quoted "detectives" saying after the inquest that Jesse James "must have been mistaken when he said he saw bonds, stocks and diamonds valued at $100,000." Ironically, the police department came to the defense of the defense lawyer by dismissing the lawyer's own sworn testimony.

It was not so easily dismissed. James's repeated statements about Zeo's valuables were quite specific and lengthy. And Eva Grundy saw them too—she testified that Zeo kept valuables in her home. She said Zeo tossed a thousand-dollar certificate on her lap the night before the murder.

And what of Eva Grundy? She was never seen as a suspect or characterized as a possible accomplice. She was a tiny woman, much smaller than Dr. Wilkins. But she believed Zeo kept a fortune in her home, and her odd behavior before and during her appearance at the inquest eluded ready explanation.

The *Kansas City Times* obtained an exclusive interview with Eva after the inquest. She repeated that it was Dr. Wilkins who asked her to leave on the night she was killed. "She told me to run all the way to the car line," Eva said.

"When I left the house," Eva added, "two negroes were approaching. I ran across the street and to the car line. I did not look back to learn whether they went into the house. When I changed cars at Thirty-First Street and Brooklyn Avenue, I thought I should call the police, but decided not to do so. When I reached home I tried to call Dr. Wilkins on the phone, as she had asked, but was unable to get her. The operator told me the receiver was off the hook.

"I believe now that Dr. Wilkins was killed within 10 minutes after I left her. She was dressed for the street when I left. But when she was found dead she did not have a coat or hat on."

Her final published remark: "I believe it was an underworld job."

Chief Walston agreed with Eva. After the inquest he came up with yet another theory on the motive of Dr. Wilkins's slayer. In a statement to reporters, Walston "recalled Dr. Wilkins' alleged connection five years ago with a group of nationally known confidence men. Chief Walston said he investigated her home at that time and discovered strong evidence of such a connection. L. A. Myers, detective, also recalled that Dr. Wilkins had figured in the investigation of a Dr. McClintock two years ago. Dr. McClintock was said to have been a fence for stolen motor cars. Dr. Wilkins is said to have had two stolen motor cars in her possession at that time, obtained through Dr. McClintock." If Zeo had dealings in the underworld beyond her liquor deal with John McNamara, the details never saw the light of day.

Within weeks of the murder, all mention of Bertillon experts and envelopes gripped with blood-stained fingers was forgotten. Nothing more was ever made of the bloody footprints or fingerprints found in her home. There was also no public disclosure of any evidence that anyone connected to Zeo Wilkins experienced a change in their fortunes after she was killed. As far as the public chapters of the investigation went, the diamonds and bonds, assuming they did exist and were in her home on the night of her murder, vanished into thin air.

The Kansas City police department eventually admitted that it could not penetrate the mystery. Even if there were slightly better evidence pointing to one particular party, such a case was not triable. The worst defense attorney in the country could have secured an acquittal for any defendant who may have gone on trial for this woman's murder. A full rendition of the list of men and women with motive to kill her would have provided a good defense attorney several hours of closing argument.

Neither the local press nor the pool reporters pressured the police to pursue the case; just the opposite. Journalists wrote *finis* on her story as though they'd heard that ending before and liked it. Mark Twain once explained that "nothing in the world affords a newspaper reporter so much satisfaction as gathering up the details of a bloody and mysterious murder and writing them up with aggravating circumstantiality."

"In the mass of evidence so far uncovered there is nothing to point to any particular person as the slayer, in the opinion of the police," said one Kansas City daily. "The woman had many friendships; and many quarrels. She was the center of intrigue and plotting in efforts to obtain money, including transactions involving some of her six [*sic*] former husbands." The *Kansas City Journal* gave up on the puzzle in its very first report on the case: "So many stories of intrigue and adventuring have been woven around Dr. Wilkins's name in the last eight years, police are left groping in a maze of innumerable hypothetical clews." Said the *Lima News* in Ohio on March 27, twelve days after Zeo was killed: "Not even her most intimate friends knew how many spectres lurked in her past. The precise details of Zoe Wilkins' murder remained clouded in sinister mist. 'They may find the man, or woman, who killed her,' whispers Kansas City. 'They may even unearth a supposed motive.' But the exact reason will elude them. It has gone to the grave with Zoe—and dead women tell no tales." The *Lima News* literally gave Zeo barrels of ink to cap off her long press run, for it would have taken ink in volumes and extra drying time to print the artwork that accompanied her last story in that publication.

The most scathing post-mortem critique of Zeo's "adventures" came from Ogden City, Utah. Its *Standard-Examiner* regularly published long true crime essays and never reserved judgment on the debauched men

The "Stalked to the Grave" illustration from the *Lima News,*
April 24, 1924. (*Lima News*)

and abandoned women who were fodder for its columns. Unapologetic
for its interest in true crime, the newspaper overtly shunned what it
called "success stories and inspirational twaddle" in favor of carefully
reported murder stories featuring blunt assessments on the causes of
"the descent and destruction of the human spirit," by which the paper
hoped to educate those interested in "the pattern of life." As it once took
on Mattie Howard in a full-page, heavily illustrated essay, it would also
disclose the baser truths about Zeo Wilkins. In the firestorm of public

outrage over the details of Zeo's life, the *Standard-Examiner* brought the firewood.

WICKEDEST MOVIE VAMPS OUTDONE IN REAL LIFE
Astonishing Career of Zeo Zoe Wilkins,
Who Trained Herself From Girlhood To Be a
Heartless Siren and Wreck Countless Lives

The ruthless, self-seeking adventuress whom Kipling christened the "vampire," is a type of woman well known to every movie goer. The scenario writers delight in weaving her wickedness into their plots and some of the greatest film actresses have scored their success in the roles of "vamps."

But neither the famous vampire of Kipling's poem nor any of the countless vampires of the movies nor those to be found in books and in dramas of the speaking stage can begin to equal the shocking iniquity of a flesh and blood woman of our own time and country—Zeo Zoe Wilkins, the beautiful young osteopath physician, who was found murdered in her home in Kansas City . . .

She was a vampire extraordinary, another Jezebel made more terrible by the very fact that she had at her command all the tools of modern civilization. From Texas to Chicago and as far west as the sunny slopes of California she claimed her victims by the score, perhaps by the hundred.

Force of circumstances, disappointment in love, adverse financial conditions, and other similar causes have often turned women from the straight and narrow path to ways of designing wickedness. It is seldom, however, that a young girl in her teens carefully plans for herself a vampire career . . .

The pathway of her life is strewn with the wrecks of human lives and fortunes, with prison terms, suicides and murders. By her own words set down in letters and diaries found since her mysterious death she stands convicted of almost every crime in the calendar.

Did Zeo Zoe Wilkins realize that, after such a life of destruction, and ruthless torture of others, there could be but one end—murder? Who it was that killed her the police cannot find out. There are so many who may have felt they had good reason for wanting to end the vampire's life.

"Who it was that killed her the police cannot find out." Given the context, it was less a statement of fact than it was a demand.

Another newspaper concluded its coverage with: "A group of kids gathered in front of the house making dares and one boy ventured as far as the front porch. The others laughed and he ran away." At the very last, a spiritualist took an interest in the scene of the murder.

A "MEDIUM" WOULD LIVE THERE.
Spiritualist, Seeking Sympathetic
Atmosphere, Applies to Owner.

Houses that have been the scenes of mysterious murders or other tragedies usually are avoided thereafter. But exactly the opposite is true in the case of the house at 2425 Park Avenue, where Dr. Wilkins was murdered. Several persons have expressed a desire to rent, lease or buy the property since it has come into public view, according to Mrs. L.F. Palmer, the owner. A spiritualist "medium" was the latest applicant, Mrs. Palmer said. The "medium" believed she would find a sympathetic atmosphere for her work, "influences" that would be attracted to the house because of recent events.

The assistant prosecutor handling the investigation, James Anderson, gave the last official published quote on the subject of the murder of Dr. Zeo Wilkins. In November 1924, he spoke to reporter Constance Brown for a piece that appeared in the *Syracuse Herald* in New York. Ms. Brown's article quoted him at length:

It will be a long hunt. At first we thought we had only to go back a few days and check up on the movements of the young woman, list her acquaintances and then find the guilty one by the process of eliminating those who could prove themselves innocent.

We soon discovered that we would have to begin our hunt away back at the time a fifteen-year-old girl [*sic*] entered a school of osteopathy at Kirksville, Mo.; that we would have to follow that girl's career through year after year of intrigue and adventure; that we would have to bring together, here and there along the trail, the tangled threads of many tragedies, suicides, other murders, bankrupt banks, broken homes and love piracies, all with pretty Zeo Zoe Wilkins as their central figure; and that we must come on down the years until that fifteen-year-old girl had married and dismissed six [*sic*] husbands, accumulated three great fortunes, and mocked a score of men whom she had first taught to love her.

Somewhere along the line we hope to find the man who did not forget, or who became afraid that he, too, would become a victim, or someone who knew the young woman had hidden away a vast amount of money. Then, perhaps, we will have solved the murder.

It may be said by some that the slaying of this strange and adventurous woman was a retribution, but her murderer must be found or all standards of Justice are flagrantly balked. It is tragic to have to believe that a man can go into the home of a woman, kill her brutally, ransack her effects, and go along in peace and security, in his very elusiveness a daily encouragement to others to plan similar crimes.

Constance Brown also reported that Anderson believed "the crime was one of revenge, and that the disappearance of the fortune was a separate affair." Anderson seems to suggest that the person who murdered Zeo Wilkins was not the same person who stole her diamonds and bonds. He seems to suggest that the theft took place long after the murder, perhaps even before. Those remarks did not make much sense.

Then again, little of what Anderson said made sense. The lengthy article written by Constance Brown was the most inaccurate account of Zeo Wilkins's life that ever saw print. Virtually every sentence contained factual errors. It appears that Anderson was a stranger to the murder victim's most basic biographical facts; in which case, one has to wonder whether he was motivated to perform his work diligently—and to look suspiciously on everything he said. That would include not only his murder-as-revenge theory but also his assertion that human blood and not horse blood was found on the boots belonging to Dillard Davies.

Still, his final remark was curious. He apparently did not state his reason for believing the theft of Zeo's fortune was separate from her murder. Did the prosecutor trace her stolen valuables to someone in particular—and did that someone try to deflect suspicion by confessing to theft while denying involvement in her death?

But why then did the killer steal her strongbox? Surely it was not empty. Surely it held something of value, or he would have left it behind. Unless the killer was as crazy as the woman he murdered.

In 1939, fifteen years after Zeo's murder, the magazine *True Detective Mysteries* delved into "Kansas City's Strange 'Zeo Zoe' Riddle." Written by an Associated Press editor, the piece recapped her career but shed no new light on the mystery.

In 1945, prolific Missouri folklorist Vance Randolph wrote a curious essay on Zeo Wilkins under a pseudonym. Vance Randolph was a prolific writer of Missouri folklore and fiction. His lifelong passion was to travel through the Ozark Mountains, where he collected folk songs, slang, insults, jokes, and legends, among them many ballads about the James boys. Randolph bragged that he knew more about the Ozarks than anyone alive.

Randolph moved to Hollywood, California, in 1933. There he worked with fellow Missouri folklorist Homer Croy, who grew up in Kearney, near the James farm, and knew more about the James family than anyone, including the James family. Croy traveled five thousand miles for Jesse James–related research and was a self-proclaimed "whirling dervish" of James lore. Croy would author a very friendly family biography in 1949.

During his first two months in Hollywood, Vance Randolph worked on a movie script set in the Ozarks for a studio and made the most money he'd ever made in his writing career. Then the movie producer for whom he worked told him his Ozark dialogue didn't sound authentic. He was fired, and his script was turned over to Homer Croy.

Vance Randolph announced his departure from California with a stream of tobacco juice shot onto the green carpet of a Hollywood producer. But during those two months, Vance must have talked to Homer. It's hard to imagine they did not discuss the case of Zeo Zoe Wilkins, since it put Jesse James Jr. in the hot seat for a time. As another James scholar, Carl Breihan, once remarked, "No particle of new information is ignored by the scholars of Jamesiana. They are keeping track of the family . . ."

Somewhere along the line Vance Randolph heard the story of Zeo Wilkins—he does not cite his sources for his essay—and one has to wonder if he picked up the tale from Homer Croy, for his rendition is fairly accurate. It is unlikely that newspaper accounts were his sole source of information; for one thing, he correctly stated the year of Zeo's birth and the locations of her various residences, details the press often got wrong, not to mention the prosecutor who handled her murder case. Randolph insisted on calling her Zoe, knowing it was her middle name, because Zeo was just too strange a moniker to repeat.

Regardless of where he heard the tale or picked up unpublished details, Vance Randolph's essay on the Zeo Zoe Wilkins case closes with a tantalizing hint:

> No motive for the killing was uncovered. Zoe's adopted son and
> her brother were presumably her heirs, but both had unshakable

alibis. The police discovered that the dead woman had been intimately acquainted with several notorious criminals, and had probably been involved in some gang activities. She had told several persons that she was likely to be murdered at any moment. But there was no evidence to connect any of Zoe's criminal associates with the killing.

The police held several men, including a Negro who had spent a great deal of time in Zoe's house, but later released them because of insufficient evidence. That was more than 20 years ago, and nobody has ever been punished for the murder of Doctor Zoe Wilkins. There are people in Kansas City today who claim to know who got Zoe's $100,000, but they are not the sort of people who are likely to tell the police about it.

So she *did* keep a fortune in her home, according to popular wisdom as Randolph had it. But he could not name the man Kansas City suspected.

If today you call up the Kansas City police department and pester them for the tenth time for some clues to the whereabouts of some very old files, a gruff desk man will grumble, "we burned all that stuff in the seventies." One day the answer might be found locked up somewhere.

The Marksheffel trust perhaps.

A small fortune in uncashable, blood-stained corporate bonds.

Vance Randolph's unpublished gossip.

Notes from a memorable conversation.

The diary of Eva Grundy.

Unless and until then nobody knows. The murder remains unsolved, and those frustrated by that fact have the victim herself to blame. Zeo Zoe Wilkins lies buried with her last secret in an unmarked grave. The knife slashes into her throat as if guided by an occult hand.

Epilogue

Jesse James on Carpet

Every klansman who commits a lawless act, or who withholds
his influence against such an act, at the same time commits
perjury. Uninformed and malicious critics have accused us
of being a whipping organization. Many crimes and cruelties
abhorrent to our every feeling, conviction and purpose have
been charged against our order calumniously. If we were a
whipping organization, with our hundreds of thousands of
ardent members spread throughout the country, and with
solemn breakers of every law, human and divine, abounding,
we should be whipping thousands of culprits every night.
They deserve it. But that is not the klan way.
— *Dr. H. W. Evans,* Imperial Wizard of the
Ku Klux Klan *(1924)*

Kansas City held its municipal elections in early April 1924. Pendergast grappled the Klan to a draw. The boss offered protection
to black voters, who thanked him with support for his Democratic Party.
Jesse James Jr.'s faction did not do all that well in Kansas City, but it
managed a few victories. The Klan unseated Judge Truman, who blamed
his one and only election defeat on a "vicious, hate-filled melee" caused
by Klansmen on election day.

Jesse James's involvement in the Klan went beyond the political
dimension. As everyone in Kansas City would learn less than six weeks
after the murder of Dr. Wilkins and a month after the election, Jesse was
not only participating in but spearheading the night rides for the Kansas
City cross-burners in 1924.

In May 1924, James approached Kansas City Police Chief William

Shreeve. He asked Shreeve to give him a "detail of patrolmen." James planned to lead the patrolmen on a "road patrol" because of recent "banditry" outside Kansas City. Chief Shreeve would later say he did not take Jesse seriously. He said he would only respond to a request from Clay County officials. James went ahead and organized an armed expedition without an official contingent. Things went horribly wrong for him.

On Saturday, May 10, around midnight, Jesse E. James was driving a hot rod Ford touring car with a rebuilt high-powered Liberty motor on the brand new highway between Kansas City and Excelsior Springs on a heavily armed Ku Klux Klan "road patrol." Next to him was a woman who was not his wife. In the rear seat was another couple. That man was married, too, though not to the woman who sat with him. Behind them was a second car built for speed, at its wheel a private detective. At his side were two more women.

Jesse stopped paying attention to his driving and hit another car. Two young men were in that car and at least one of them was hurt. He happened to be the son of a James family friend, Dr. John Sheldon.

James took the young men to the medical office of a physician in Excelsior Springs, Dr. Ernest Lowry. Dr. Lowry had known Frank James. Dr. Lowry apparently felt that young Sheldon needed to be taken to the hospital. Somehow local authorities learned of the crash and came to investigate. At some point a bulge was seen in Jesse's pockets, and the police discovered that James and his companions were all carrying loaded weapons. Jesse carried at least three weapons with him, two handguns and a shotgun. All three had once belonged to his father, or so he said.

The police were not amused. As far as law enforcement was concerned, Jesse James was never going to ride again in Clay County. They questioned James on the night of the accident with the intention of charging him with carrying a concealed weapon. One news account described James as "highly nervous" and "confused."

The accident could not remain a secret. The incident caused

"considerable excitement" in the state. It was first revealed in a piece in the *Excelsior Springs Daily Herald* on May 11, 1924:

JESSE JAMES WRECKED ARMED TO TEETH.

News of the crash later appeared on page one of all the local papers. Jesse James Jr. became widely known as a sectarian leader of the Klan at the height of its violence, as well as being a confirmed womanizer. The details appeared at the top of page one of the *Kansas City Star* on May 12, 1924:

JESSE JAMES "ON CARPET"

CLAY COUNTY PROSECUTOR PROBES

ARMED ROAD PATROL.

It appeared this afternoon the hearing for Jesse James, Kansas City lawyer, set for 1 o'clock at Excelsior Springs, would not be held today.

James and his companions, who were found heavily armed after they figured in a motor car crash on the Excelsior Springs road early Sunday morning, failed to appear at the hearing ordered by the Clay County prosecutor.

William Payne, night marshal of Excelsior Springs, said James was in one car with another man and two women. . . . Mrs. James is said to be in California.

James accounted for the revolvers which he carried and those of his companions by saying he was patrolling the road for outlaws . . . . Explaining the presence of the revolvers and a shotgun, James said he had been asked by the Kansas City police department and Clay County authorities to form the patrol as a protection against bandits. . . . The Kansas City police department did not authorize James to patrol the Clay County roads, William A. Shreeve, chief of police, said today. . . . "We did not even consider his request seriously," Chief Shreeve said . . .

KLAN BACK OF THE PATROL

Dr. John G. Sheldon, Kansas City surgeon, said today Jesse James told him the patrol of Clay County roads was an activity sponsored by the Ku Klux Klan, with which James has been identified lately . . .

According to Dr. Sheldon, James found himself in another kettle of hot water when he was in the presence of Dr. Lowry, because Dr. Lowry is a leader in an active anti-klan movement in Excelsior Springs.

"I don't know whether you boys had better try to go back to Kansas City tonight. The Kluxers might get you and beat you up," Dr. Sheldon said Lowry told [them].

Then James stepped forward and declared he was a Klansman and that he would see that the son of his old friend, Dr. Sheldon, and [his companion Donald] Quinn would be escorted safely back to Kansas City. Then it was seen that James and his companions of the patrol were armed. Questions were plied, but through the influence of Dr. Lowry, James and the others were allowed to go.

Dr. Ernest Lowry charged a high price for his services that night. The doctor was, as it turned out, a fervent collector of James Gang memorabilia. Jesse turned over his father's pistols and shotgun to Dr. Lowry. The terms of the transaction were never quite clear.

And yet Clay County officials weren't satisfied to let the matter rest. The county prosecutor demanded an accounting from Jesse James. He threatened that if James did not come to Excelsior Springs to explain himself, "he would be sent for and taken by force."

The next day, James limped into a courtroom full of spectators in Excelsior Springs with his arm in a sling. He said his arm was broken in two places, although Dr. Sheldon had said it was a minor injury. Dr. Lowry appeared to say James was suffering from a "nervous breakdown" and needed to be hospitalized. Added the doctor: "James had been extremely nervous some time prior to the motor wreck . . . in which he figured while acting as a self-appointed armed patrol on the new Excelsior Springs–Kansas City Highway." Dr. John Sheldon also appeared, as did the Clay County attorney, sheriff, and justice of the peace. At the conclusion of the hearing, which had become a "friendly consultation," remarked the *Kansas City Journal*, they agreed to halt their investigation if James sought treatment.

One reporter described James as "reticent" to disclose which police authorities approved his bandit patrol. James finally said he was doing the "patrolling" at the request of certain prominent citizens in Excelsior Springs and Liberty. He was asked to identify the two men who were known to be with him on his patrol. The *Kansas City Star* said one of them was his brother-in-law. James would only name Alex Johnson, a friend and former house detective at the Muehlebach Hotel.

Commitment proceedings were then begun in Kansas City. A judge reportedly signed an order committing Jesse E. James to a mental hospital. That is how the case was reported in the *Star* when James checked into Dr. Sheldon's Vineyard Park Hospital for a week of "needed rest." When James left Vineyard Park that Saturday Dr. Sheldon announced, "James said he was going fishing and intended to get a complete rest."

Within days, he suffered another complete breakdown. James went to the Simpson-Major Sanitarium for several more weeks of rest. On May 21, Dr. Herbert S. Major reported another relapse. "Mr. James is suffering from grandiose hallucinations as a result of his breakdown. With rest and careful treatment he probably will recover, but his condition still is serious."

At the time Jesse James Jr. crashed his car on the Klucker "patrol," his wife was visiting in California, but she hurried to his side. "Shortly afterward," James chronicler Carl Breihan noted, "the recuperating young Jesse and his wife left Missouri for a visit to California, and they settled there." Stella called it "a long vacation." She blamed his illness on the outcome of his *Under the Black Flag* venture. As Stella would later say, the failure of the movie cost him dearly both "in peace of mind and eventually broken health."

Like his father before him, Jesse Woodson James, who eased his bullet-ridden body into the hot sulphurous mud springs at his uncle's famous health resort south of Paso Robles, California, Jesse Jr. also turned to the sunny climate of California to heal his wounds and escape his troubles in Missouri. As best as can be determined, Jesse Edwards James didn't set foot in the state again for more than a decade. For a good ten years, he absented himself from Missouri, on whose soil his father fought and bled and suffered and was martyred.

The Jameses decided to move to Los Angeles, as more than a million other Americans did in the 1920s. They made the decision to try to remain anonymous, officially moving to a nice tract home in Los Angeles at 1555 W. 48th Street in October 1926. In that, Stella succeeded where Zee James never could. Zee also tried over the years to persuade her husband to abandon his outlawry and find some remote part of the country or continent where nobody knew them. Her husband never agreed, and Robert Ford finally made the dream impossible.

Jesse's mental health improved markedly after the move out of Kansas City. But even in California, Jesse could not escape his father's shadow. The *L.A. Times* learned that the son of Jesse James was living in Los Angeles and ran a feature story on him in April 1927.

That same year, he joined the California bar. He called himself Jesse E. James again. He rented an office and listed himself as a lawyer in the city phone book. In May 1927, he let the *L.A. Times* take his photograph. The *Times* man asked him to comment on the murders his father committed. Jesse gave the same reply he'd used for thirty years: "With all that has been written about father, no one has ever, to my knowledge, accused him of cowardice or of breaking his word."

James made fresh headlines across California when he appeared in the Pasadena Justice Court to defend a man on an armed robbery charge. The "son of a friend" was accused of attempting to rob a grocery

Jesse and Stella James pose in front of their new home. (*Missouri Valley Special Collections, Kansas City Public Library, Kansas City, Missouri*)

store clerk. The clerk said the defendant beat him on the head with a gun and knocked him down, then sped away in a car while firing two shots at the prostrate clerk.

James thought his client was overcharged. He pointed out to the judge that the defendant was only accused of saying "stand back there," and that was not enough to indicate that he was attempting a robbery.

"Now if you had made the charge 'assault with a deadly weapon,' it would have been more reasonable," James argued.

"That's a good suggestion," replied the judge. "We'll hold the prisoner on that charge, too, as well as the attempted robbery charge."

In the courthouse hallway after the hearing, James was heard to tell his client he was an amateur. "My father would have been ashamed of you," he said.

In 1927, James re-entered the motion picture business amid high expectations. Paramount Studios planned to make a movie about Jesse James starring popular western actor Fred Thomson in the lead role. The studio hired the outlaw's son as a consultant on the film. The plot, according to film historian J. W. Williamson, was "as phony as a banker's religion."

Filming began in June 1927, and Jesse's involvement piqued interest in the picture. Several journalists interviewed him, and features ran in the *New York Times,* the *L.A. Times,* and many newspapers in between. Jesse brought his two daughters to the movie set daily. He watched the production and hoped to secure a part for his daughter Josephine. She wanted to play her great-grandmother. After a brief conversation with the director—the exact words would become the object of dispute—Jo was under the impression she had the part. The wire services ran photos of Jo and her father and sister over an announcement that Jo would play Zerelda Samuel in the motion picture. Weeks later she was given a bit part.

Paramount released the movie on October 22, 1927, as "Jesse James" in the United States and as "Rebel Rider" in Canada. It was a modest hit with audiences expecting action in their westerns, but critics were harsh. The lead actor "gives small suggestion of the man he impersonates," wrote *Variety.* "He is merely an exceptional horseman trying his best to act like a dashing swashbuckler, and not making a very good job of it. . . . 'Jesse James' is not an important contribution to the historical cinema, but it is a capital action drama, and will be appreciated as such." Hollywood briefly cut back on its production of western films after 1927.

Producers declared that suitable stories were hard to find and there was no interest in the genre in the eastern part of the United States or in the deluxe theaters. Westerns were simply not considered "classy enough." In January 1928, *Variety* reported that western films were on the slide.

The publicity that attended the picture emphasized that the James family supervised the filming and Jesse James Jr. approved the picture. But it wasn't enough that Hollywood portrayed his father as a hero. James felt cheated by Paramount Studios and wanted his cut. He decided to file suit on behalf of his daughter and himself. Initially he asked for nine thousand four hundred dollars, but later bumped it up to a demand for seventy-five thousand dollars against Paramount. James wanted payment for suggesting the scenarios, furnishing costumes and arms, and for the broken promise to Jo that she would play her great-grandmother. It was nearly the same amount paid to the star. Fred Thomson reportedly received a hundred thousand dollars for the picture.

The claim was dismissed because Jesse had no evidence of any broken agreements nor proof that Jo was ever promised more than a screen test. James then went after Fred Thomson, naming him personally as a defendant in another suit. But James blew the statute of limitations on the claim by waiting too long to file it, and his suit was dismissed. When Fred Thomson died suddenly on Christmas 1928, leaving a devastated widow and several small children, James brought a claim against the late actor's estate, demanding nine thousand four hundred dollars from his heirs for furnishing publicity and advice for the dead actor's next-to-last film. Because of Jesse's mental illness, the suit was filed in Stella's name as his guardian. That case, too, was dismissed, but not before the *L.A. Times* remarked, "The plaintiff, James, is admitted to be of unsound mind but not entirely without understanding, and with a particularly perfect recollection of his father."

The lawsuit against Paramount was a bad move for the family's reputation in California. The Jameses would become known throughout Hollywood as litigious. In case after case, the James family sought money from production companies. Repeated scenes of courthouse defeats in Los Angeles took their toll. They became caustic toward the movie business because they never won any of their lawsuits and never made as much as they felt they should have from any of the films and later television shows on the James Gang. "Always giving without receiving isn't exactly in the Jesse James tradition," as Homer Croy observed.

Jesse could not practice law much longer. In 1928, *Variety* magazine reported that Jesse James Jr. was broke, had suffered another nervous breakdown, and was closing his California office. He apparently made his last appearance as an attorney in a probate case in Bedford, Iowa, in a visit widely reported throughout that state in December 1929. But still he did not visit Missouri.

In 1930, Jesse's health improved again. He opened a small café in Los Angeles he called the "Jesse James Cabin" and displayed his father's cartridges, belt, boots, spurs, and other memorabilia. His last known conversation with the press resulted in a brief piece in the *Los Angeles Times* in the summer of 1930. Jesse told the astonished reporter that two of his daughters worked in banks. "All trace of banditry are gone from the family, I can assure you." Beyond that, he asked to be left alone. The *Times* headline declared: JESSE JAMES'S SON SEEKS QUIET LIFE.

His wish was granted. Many back in Missouri asked about Jesse, still wondering after all these years about the life of the outlaw's son. All inquirers were told that he was gravely ill. Jesse had no law practice and no income. His family moved frequently, taking several houses in Los Angeles and Long Beach. He was not known to have been in contact with anyone except his friend Harry Hoffman.

His wife Stella wrote a letter to Harry describing how upset Jesse became when old men paraded around the country masquerading as Jesse James. Sometimes these phony outlaws drove him to another hospitalization. So many folk in the Midwest wished Jesse James well that they wished him back to life, and impostors flourished on that sentiment. Many a lonely old man enjoyed a free lunch with a bogus story.

Texas seemed to produce a new and authentic living legend every few years. The one man who could discount their silly stories, the man who himself had witnessed the assassination of Jesse James as a child, was trying to ignore them. He was trying to live in obscurity, but they would not let him. One story that particularly disturbed Jesse involved a man who said he was the real outlaw Jesse James and had a hundred thousand dollars hidden away that he wanted Jesse Jr. to have. He was bent on visiting Jesse. "We wanted no part of the old man," Stella said. Jesse suffered another breakdown. Stella reported that it took several people to restrain him and "they have to strap him down at times."

In 1932, Stella James brought a lawsuit in Missouri against Dr. Lowry to recover the pistols he took from her husband after his motor wreck in May 1924. It's not clear if she ever got the real guns back. Jesse was too sick to go. She also attended court proceedings in Missouri concerning a Jesse W. James impostor. Her husband appeared only by affidavit.

Many people craved his company, especially journalists, but he would not speak to many of them, not even the friendliest of his father's biographers. The most enthusiastic enjoyed a brief correspondence. A member of the Crittenden family, writing in 1936, reported, "The writer understands that he is now living in California and is in very poor health." Added Mattie "Agate Eyes" Howard in her 1937 autobiography, still hateful after all those years: "This lawyer is now in a rest home in California, due to his mental condition. Is it his punishment for not doing his duty towards saving this innocent girl from spending the best part of [my] young life behind prison bars? It is known that he collected a larger fee through [my] conviction than he would have obtained by winning [my] case."

Added Homer Croy, writing in 1949: "His health is not good. Once he had to go to a hospital. This was published in the newspapers, and for the first time the public learned he was living in that part of California. So great was the interest that people came and stood in the hospital yard and stared up at the window where he was supposed to be." Stella

James wrote a letter to Homer Croy that echoed others written by James women over the years: "We have Mr. James in the Hospital again, and believe me, I am just about broke."

James spent the last half of his life suffering from profound mental illness. He was "wild and hard to manage," Stella said. In another letter to Jesse's best friend Harry Hoffman, written in 1948, Stella remarked that "He will not eat. They force feed him. He fights ever [*sic*] thing and says he wants to die. He is so very thin and weak. He has turned agains [*sic*] me, which nearly kills me."

"In later decades," remarked James historian Ted Yeatman, "with advances in medical knowledge and treatments, Jesse Jr. might have resumed something of a normal life."

Perhaps the only surprising aspect of the collapse of his psyche is the length of time he held himself together until his breakdown. Jesse James was not for him merely a name. It was a memory of a loud blast and blood and the smell of gunpowder. It was a life sentence. As a father he hoped to pass it on, but he never had a son. As a train robber, actor, and Klansman, he tried to live up to it. As a lawyer he tried to live it down. Failure met his every effort.

Jesse Edwards James shuffled off this mortal coil on March 26, 1951, at his home in California at the age of seventy-five. Brief obituaries circulated throughout the country, but few remembered any details of his life.

Even Kansas City had a short memory. Jesse had lived his last twenty-five years in exile. His legal career, his famous murder cases, his movie, his train robbery trial, his Klan shenanigans, everything else he'd done, good and bad, all the ways he'd tried to imitate his father, all the ways he'd tried to repudiate him—all of it was forgotten. To this day, his middle name is more often misspelled than not, and his life, though twice as long as his father's, is usually rendered as little more than a foot-note in tributes to the legendary exploits of the elder James.

Jesse made no known deathbed confession to the murder of Zeo

Wilkins. Like many other men who knew her, he will probably always remain a suspect in her brutal death. If he did murder her, then shame rained down on him, if from no one else then from himself. He was not war-hardened, as his sire was. Even his father might have hung his head after murdering an unarmed woman with bare hands and a dull knife, be she extraordinarily wicked or not. His complete mental collapse followed the death of Dr. Wilkins by six weeks. Is that how long it took him to spend his unholy gain? Did he then pay for the crime with his peace of mind?

Jesse did not keep the files from his law practice. He was never known to speak or write of any of the cases he handled. Late in his life he must have been pleased to learn that his grandson, James Ross, would take up the study of law. His grandson would remember him as "an extremely pampered and spoiled individual." As Ross would later recall, "I kidded him when I was younger by saying, 'With the name Jesse James Jr. you didn't have any problem getting clients.' He would just smile.

"But he did not want me to go into criminal law. He said you get into that bad element. It's good to stay away from it."

SELECTED NECROLOGY

Dr. Arthur F. Blanchard—Suffering from a number of diabetic complications, he developed an abscess on his back in the summer of 1925 and entered a sanitarium. He died on August 17, 1925.

Grover Burcham—He remarried and lived in California until his death in Santa Monica in 1966.

Bates B. Burnett—He died in 1925, but his Main Street mansion in Sapulpa still clings to life.

Tom Cunningham—After scraping together his post-Zeo assets, he organized a new bank and led a campaign to improve the road network in Jasper County. He died on April 11, 1922.

Dillard Davies—He resumed his life in Kansas City, remarried, and died in 1947.

Dr. Charles Garring—After his marriage to Zeo ended, he moved from one frontier town to another, practicing medicine in Atoka, Oklahoma; Brady, Texas; and Orange, Texas. He died in Orange on August 26, 1922, of a hemorrhage in his stomach, an illness often but not always associated with alcoholism. His death certificate identified him as a widower.

Mattie Howard—She served more than seven years of her sentence and emerged from prison on May 17, 1928. One lonely day she answered an altar call broadcast on the radio, became a born-again Christian, started attending revival meetings, and began a new career as an evangelist. From the 1940s to the mid-1960s, she preached in every state in the Union and hosted a popular radio show. She forgave everyone connected to her long prison stay, including the judges, jurors, and witnesses, save one. She reserved all her brimstone for her trial lawyer. Mattie's old friends marveled at the success of her "new racket."

Roy Hartman—A man by that name committed suicide at a Civilian Conservation Corps camp in Missouri in 1937 by hanging himself in the woods.

Stella James—She outlived her husband by two decades and was as beautiful a widow as she was a bride.

John Kennedy—Following his conviction on train robbery charges in 1899, he went to prison for many years. Jesse James Jr.'s one-time compadre was eventually paroled only to be shot and killed during a train robbery in Wittenberg, Missouri, in 1922. The press called him "the last of the daring western hold-up men."

Albert Marksheffel—He continued his civic boosting for Colorado Springs and eventually became a member of the Colorado State Highway Advisory Board. He died in August 1938 at the age of fifty-seven.

Benjamin Franklin Tarpley—He outlived two wives and died at age eighty of heart disease in 1956.

Tabitha Taylor—Even after his divorce from Zeo Wilkins, Tom Cunningham still refused to marry Tabitha. She repeatedly threatened to kill him. In October 1917 she fired at him with a rifle and put a bullet in the wall. He swore out a warrant and had her arrested. After the charges were resolved, she moved out of the apartment above his bank. She lived out her days on Pearl Street in Joplin and died just shy of her eighty-seventh birthday in 1933.

Charles Wilkins—He disappeared from public view after his release from jail. Arthur said his brother Charlie was born on April 5, 1875, and lived for about fifty years, but "nobody can remember if he died, was killed, or committed suicide." Wherever he met his end, it wasn't in Missouri.

Arthur Wilkins—He stayed in the liquor trade and his intemperate career sent him to the Colorado State Penitentiary in 1929. He was paroled in 1930 and remained with wife Laura in Colorado Springs. He died in 1959 shortly after he granted an interview to a local historian on the subject of his sister Zeo Zoe Wilkins, their family life in Ohio, and her career as an adventuress. All those years later he was still mad at his sister. "Thank God. I'm glad she's dead. She was the orneriest bitch that ever lived. . . . What a rat she was."

SOURCES

BOOKS

Adams, Samuel Hopkins. *The Great American Fraud: Articles on the Nostrum Evil and Quacks*. Chicago, Illinois: American Medical Association, 1907.

Angel, Myron. *History of San Luis Obispo County, California*. Oakland, California: Thompson & West, 1883.

Bell, Edward Price. *Is the Ku Klux Klan Constructive or Destructive?* Girard, Kansas: Haldeman-Julius Publications, 1924.

Bloom, Harold, Ed. *The Best Poems of the English Language: From Chaucer Through Frost*. New York: HarperCollins Publishers, 2004.

Breihan, Carl W. *The Escapades of Frank and Jesse James*. New York: Frederick Fell Publishers, 1974.

Clifford, Amber R. "Prostitution and Reform in Kansas City." *The Other Missouri History: Populists, Prostitutes, and Regular Folk*. Thomas M. Spencer, ed. Columbia and London: University of Missouri Press, 2004.

Crittenden, H. H., ed. *The Crittenden Memoirs*. New York: G. P. Putnam's Sons, 1936.

Cochran, Robert. *Vance Randolph, An Ozark Life*. Urbana and Chicago: University of Illinois Press, 1985.

Croy, Homer. Introduction to *The Complete and Authentic Life of Jesse James* by Carl W. Breihan. New York: Frederick Fell Publishers, 1953.

Croy, Homer. *Jesse James Was My Neighbor*. New York: Duell, Sloan and Pearce, 1949.

Fanebust, Wayne. *The Missing Corpse: Grave Robbing a Gilded Age Tycoon*. Westport, Connecticut: Praeger, 2005.

Fink, Leon. *Progressive Intellectuals and the Dilemmas of Democratic Commitment*. Cambridge, Massachusetts: Harvard University Press, 1997.

George, Todd Menzies. *Just Memories and Twelve Years with Cole Younger*. Privately published, 1959.

Green, George Fuller. *A Condensed History of the Kansas City Area, Its Mayors and Some VIPs*. Kansas City, Missouri: Lowell Press, 1968.

Gotham, Kevin Fox. *Race, Real Estate, and Uneven Development: The Kansas City Experience, 1900–2000*. Albany: State University of New York Press, 2002.

Habe, Hans. *The Countess*, New York: Harcourt, Brace & World, 1963.

Hartmann, Rudolph H. *The Kansas City Investigation*. Robert H. Ferrell, ed. Columbia: University of Missouri Press, 1999.

Howard, Mattie, writing as M. Harris. *The Pathway of Mattie Howard*. Privately published, 1937.

Hemingway, Ernest. *Across the River and into the Trees*. New York: Charles Scribner's Sons, 1950.

James, Jesse Edwards, writing as Jesse James Jr. *Jesse James, My Father, The First and Only True Story of His Adventures Ever Written*. Independence, Missouri: Sentinel Publishing Co., 1899; New York: Frederick Fell, 1955.

James, Stella Frances. *In the Shadow of Jesse James*. Thousand Oaks, California: Dragon Books, 1990.

Jesse, F. Tennyson. *Murder and Its Motives*. New York: Alfred A. Knopf, 1924.

Kelley, Henry S. *A Treatise on Criminal Law and Practice: Comprising Generally the Statutes of Missouri Defining Criminal Offenses*. Kansas City, Missouri: Vernon, 1913.

Kelley, Mary L. *The Foundations of Texas Philanthropy*. College Station: Texas A&M University Press, 2004.

Kimes, Beverly Rae. *The Cars That Henry Ford Built: A 75th Anniversary Tribute to America's Most Remembered Automobiles*. Princeton, New Jersey: Automobile Quarterly Publications [distributed by E. P. Dutton], 1978.

Kirkendall, Richard S. *A History of Missouri, Vol. V, 1919–1953*. Columbia: University of Missouri Press, 1986.

Ku Klux Klan. *Installation Ceremonies of the Knights of the Ku Klux Klan*. Privately published, 1924.

Litton, Gaston. *History of Oklahoma: At the Golden Anniversary of Statehood, Vol. II*. New York: Lewis Historical Pub. Co., 1957.

Love, Robertus. *The Rise and Fall of Jesse James*. New York: G. P. Putnam's Sons, 1926.

MacLean, Nancy. *Behind the Mask of Chivalry: The Making of the Second Ku Klux Klan*. New York: Oxford University Press, 1994.

Martin, Asa E. *Our Negro Population: A Sociological Study of the Negroes of Kansas City, Missouri*. Kansas City, Missouri: Franklin Hudson Publishing Co., 1913.

Members of the Staff of the Denver Public Library. *Colorado Marriages, 1858–1939*. Denver: The Colorado Genealogical Society, 2005.

Members of the Staff of the *Kansas City Star, William Rockhill Nelson, The Story of a Man, a Newspaper, and a City*. Cambridge, Massachusetts: Riverside Press, 1915.

Meyer, Lewis. *Preposterous Papa, A Hilarious and Affectionate Portrait by His Son*. Cleveland, Ohio: World Publishing Co., 1959.

Mitchell, Franklin D. *Harry S. Truman and the News Media: Contentious Relations, Belated Respect*. Columbia: University of Missouri Press, 1998.

O'Connell, Jay. *Train Robber's Daughter: The Melodramatic Life of Eva Evans, 1876–1970*. Northridge, California: Raven River Press, 2008.

O'Donnell, Bernard. "The Vampire of Kansas City." *The World's Worst Women (of the Twentieth Century)*. London: W. H. Allen & Co., Ltd., 1953.

Ottenheimer, Martin. *Forbidden Relatives: The American Myth of Cousin Marriage*. Urbana and Chicago: University of Illinois Press, 1996.

Patterson, Richard M. *The Train Robbery Era: An Encyclopedic History*. Boulder, Colorado: Pruett Publishing Co., 1991.

Petrone, Gerard S. *Judgment at Gallatin: The Trial of Frank James*. Lubbock: Texas Tech University Press, 1998.

Political History of Jackson County. Kansas City, Missouri: Marshall & Morrison, 1902.

Quigley, Martin. *Mr. Blood's Last Night—End of an Era in Journalism: A Reporter Remembers Kansas City and The Times in the Late Thirties*. St. Louis, Missouri: Sunrise Publishing Co., 1980.

Randolph, Vance, writing as Anton S. Booker. *Wildcats in Petticoats: A Garland of Female Desperadoes*. Girard, Kansas: Haldeman-Julius Publications, 1945.

Reddig, William M. *Tom's Town: Kansas City and the Pendergast Legend*. Philadelphia and New York: J. B. Lippincott Co., 1947.

Rice, Arnold S. *The Ku Klux Klan in American Politics*. Washington, D.C.: Public Affairs Press, 1962.

Rister, Carl Coke. *Oil! Titan of the Southwest*. Norman: University of Oklahoma Press, 1949.

Sappol, Michael. *A Traffic of Dead Bodies: Anatomy and Embodied Social Identity in Nineteenth-Century America*. Princeton, New Jersey: Princeton University Press, 2002.

Schirmer, Sherry Lamb. *A City Divided: The Racial Landscape of Kansas City, 1900–1960.* Columbia and London: University of Missouri Press, 2002.

Sprague, Marshall. *Newport in the Rockies, The Life and Good Times of Colorado Springs,* rev. ed. Chicago, Illinois: Sage Books, 1971.

Steele, Phillip W. *Jesse and Frank James: The Family History.* Gretna, Louisiana: Pelican Publishing Co., 1989.

Stiles, T. J. *Jesse James: Last Rebel of the Civil War.* New York: Random House, 2002.

Truman, Harry S. *The Autobiography of Harry S. Truman.* Robert H. Ferrell, Ed. Boulder, Colorado: Colorado Associated University Press, 1980.

Truman, Harry S. *Memoirs.* Garden City, New York: Doubleday & Co., 1956.

Truman, Margaret. *Bess W. Truman.* New York: Macmillan, 1986.

Truman, Margaret. *Harry S. Truman.* New York: William Morrow & Co., 1973.

Underhill, Robert. *The Truman Persuasions.* Ames: Iowa State University Press, 1981.

Williams, Walter. *The State of Missouri: An Autobiography.* Columbia: Press of E. W. Stephens, 1904.

Williamson, J. W. *Hillbillyland: What the Movies Did to the Mountains and What the Mountains Did to the Movies.* Chapel Hill: University of North Carolina Press, 1995.

Yeatman, Ted P. *Frank and Jesse James: The Story Behind the Legend.* Nashville, Tennessee: Cumberland House, 2000.

PUBLIC RECORDS & LEGAL SOURCES

Census records, various.

City directories, various.

Huron County, Ohio Birth Registry; Sherman Township Atlas, circa 1891.

State of Colorado Division of Vital Statistics, Marriage Record Report No. 15519.

Cuyahoga County Archives, Marriage License Applications, Application No. 38895, July 1904, Vol. 59, p. 224.

Burnett litigation: *Bates B. Burnett et al. v. State,* 8 Okla. Cr. 639 (1913); *Burnett v. Davis,* 27 Okla. 124 (1910); *Burnett v. Jackson, Judge,* 27 Okla. 275 (1910); *Hengst v. Burnett,* 40 Okla. 42 (1913); *Berryhill v. Jackson,* 70 Okla. 16 (1918); *Hill v. Burnett,* 69 Okla. 54 (1918); *Indiahoma Oil Co. v. Thompson Oil & Gas Co.,* 38 Okla. 140 (1913).

State of Missouri v. Charles Ford and Robert Ford, Archives of the Court of Buchanan County, Missouri.

Missouri's early fingerprint use: Secs. 4140–4143, 8955, 8964 of the Revised Statutes of 1919; *Irons v. Am. Ry. Express Co.,* 318 Mo. 318 (Mo. Banc 1927); *Bennett v. Gerk,* 230 Mo. App. 601 (1933) (first Missouri appellate case to mention fingerprints); *State v. Pinkston,* 336 Mo. 614 (1935) (first Missouri appellate case to cite the evidence of a fingerprint expert).

State of Missouri v. Albert Crone, 209 Mo. 316, 108 S.W. 555 (Mo. 1908) and *State of Missouri v. Mattie Howard,* 231 S.W. 255 (Mo. 1921), Trial Transcripts and Pleadings, Missouri Supreme Court Historical Database, Missouri State Archives, Jefferson City.

Jesse E. James's civil appellate cases: *Harmon v. Fowler Packing Co.,* 129 Mo. App. 715, 108 S.W. 610 (1908); *Bilhimer v. Metropolitan St. Ry. Co.,* 137 Mo. App. 675, 119 S.W. 502 (1909); *Wasmer v. Missouri Pac. Ry. Co.,* 166 Mo. App. 215, 148 S.W. 155 (1912); *Kalver v. Metropolitan St. Ry. Co.,* 166 Mo. App. 198, 148 S.W. 130 (1912); *Danielson v. Metropolitan St. Ry. Co.,* 175 Mo. App. 314, 162 S.W. 307 (1913); *Stockton v. Metropolitan St. Ry. Co.,* 177 Mo. App. 286, 164 SW 176 (1914).

Missouri law on the parol evidence rule: *Scrivner v. American Car & Foundry Co.,* 330 Mo. 408, 431 (Mo. Banc 1932) (describing the circumstances under which parol testimony can be admitted to establish the terms of a lost contract); *Metropolitan Discount Co. v. Indermuehle,* 217 Mo. App. 326 (1925) (where a written contract is properly proven to be lost or destroyed, witnesses will be permitted to testify to what they recall its provisions to be).

McNamara vs. Marksheffel, U.S. District Court, Western District of Missouri, Kansas City, Case No. 5027, Record Group 21, Vol. 3, 1920–28, Law & Equity Index, Box 504, National Archives and Records Administration—Central Plains Region.

Jesse E. James v. Stella F. James, Case No. 53560, Jackson County Circuit Court Archives, Kansas City, Missouri.

James v. Paramount-Famous-Lasky Corp., 138 Cal.App. 585; 33 P.2d 63 (1934); *James v. Screen Gems, Inc.,* 174 Cal.App.2d 650; 344 P.2d 799 (1959).

Colorado State Archives, Record of Arthur Wilkins, Convict No. 15320, Colorado State Penitentiary.

Homer Croy Collection, Western Historical Manuscript Collection, State Historical Society of Missouri, Columbia, Mo.

Frank P. Walsh Papers, Manuscripts and Archives Division, New York Public Library.

Archives of the Still National Osteopathic Museum: Bulletin of the American School of Osteopathy, June 1903; ASO Student Ledger, 1905–1909; ASO Student Records Book and Student Register, 1899–1903; Catalogue of the

American School of Osteopathy, Vol. 1, No. 1, June 1903; Tenth Annual Commencement, Session of 1902–1903; Twelfth Annual Announcement and Annual Catalogue, 1904–05; Thirteenth Annual Catalogue, 1905–06; Directory of Members of the American Osteopathic Association, November 1904; "New February Class in the A.S.O.," *Journal of Osteopathy,* March 1902; "By Their Works," *Journal of Osteopathy,* March 1902; "Commencement Week at the A.S.O.," *Journal of Osteopathy,* June 1905; "Personal Mention," *Journal of Osteopathy,* November 1905; "Catechism of the Electronic Methods of Dr. Albert Abrams" (pamphlet), circa 1922; "Personals," *Journal of Osteopathy,* April 1924; "In D.O. Land," *The Osteopathic Physician,* April 1924; American Osteopathic Association Member Directory, 1924–1925; Osteoblast Yearbook, 1926.

MAGAZINES

Jordan, Philip D. "The Adair Train Robbery," *The Palimpsest,* February 1936.

MacLean, Angus. "The Ghosts of Frank and Jesse James," *Golden West,* November 1965.

McClaughry, Matthew W. "History of the Introduction of the Bertillon System," *Fingerprint Magazine,* April 1922.

Moving Picture World: "New Company in Missouri Producing 'Jesse James Under the Black Flag'," Oct. 2, 1920; "Make Scenes in New Mexico for 'Jesse James' Picture," Nov. 20, 1920; "'Jesse James Under the Black Flag' Nears Completion in Chicago Studio," Dec. 18, 1920; no title (scenes from *Under the Black Flag*), Dec. 25, 1920; "Thomson's First Is 'Jesse James'," Apr. 16, 1927; "In The Heyday of Banditry," Aug. 27, 1927; "Paramount Has Scheduled Ten Productions," Oct. 1, 1927; "Jesse James," Oct. 8, 1927; "Through the Box-Office Window," Oct. 22, 1927.

"A New Crime Law," *Opportunity: A Journal of Negro Life,* December 1926.

Patterson, Richard. "The Trial of Jesse James, Jr.," *Old West,* Summer 1987.

Quinn, Allen. "Kansas City's Strange 'Zeo Zeo' Riddle," *True Detective Mysteries,* January 1939.

Variety: "Just How and Why 'Western' Films Commenced to Slide—And Now!" Jan. 25, 1928; "Jesse James' Children Suing Paramount," Apr. 17, 1929; Par. Denies Allegations of J. James' Granddaughter," May 1, 1929; "James Girl's Demurrer," May 22, 1929.

Wayman, Illinois State's Attorney. "The Law Student's Helper," November 1912.

PRIVATE PAPERS

Archives of the James Farm, Kearney, Missouri.

Englert, Lorene, and Englert, Kenny. *Zeo Zoe The Scarlet Harlot*. Unpublished manuscript, December 1960. Kenneth Englert Papers, Special Collections, Pikes Peak Library District, Colorado Springs, Colorado.

Funeral Home Records, Eylar Bros. Chapel, Kansas City, Missouri.

Personal correspondence with Judge James Ross.

NEWSPAPERS

Ada (Oklahoma) *Evening News:* "Grand Sec'y Chauncey Takes In Sapulpa," Oct. 18, 1909.

Arkansas City (Kansas) *Traveler*: "Amos Gipson, Former Owner of Gladstone Hotel, Commits Suicide," Nov. 12, 1921.

Atlanta (Georgia) *Constitution:* "Young Jesse James's Strange Luck," attributed to the *St. Louis Chronicle,* Oct. 15, 1888; "Sandwiches May Bare Slayer Of Ardent Devotee of Cupid," Mar. 20, 1924; "Marital Adventuress, Bride of Six Men, Lies in Morgue Unclaimed by Anyone," by Arthur F. DeGreve, Mar. 21, 1924; "Jesse James' Wicked Pistols Land His Son in Sanitarium," by Arthur F. DeGreve, May 14, 1924.

Bedford (Pennsylvania) *Gazette:* "Wife of a Bandit's Son," Apr. 13, 1900.

Billings (Montana) *Gazette:* "Trio Held In Murder of Love Adventuress," Mar. 20, 1924; "Slain Woman Awaited Murder," Mar. 21, 1924.

Boston (Massachusetts) *Daily Globe:* "GLOBE EXTRA! 5 O'Clock Trial Is On," Feb. 24, 1899.

Bridgeport (Conn.) *Telegram:* "Feared Brother Would Slay Her, Attorney's Clue," Mar. 22, 1924.

Brownsville (Texas) *Herald:* "Visitor Recalls Being Neighbor of Jesse James," Mar. 27, 1939.

Charleston (South Carolina) *Gazette*: "Fred Thompson [*sic*] in 'Jesse James' To Be Seen at Rialto," Jan. 22, 1928.

Chester (Pennsylvania) *Times:* "A Woman's Day" by Allene Sumner, Jan. 31, 1930.

Chicago (Illinois) *Daily Tribune:* "Take Alleged Train Robber," Oct. 2, 1898; "Jesse James Jr. Arrested," Oct. 12, 1898; "Jesse James Out On Bail," Oct. 13, 1898; "Arrest of Jesse James Jr. Affords A Study In Heredity," Oct. 23, 1898; "Election Turns On Jesse James," Oct. 31, 1898; "James Trial Is Deferred," Nov. 1, 1898; "Jesse James Jr. May Go Clear," Nov. 2, 1898; "Queer Campaign to End Tonight," Nov. 7, 1898; "Fail To Shake Lowe's Story," Feb. 25, 1899; "Jesse James Tells His Side," Feb. 28, 1899; "See A Star In Jesse James," Mar. 4, 1899; "Jesse E. James is Married," Jan. 25, 1900;

"In A Tangle," Feb. 8, 1917; "A Dashing Young Osteopath Comes Into Life and Lucre Of Cincinnati Man," Feb. 8, 1917; "Hypotenuse of $3,000,000 Case Sues Husband," Jan. 30, 1919; "Zoe Wilkins' Will Sought; Brother Held," Mar. 20, 1924; "Zoe's Last Days Were Haunted By 4 Avengers," by the Associated Press, Mar. 21, 1924.

Chicago Herald: "Young Jesse James," attributed to the *Chicago Herald,* circa 1888, in *Historic 1890 Murders, Disasters & Lawlessness Scrapbook.* Charlie Crowell, ed. Privately published, 2002.

Chillicothe (Missouri) *Constitution (Constitution Tribune, Morning Constitution, Daily Constitution):* Untitled (Jesse James Jr. robbed), Oct. 9, 1905; "Joplin Banker Makes Up With Housekeeper," Feb. 9, 1917; "Cunningham Secured License in Gallatin," Feb. 15, 1917; "Jesse James Will Perform," Aug. 10, 1920; Display ads, Jun. 16 and 21, 1921; "62 Names In Book Found In Wilkins Home," Mar. 20, 1924; "Dr. Wilkins Was Assaulted Before the Murder Was Committed," Mar. 21, 1924; "Jesse James Carried Arsenal," attributed to the *Excelsior Springs Standard,* May 13, 1924; "Negro Faces New Trial in Zeo Zoe Wilkins Case," Sept. 13, 1924; "Jesse E. James Seeks To Join California Bar," May 20, 1927.

Clearfield (Pennsylvania) *Progress:* "Janitor Involved in Murder of Mrs. Dr. Zeo Williams [*sic*]," Mar. 21, 1924.

Colorado Springs Gazette: Wedding announcements, Jul. 6, 1902; "News of the Local Courts," Mar. 9, 1907; "The Awful Price of Speed," Sept. 18, 1907; "Marksheffel Is Held," Sept. 19, 1907; "Criminal Docket for Sept. Term," Sept. 2, 1908; "Boy Slightly Hurt By an Automobile," Oct. 21, 1909; "Chief of Police Burno Asks City to Help in Campaign Against Social Evil," Jan. 17, 1914; "Married," May 11, 1917; "Zoe Zeo Wilkins [*sic*] Murdered In Kansas City," Mar. 19, 1924; "Hold 3 Men For Investigation In Probe of Wilkins Murder," Mar. 20, 1924; "Zoe Zeo Wilkins [*sic*] Died In Fear of Four Avengers, Woman Declares," Mar. 21, 1924.

Coshocton (Ohio) *Tribune:* "May Employ Truth Serum On Suspect in Mystery Crime," Mar. 25, 1924.

Creede (Colorado) *Candle:* "Colorado State News," Dec. 18, 1920.

Danville (Virginia) *Bee:* "Bandit Jesse Her Granddad," Nov. 3, 1923; "Three Charged With Murder of Wilkins," by the Associated Press, Mar. 25, 1924.

Davenport (Iowa) *Daily Republican:* "Osteopaths Rejected; State Board of Health Refuses to Give Them Certificates," Dec. 30, 1898; "Jesse James Widow Dead," Nov. 20, 1900.

Davenport (Iowa) *Gazette:* "Horrible Death of an Aged Lady," Oct. 16, 1886.

Decatur (Illinois) *Review* and *Daily Review:* "Doctor Had Fear of Sudden Death," Mar. 21, 1924; "Jesse James Gets Into Films," Jul. 21, 1927.

Denver (Colorado) *Post:* "His Millions Are Now Mine, Says Wife of Aged Ex-Banker As Common-Law Rival Sues," Jan. 21, 1917; "Cunninghams Disappear When Plot Thickens," Jan. 26, 1917; "Cunningham To Pay $250,000 to Woman of 72 Who Asked Million As Common-Law Wife," Jan. 28, 1917; "Petition Shows 2 Marriages of Cunninghams," Feb. 28, 1917; "Rich Springs Divorcee Slain By Mystery Looter of Home," Mar. 19, 1924; "Matrimonial Adventuress Is Mysteriously Murdered," Mar. 19, 1924; "Mystery Woman Being Sought As Trio Are Held In Slaying of Springs Marital Adventuress," Mar. 20, 1924; "Arrest of Denver Man Is Asked In Mystery Murder of Widow," Mar. 21, 1924; "Zoe Wilkins [*sic*] Victim of Own Intrigue and Dope, Relatives Say," Mar. 21, 1924.

Des Moines (Iowa) *Capital:* "Colorado Springs Located on Spinal Column of America," May 7, 1915.

Durango (Colorado) *Democrat:* "The Fast Chauffeur Arrested," Sept. 19, 1907.

Durant (Oklahoma) *Daily Democrat:* "Seek Fortune As Clue to Slaying of Wealthy Woman," Mar. 19, 1924; "Slain Woman Once Lived in Durant," Mar. 20, 1924.

Edwardsville (Illinois) *Intelligencer:* "Jesse James Jr. In Person," Sept. 2, 1921.

Elyria (Ohio) *Chronicle Telegram:* "Bad Guys Married Good Girls: Were Wild West Outlaws Not So Villainous?" by Eleanor Berman, Nov. 20, 1977.

Emery County (Utah) *Press:* "Chauffeur Charged With Manslaughter," Sept. 28, 1907.

Excelsior Springs (Missouri) *Daily Standard:* "Jesse James Wrecked Armed To Teeth," May 11, 1924; "Jesse James Is Adjudged Nervous," May 12, 1924; "Jesse James To A Sanitarium," attributed to the *Kansas City Times*, May 20, 1924; "Jesse James' Trouble," attributed to the *Kansas City Post*, May 23, 1924.

Excelsior Springs Standard: "The Misfortune of Excelsior Springs," Aug. 9, 1925; "State to Investigate Tragedy of Friday," Aug. 10, 1925; "Gathering Names For Grand Jury Hearing," Aug. 11, 1925; "Dr. Blanchard Very Low," Aug. 12, 1925; "Indictments Doubtful In Lynching Probe," Aug. 19, 1925; "Funeral of Dr. Blanchard," Apr. 20, 1925.

Fayetteville (Arkansas) *Daily Democrat:* "Suspect Arrested for Murder of Dr. Zoe Zoe [*sic*] Wilkins," May 8, 1924.

Fort Wayne (Indiana) *Daily Gazette:* Untitled (Jesse James Jr. at 7), May 3, 1882.

Fort Wayne Sentinel: "Jesse James Lost Case," Feb. 9, 1907.

Fort Wayne Sunday Gazette: "The Sad Story of Jesse James," Feb. 5, 1899.

Fort Worth (Texas) *Star Telegram:* "Woman Doctor Found Slain in Kansas City," Mar. 19, 1924; "Slain Kansas City Osteopath Visited Fort Worth 2 Years Ago, Asserts Her Sister Here," Mar. 20, 1924; "Mystery Woman Enters Baffling Slaying Case," Mar. 20, 1924; "Slain Woman Distraught From Fear of Plots Says Lawyer," Mar. 21, 1924; "Negro May Be Charged in Kansas City Woman's Death," Mar. 22, 1924; "Osteopath Who Was Cruelly Killed," Mar. 23, 1924.

Frederick (Maryland) *News:* "Jesse James, Jr., As a Lawyer," Feb. 9, 1907.

Frederick (Maryland) *Post:* "Death Bares Wild Career," Mar. 25, 1924.

Fresno (California) *Bee:* "If Men Understood Women," by Dorothy Dix, May 5, 1930.

Fresno Weekly Republican: "Convicted of Train Robbery," June 22, 1899.

Galveston (Texas) *Daily News:* "The Romance of the Glenn Pool," by Frederic J. Haskin, Nov. 9, 1907; "Morris-Schreck Fight," Mar. 5, 1911.

Gettysburg (Virginia) *Times:* "Pretty Doctor Is Slashed to Death," Mar. 20, 1924.

Hamilton (Ohio) *Evening Journal:* "The Gold-Digger's Spade," by Jack Lait, Apr. 7, 1923.

Henryetta (Oklahoma) *Daily Free-Lancer:* "Slain Woman Former Wife [Of] Millionaire," May 19, 1924; "Tracing Clues in Murder Case," Mar. 20, 1924; "Great Mystery in Murder Case," Mar. 21, 1924; "Say Murdered Woman Insane," Mar. 22, 1924.

Humeston (Iowa) *New Era:* "A Great Institution," Nov. 9, 1904.

Independence (Missouri) *Examiner:* "The True Story of Jesse James and Son," by Donna Biddle, Jul. 24, 1987.

Indiana (Pennsylvania) *Weekly Messenger:* "An Outlaw's Son," Nov. 4, 1896.

Indiana (Pennsylvania) *Evening Gazette:* "Not Like Noted Pa," Nov. 30, 1906.

Indianapolis (Indiana) *Star:* "Jesse James Kidnaps Baby," Oct. 15, 1910.

Iowa City Daily Press: "Bandit's Son At Bar," Jun. 25, 1907.

Iowa City Press Citizen: "Woman Sought In Wilkins Slaying," Mar. 20, 1924; "Trio Held In Love Slaying," Mar. 21, 1924.

Iowa Recorder: "Jesse James, Jr., Visits Iowa," Dec. 11, 1929 (and in the *Spirit Lake Beacon,* Dec. 12, 1929 and *Marble Rock News,* Dec. 11, 1929).

Joplin (Missouri) *Globe:* "Cunningham Bank Sold to Amos Gipson; Wife Closes Deal," Jan. 14, 1917; "As Common Law Wife, Files A Suit Against Banker," Jan. 16, 1917; "Mrs. Cunningham Refuses To Discuss Her Marriage," Jan. 17, 1917; "Cunningham Denies Charges Made by Mrs. Taylor—'Won't Get My Money,' He Asserts," Jan. 20, 1917; "Cunningham Bank Now Only History," Jan. 21, 1917; "Mrs. Taylor Denies 'Settlement'," Jan. 30, 1917; "We Will Fight To End, Says Mrs. Cunningham," Jan. 31, 1917; "Cunningham's Whereabouts Is [*sic*] A Mystery," Feb. 1, 1917; "Tom Cunningham In Chicago Guarded Against Interviews," Feb. 3, 1917; "Ask Guardian for Tom Cunningham," Feb. 6, 1917; "Cunningham Confronted by Aged Woman Who Sues Him For Million," Feb. 7, 1917; "Cunningham's Not Worried Over Sale of His Bank Stock," Feb. 9, 1917.

Joplin News-Herald: "Wedding of Cunningham to Be Contested?" Jan. 15, 1917; "Cunningham Is Defendant In Divorce Suit," Jan. 16, 1917; "Announcement," Jan. 18, 1917; "Mrs. Taylor in Suit To Tie Up Banker's Land," Jan. 19, 1917; "Mrs. Cunningham in Kansas City Meets Attorneys," Jan. 24, 1917; "Agreement May Be Sought In Cunningham Case," Jan. 25, 1917; "Cunningham Will Pay Mrs. Taylor $250,000 To Keep Young Bride," Jan. 28, 1917; "Walsh, Attorney Against Thaw, Retained By Mrs. Cunningham," Jan. 29, 1917; "Cunningham in Trade for 6,000 Acres of Land," Jan. 30, 1917; "Cunningham Believes He Has A Sound Mind," Feb. 7, 1917; "Old Couple Are Together Again," Feb. 8, 1917; "Mrs. Cunningham, in Chicago, Plans to Fight On Divorce," March 1, 1917; "Divorced Wife of Tom Cunningham Weds Again," May 11, 1917.

Kansas City Call: "No Bond For Dillard Davies," Apr. 18, 1924; "Wilkins Quiz Continued," May 16, 1924.

Kansas City Journal: "Lowe's Story," Oct. 14, 1898; "Young Wife Ready For Legal Battle," Jan. 31, 1917; "Joplin Millionaire Is Detained Here," Feb. 7, 1917; "Cunningham and Housekeeper Embrace," Feb. 8, 1917; "Cunningham Says He'll Fight Case," Feb. 9, 1917; "Dr. Zeo Zoe Wilkins, Five Times Married, Slashed to Death," Mar. 19, 1924; "Death of Zoe Wilkins Closes Career of Love, Plots and Litigation," Mar. 19, 1924; "Scene of Slaying, Victim, and Discoverer of Body," Mar. 19, 1924; "Beautiful Divorcee, Six Times Married, Slain," Mar. 19, 1924; "Dr. Zeo Wilkins' Nurse and Negro Janitor Tell of Tarpley's Many Calls," Mar. 20, 1924; "Police Grill Dr. Wilkins' Friend," Mar. 20, 1924; "Dr. Wilkins' Slayer Now Believed One of 'Avenging Four,'" Mar. 21, 1924; "Desire for Abrams Machine New Theory In Wilkins Slaying," Mar. 21, 1924; "Shadow Of Death Seen By Dr. Wilkins Before Ghastly End, Says Woman," Mar. 22, 1924; "Chain of Evidence Tightens Around Wilkins' Janitor," Mar. 22, 1924; "Basis for New Wilkins Slaying Theory," Mar. 22, 1924; "Negro's Alibi Punctured in Wilkins Case," Mar. 24, 1924; "New Wilkins Clews Point to Janitor," Mar. 24, 1924; "Three Held For Death of Dr. Wilkins," Mar. 25, 1924; "Blanchard 'Grilled' By Detectives," Mar. 26, 1924; "Bloody Hand Tips Still Unverified," Mar. 27, 1924; "Zoe's Effort To Quit High Life," Mar. 27, 1924; "Zoe's Slayer Should Hang, Davies Says," Mar. 27, 1924; "Woman Offers New Clew In Wilkins Case," Mar. 28, 1924; "James Goes To Hospital For 'Nerves,'" May 13, 1924.

Kansas City Post: "Banker Sued By Aged Joplin Woman Is Found In Seclusion With Young Wife," Jan. 20, 1917; "Mrs. Cunningham To Fight Bitterly for Husband," Jan. 30, 1917; "Mystery Deepens As to Whereabouts of Wealthy Banker," Feb. 4, 1917; "Banker's Sanity Is to Be Tested," Feb. 7, 1917; "Aged Housekeeper, Reunited With Millionaire," Feb. 8, 1917; "Rich Man's Young

Wife Vanishes," Feb. 9, 1917; "County Seeks Cunningham Millions," Feb. 10, 1917; "Joplin Rallies To Cunningham's Aid," Feb. 11, 1917; "Gun and Jail Figure in Cunningham Case," Oct. 15, 1917; "Introducing Kansas City's Hollywood Plus," July 10, 1921; "Threats of Death to Dr. Wilkins, Bared By Attorney," Mar. 19, 1924; "Dr. Wilkins' Fear of Death At Brother's Hand Told By Friend," Mar. 20, 1924; "Coroner's Inquest Into Wilkins Slaying Begins," Mar. 21, 1924; "Visits to Zeo's Home New Clew," Mar. 24, 1924; "Blanchard Slated For Grilling As Net In Zeo's Slaying Grips Doctor," Mar. 25, 1924; "Blood Clew In Murder Probe," Mar. 26, 1924; "Probe Shifts In Wilkins Slaying," Mar. 27, 1924; "Davies Held In Murder," Apr. 12, 1924; "Wilkins' Suspect Held," May 8, 1924; "Wilkins Quiz Goes On," May 10, 1924; "James Ready To Explain 'Patrol'," May 12, 1924; "James Departs From Hospital," May 19, 1924; "James Is No Better," May 21, 1924.

Kansas City Star: "The State Rests Its Case," Feb. 26, 1899; "He Won't Go On the Stage," Mar. 3, 1899; "Women Have Guided Tom Cunningham To Success," Feb. 11, 1917; "Aged Banker Is Reunited," Feb. 17, 1917; "The Marksheffels Fall Out," Jan. 29, 1919; "Jewel Thief Slays," Oct. 23, 1919; "To Agate Eyes, 12 Years," Oct. 26, 1919; "Witness Diagrams A Den," Mar. 24, 1920; "A Life Term for Majors," Mar. 25, 1920; "Mrs. Mamie Allen Asks Heart Balm," Mar. 19, 1924; "Zeo's $100,000 is Missing," Mar. 19, 1924; "Negro Had the Knife," Mar. 20, 1924; "Brother Plots My Life," Mar. 21, 1924; "Knew Death Was Near," Mar. 22, 1924; "Into 'Plot Against Zeo,'" Mar. 23, 1924; "Tarpley Tells His Story," Mar. 24, 1924; "Call Dr. Blanchard Again," Mar. 25, 1924; "More For Davies To Explain," Mar. 26, 1924; "Saw Negroes Near Zeo's Home," Mar. 26, 1924; "Zeo Wilkins Found Slain," Mar. 26, 1924 (weekly edition); "Divorces to Thirty-Four," Mar. 27, 1924; "Zeo Wilkins Hearings Later," Mar. 29, 1924; "Tarpley Released On Bond," Mar. 30, 1924; "Maysville Mob Thwarted," Mar. 30, 1924; "Charles Wilkins Gives Bond," Apr. 1, 1924; "Bond for Two in Wilkins Murder," Apr. 2, 1924; "Hold Negro In Wilkins Case," Apr. 12, 1924; "In A Year, 2,459 Divorces," May 5, 1924; "Says He Lived At Zeo's Home," May 8, 1924; "Jesse James 'On Carpet,'" May 12, 1924; "Jesse James In Hospital," May 13, 1924; "Jesse James Case Up Later," May 17, 1924; "James Out of Hospital," May 19, 1924; "The Real Jesse James Emerges After Homer Croy's Travels," Jun. 5, 1949.

Kansas City Sun: "Davies Hearing Apr. 12th; Defence Fund Raised," Apr. 5, 1924; "Davies Released On Bond; Trial Set For Apr. 26," Apr. 19, 1924; "Why Is Davies Held?" Apr. 19, 1924.

Kansas City Times: "Mrs. Samuels Talks of The James Boys' Adventures," attributed to the *Boston Herald,* Oct. 24, 1897; "Aged Banker In Custody," Feb. 7, 1917; "Zeo Z. Wilkins Is Slain," Mar. 19, 1924; "New Paths in Death

Maze," Mar. 20, 1924; "Now, A 'Mystery Woman'," Mar. 21, 1924; "Insane, Zeo's Family Says," Mar. 22, 1924; "New Puzzle in Zeo Case," Mar. 24, 1924; "Charge Three in Zeo Case," Mar. 25, 1924; "New Clew Hits At Davies," Mar. 26, 1924; "Saw Negroes Near Zeo's Home," Mar. 27, 1924; "Zeo's Diary Bares Life," Mar. 28, 1924; "Wilkins Death Hearing Today," Apr. 12, 1924; "Kansas City Sin-Soaked; Evangelist 'Mel' Trotter Points to Lack of Morality Here," Apr. 7, 1924.

Kirksville (Missouri) *Daily Express*: "Woman Known Here Slain In Office," Mar. 19, 1924; "Knife Used In Wilkins Murder Is Identified," Mar. 20, 1924; "Dr. Zeo Wilkins' Friends Quizzed By The Police," Mar. 20, 1924; "Dr. Wilkins' Kin Says She Was Insane," Mar. 23, 1924; "Dr. Blanchard Arrested In Wilkins Case," Mar. 25, 1924; "Three Men Charged With Wilkins Murder," Mar. 25, 1924.

Kirksville Weekly Graphic: No title (Wilkins murder), Mar. 21, 1924.

La Crosse (Wisconsin) *Tribune*: "Son of Jessie [sic] James Is A Rising Young Lawyer," Jul. 21, 1906.

Lima (Ohio) *News*: "Behind the Curtains of the Slain Butterfly," by the International Feature Service, Apr. 22, 1923; "Rich Woman Is Murdered in Her Home," Mar. 19, 1924; "Mystery Woman: Police Fail to Solve Murder of Dr. Williams [sic]," Mar. 20, 1924; "Stalked to the Grave By the Ghosts of Her Wild Career," Mar. 27, 1924.

Lincoln (Nebraska) *State Journal*: "Slain Beauty Had Fortune; Dr. Zoe Wilkins Divorced Six Rich Men," Mar. 19, 1924; "No Clue To The Slayer," Mar. 20, 1924; "Think Negro Slew Beauty," Mar. 21, 1924; "Seized in Murder; Arrest Doctor in Death Case," Mar. 25, 1924; "Granddaughter of Jesse James Declares He Was A Gentleman," Jul. 5, 1938.

Long Beach (California) *Independent*: "Jesse James Jr., 75, Who Saw Dad Slain, Dies in L.A.," Mar. 28, 1951.

Los Angeles Times: "Jesse James; Noted Train-Robber's Son Under Suspicion," Oct. 2, 1898; "Jesse James Jr. Is Thought To Be Up To His Pa's Old Tricks," Oct. 12, 1898; "Keeping His Hand In; Train-Robber Lowe Adds To His Confessions," Oct. 14, 1898; "Jesse James's Trial: Judge Wofford Sworn Off Bench," Oct. 27, 1898; "Jesse James Jr. Wearied By The Attention of Pretty Girls Who Call on Him," Feb. 5, 1899; "Chip of [sic] the Old Block," Feb. 26, 1899; "Cracker Neck Conviction," Jun. 21, 1899; "Held in Woman Slaying," by Associated Press Night Wire, Mar. 20, 1924; "Jesse E. James Now Residing in L.A.," Apr. 9, 1927; "Famous Bandit's Son Bar Member," May 24, 1927; "Jesse James Pleads Case," Jun. 3, 1927; ""Shades of Early Bandit May Rise in Local Court," Feb. 20, 1929; "Jesse James's Son Seeks Quiet Life," Jul. 31, 1930; "Film Suit Lost By James Girl," Sep. 17, 1930; "James Suit Dismissed

By Court," Sep. 24, 1930; "New Suit Filed By Bandit's Son," Nov. 25, 1930; "Jesse E. James, Jr. Died at 75 at His Home Yesterday," Mar. 28, 1951.

Lowell (Mass.) *Sun*: "Mary Pickford's Case Dooms The Quick Divorce Law," Apr. 30, 1920; "Amusement Notes," Dec. 28, 1927.

Manitoba Morning Free Press: "Outlaw's Son Succeeds As Lawyer," by Leigh Mitchell Hodges, May 11, 1907; "Rebel Rider On Province Screen," May 19, 1928.

Mansfield (Ohio) *News*: "Was Young Girl's Slave Says Aged Millionaire," Feb. 24, 1917; "Murder Proves Police Puzzle," Mar. 19, 1924; "Sportsmen Hold Huron Fish Fry," May 4, 1933.

Marion (Ohio) *Daily Star*: "Stopped In Robbers' Cut," Aug. 30, 1890; "Book By Jesse James," Jun. 23, 1899; "Kansas City Widow Killed," Mar. 20, 1924.

Mexia (Texas) *Daily News*: "Sixty Two Are Named On List In Murder Quiz," Mar. 21, 1924; "Man Arrested In Connection With Wilkins Murder," May 8, 1924.

Moberly (Missouri) *Weekly Monitor*: "Bandits' Bodies Lie Unclaimed," by the Associated Press, Nov. 9, 1922.

Modesto (California) *News-Herald*: "What the Paris Criminologists Have Learned About Love Murders" by Minott Saunders, May 23, 1931.

Monessen (Pennsylvania) *Daily Independent*: "Jesse James Jr.," Nov. 4, 1916.

Nebraska State Journal: "Jesse James Asks Divorce," Sept. 23, 1910.

Nevada State Journal: "Throat of 'Adventuress' Cut," Mar. 19, 1924; "Negro Held in Woman's Death," Mar. 21, 1924; "Last Fear Tortured Hours of Adventuress Pictured," Mar. 23, 1924; "3 Held in Death of Kansas City Doctor," Mar. 25, 1924.

New Castle (Pa.) *News*: "Daily NewsLetter," by John D. Mueller, Apr. 20, 1923.

Newark (Ohio) *Daily Advocate*: "Devoured By Hogs," May 22, 1886; "Jesse James Married," Jan. 26, 1900.

New York Evening Post: "Crime Wave" by Dashiell Hammett, June 7, 1930.

New York Times: "Jesse James's Murderers," Apr. 19, 1882; "Trial of Jesse James, Jr.," Oct. 27, 1898; "Jesse James Acquitted by Jury," Mar. 1, 1899; "Train Robbery Cases Dismissed," Mar. 2, 1899; "Jesse James, Jr., Loses Case," Feb. 10, 1907; "President a Suicide, Joplin Bank Closed," Nov. 13, 1921; "An Ultimate Test of Credulity," Jan. 16, 1924; "Held For Slaying Woman," Mar. 25, 1924; "Diary Bares Tale of Love and Fraud," Mar. 30, 1924; "Klan in Missouri Election," Apr. 3, 1924; "Jesse James and Son," Jul. 31, 1927; "Jesse James Becomes Candidate For Statue," Sept. 25, 1927.

Oakland (California) *Tribune*: "Bandit's Son Now A Lawyer," Jul. 8, 1906; "Mad Flight of Auto Hurls Four to Death," Sept. 17, 1907; "Only A Woman" by Winifred Black, Mar. 20, 1919; "Meet James' Son Jesse," Jul. 31, 1930.

Ogden City Standard-Examiner: "The 'Girl With The Agate Eyes'," by Clifford Butcher, Feb. 5, 1922; "Famous Gold Diggers of History and How They Dug," by Louise Fazenda, Nov. 22, 1923; "Wickedest Movie Vamps Outdone in Real Life," May 4, 1924.

Oklahoma Leader: Untitled (James Gang gold), Jan. 18, 1917.

The Oklahoman: "Burnett Indebted to Former Wards," Nov. 2, 1911; "Big Land Suit Filed By Negro," Aug. 13, 1912; "Bank Failure is Receiver Cause," Sept. 12, 1912; "Bankers Ordered To Produce Books," Feb. 16, 1913; "Sapulpa Bankers Behind the Bars," Feb. 22, 1913; "Sapulpa Banker Held Not Guilty," May 15, 1913; "Indian Girl Dances to Help Red Cross," Jun. 30, 1918; "Policeman Slain By Former Chief," Mar. 4, 1918; "Aged Banker's Wife Is Slain," Mar. 19, 1924; "Love Piratess Felt Avenging Death At Hand," Mar. 21, 1924; "Clew Found In Woman's Death," Mar. 26, 1924; "Zeo Zoe's Brother Released On Bond," Apr. 2, 1924; "Treasured Family Home," Jul. 30, 1984; "Memories Linger In Oilman's Restored Home," Aug. 25, 1985; "Blaze Damages Burnett Mansion," Aug. 14, 2004.

Oshkosh (Wisconsin) *Daily Northwestern*: "A Horrible Fate," Oct. 16, 1886; "Trial of Jesse James, Jr.," Nov. 16, 1898; "Jesse James Weds," Jan. 25, 1900.

Plattsburg (Missouri) *Leader*: No title (*Under the Black Flag*), Mar. 18, 1921.

Port Arthur (Texas) *News*: "Things I Never Knew 'Til Now About Bandits," by Walter Winchell, Jan. 31, 1939; "Claim Brother Is Not Slayer," Mar. 23, 1924; "Osteopath Sought In Woman's Death," Mar. 25, 1924; "Osteopath Released in Woman's Death," Mar. 26, 1924; "Zoe Wilkins' Negro Janitor Is Held," Apr. 13, 1924.

Racine (Wisconsin) *Daily Journal*: "Defended by Jesse James Jr.," Feb. 9, 1907.

Racine Journal-News: "Chit-Chat," by Ruth Cameron, Nov. 6, 1913.

Richwood (Ohio) *Gazette*: "Horrible Fate. An Aged Lady Devoured by a Drove of Hogs," Oct. 21, 1886.

Riverdale (Illinois) *Pointer*: "Display of Jesse James Relics," Aug. 10, 1923.

Rocky Mountain (Colorado) *News*: "Zoe Z. Wilkins [*sic*] Killed In Home At Kansas City," Mar. 19, 1924; "Ex-Convict Jailed In Wilkins Knife Murder," Mar. 20, 1924; "Fear Overshadowed Last Tragic Hours of Dr. Zoe Wilkins," Mar. 21, 1924; "Dr. Wilkins Lived In Fear of Plot Against Her Life," Mar. 22, 1924; "Blood-Stained Note In Wilkins Home New Clew to Slaying of Adventuress," Mar. 24, 1924.

San Antonio (Texas) *Light*: "Jesse James Marries His Divorced Wife," Sept. 17, 1911; "Jesse James, Jr., Talks," Nov. 28, 1921; "Ask Dr. Brothers," by Dr. Joyce Brothers, May 24, 1972.

Sandusky (Ohio) *Star-Journal*: "Eternal Triangle Bared When Housekeeper, 71, Sues Aged Millionaire After His Marriage to Kansas City Beauty," Feb. 17, 1917.

Sapulpa (Oklahoma) *Herald*: "Slain Woman Was Wealthy," Mar. 19, 1924; "Woman's Death a Deep Mystery," Mar. 20, 1924; "Negro May Be Slayer of 'Dr. Zoe'," Mar. 24, 1924.

Sheboygan (Wisconsin) *Press-Telegram*: "Seek Treasure As Clew To Murderer of Wealthy Victim," Mar. 19, 1924.

Sioux City (Iowa) *Herald*: "Oil Wonder of the World," Jan. 15, 1908.

St. Louis (Missouri) *Post-Dispatch*: "Brother Held In Hunt For Slayer of Zoe Wilkins," Mar. 19, 1924; "Identifies Knife Used By Slayer of Zoe Wilkins," Mar. 20, 1924; "Brother Feared By Zoe Wilkins, Attorney Asserts," Mar. 21, 1924; "Says Zoe Wilkins Was A Victim of Own Intrigues," Mar. 22, 1924; "Woman Pictures Last Moments of Zoe Wilkins," Mar. 23, 1924; "Three, Including Brother, Held For Wilkins Murder," Mar. 25, 1924; "'Now I've Money, I'll Have Fun,' Wrote Zoe Wilkins In Her Little Brown Diary," Mar. 28, 1924; "Zoe Wilkins, 20 Years on the Down Grade, Meets Her Last Adventure," Mar. 30, 1924.

Statesville (North Carolina) *Semi-Weekly Landmark*: No title (robbery of James residence), Nov. 26, 1901.

Syracuse (New York) *Herald*: "Maze of Evidence Fails To Trap Slayers of Kansas City Girl," by Constance Brown, Nov. 2, 1924.

Syracuse Herald-American: "Outlaw's Kin Wants True Story Told," Aug. 27, 1989.

Tulsa Daily World: "Banker's Widow Found Murdered," Mar. 19, 1924; "Dead Mates, Broken Hearts Mark Wake of Zoe Wilkins, Former Tulsa Cigar Girl," Mar. 20, 1924; "Unnamed Woman Tells of Fears of Zoe Wilkins," Mar. 21, 1924; "Hidden Fortune Proved Undoing of Zoe Wilkins," Mar. 22, 1924.

Tulsa Tribune: "Former Tulsa Adventuress Is Slain," Mar. 19, 1924; "Seek Woman in Zoe Wilkins Murder," Mar. 20, 1924.

Van Wert (Ohio) *Republican*: "Additional News," Oct. 21, 1886.

Wall Street Journal: "First National of Joplin Reopens," Nov. 21, 1921.

Washington Post: "After Train Robbers," Oct. 2, 1898; "Jesse James and Others Indicted," Oct. 18, 1898; "Indicted For Murder; One of Roosevelt's Rough Riders Charged With Killing A Woman," Oct. 29, 1898; "Jesse James Acquitted," Mar. 1, 1899; "Prosecutor Reed Disgusted," Mar. 2, 1899; "Jesse James, Outlaw's Son, Redeems the Family Name," by Allen Bethel, Jul. 8, 1906; "Divorces Jesse E. James," Jan. 12, 1911; "Would Check Divorce," Dec. 9, 1911; "Why Juries Never Convict Pretty Women," by Professor James E. Lough, May 9, 1915; "Plucky Old Mrs. Cunningham and the Siren," Mar. 25, 1917; "Banker's Divorced Wife Found Slain," Mar. 19, 1924; "Post-Scripts" Column by George Rothwell Brown, Mar. 20, 1924; "Police Hold Three In Probe of Murder of 4-Time Divorcee," Mar. 20, 1924; "Maze of Wilkins Clews," Mar. 21, 1924; "Dr. Wilkins' Brother Declares Her Insane,"

Mar. 23, 1924; "Woman Threatened in Wilkins Murder," Mar. 24, 1924; "Three Men Accused of Wilkins Murder," Mar. 25, 1924.

Waterloo (Iowa) *Times-Tribune*: "Travelette: Colorado Springs," by Niksah, Jul. 20, 1915.

Waterloo Daily Courier: "Parkersburg Man of 83 Sticks to Claim that Famous Outlaw Jesse James is Dead," Oct. 17, 1948.

Wisconsin State Journal: "Girls Men Should Shun," by Beatrice Fairfax, Feb. 6, 1933.

Zanesville (Ohio) *Times Recorder*: "Did One Of Doctor's Admirers Slay Her in Kansas City Home?" Mar. 24, 1924.

INTERNET RESOURCES

The American Osteopathic Association, http://www.osteopathic.org/.

Ancestry.com.

Newspaperarchive.com.

Missouri State Archives' Death Certificate Database, http://www.sos.mo.gov/ archives/resources/deathcertificates/

Chronicles of Oklahoma, Volume 17, No. 4, December, 1939, Southwestern Oil Boom Towns, by Gerald Forbes, http://digital.library.okstate.edu/ Chronicles/v017/v017p393.html

NOTES

The author's copies of many of the resources relied on for this book have been donated to the Milton F. Perry Research Library at the Jesse James Farm & Museum, Kearney, Missouri, and are available for viewing upon appropriate request.

PROLOGUE: A TERRIFIC FIGHT

The reconstruction of the murder of Zeo Wilkins was based on the autopsy report of Deputy Coroner H. E. Moss, M.D., which was reprinted in the press, as well as descriptions of the murder scene given by detectives and written by journalists allowed to enter 2425 Park Avenue. See the *Kansas City Journal, Kansas City Post, Kansas City Star, Kansas City Times,* and Associated Press and United Press coverage, March 19–22, 1924. The house still stands today, unoccupied.

CHAPTER 1: HOGGIE! HOGGIE! HOGGIE!

For articles about hog pen deaths see the *Van Wert Republican, Richwood Gazette, Davenport Gazette, Newark Daily Advocate,* and *Oshkosh Daily Northwestern.*

The story of Zeo's hog pen tantrum was told repeatedly by her brothers. Arthur Wilkins recalled it as an old man when he gave a long interview to an historian in Colorado Springs about his sister (see Englert). Horace Wilkins told the same story to a room full of newspaper reporters. Zeo also mentioned it in her diary. See the *Syracuse Herald*, *New York Times*, *St. Louis Post-Dispatch*, *Kansas City Times*, etc. Though it was widely quoted after her death, Zeo's original diary did not surface in this author's research.

Arthur read a roll of his siblings and their birth and death dates from the Wilkins family Bible to the same historian. The direct quotes that begin this chapter are Arthur's commentary for the occasion. According to Arthur's account, Zeo was the eleventh child of the family. None of their names appear where they should in the Huron County, Ohio, birth registries, though they do appear in other local records. Zeo herself told friends and acquaintances (and at least one newspaper reporter) that she was the thirteenth child of her family. But she also said she was born and raised in Lamar, Missouri, which was untrue. See the *Washington Post*.

CHAPTER 2: SOMEDAY I'M GOING TO BE RICH, RICH, RICH

This chapter relied on the *Chester Times* (Allene Sumner), *Davenport Daily Republican* (on acceptance of osteopathy), and *Mansfield News* (on Horace Wilkins). For the story of the grave robber gang of Cleveland Homeopathic and medical grave robbery in the era, see Fanebust and Sappol. The description of Zeo's medical school career from inception to graduation is based on the carefully kept archives of the American School of Osteopathy, now housed at the Still National Osteopathic Museum and National Center for Osteopathic History in Kirksville, Missouri.

CHAPTER 3: I WILL LET HIM KISS ME

The resources relied on for this chapter include O'Donnell, Quinn ("queen among the co-eds," "glamor and daring"), and the *Humeston New Era* (on the ASO), *St. Louis Post-Dispatch*, and *Washington Post*. Decades after their graduation, Zeo and her sister Gertrude were still remembered in Kirksville as "quite popular." See the *Kirksville Weekly Graphic*.

There are many different accounts of Zeo's first marriage. Zeo's brother Charles Wilkins spoke to journalists in Kansas City after her murder about some of her marital adventures, mentioning that her first husband's name was Richard Dyer. British true crime author Bernard O'Donnell wrote a brief essay about Dr. Wilkins that was published in the 1950s and reprinted many times since. Without revealing his sources, O'Donnell identified Zeo's first husband as Richard Dryer, son of a banker in Montana. The obituary for Zeo Wilkins that ran in the *Osteopathic Physician Magazine* identified her first husband as "a man named Dryder, a fellow student at the A.S.O. from whom she separated because he refused to allow her to continue her practice." There is no ASO record of a student with that name or a like one, nor any corresponding census record, and no marriage license could be found.

CHAPTER 4: DR. G. JUST ADORES ME

The story of the Garrings' marriage was found in Englert (for the quotes attributed to Arthur Wilkins), Litton (on the Indian Territory osteopathy law), O'Donnell, Quinn ("in court he stated"), *Durant Daily Democrat, Fort Worth Star Telegram, Hamilton Evening Journal* (Jack Lait), and the Still National Osteopathic Museum archives. Charles K. Garring described his reasons for studying osteopathy to a writer for the *Journal of Osteopathy* three weeks after he began his studies.

Some sources stated that Zeo shot Charles Garring not in Durant but in San Antonio. Zeo's brother-in-law, Kibby J. Clements, D.O., told the *Tulsa Daily World* that the Garrings stayed for a time in San Antonio. One source—Arthur Wilkins in his old age—said that Gertrude Wilkins-Clements encouraged Zeo to shoot Charles and was present at the time, but no other source mentioned or confirmed this. A scan of the headlines for the Durant and San Antonio dailies failed to turn up any coverage around the time it might have occurred.

While a marriage record was found for Zeo and Charles Garring, no divorce records could be found in archives of the Indian Territory nor in Bexar County, Texas (San Antonio), so the date of their divorce and the particulars could not be better fixed. In November 1905, Dr. Charles Garring ran a classified ad in the Journal of Osteopathy that said: "PRACTICE FOR SALE—In town in Indian Territory, population 7,000; no negroes and growing rapidly; a good business for two. Address C.K. Garring, Durant, Ind. Ter.," which would suggest they fell out that year. All of this assumes, of course, that they were actually divorced.

CHAPTER 5: POOR B.B.

The resources relied on for this chapter include Meyer (on Max Meyer), Quinn ("to go riding"), and the *Ada Evening News* ("A few strenuous hours"), *Galveston Daily News* (on the Glenn Pool), *The Oklahoman* (on the murderous police chief and coverage of the cases against B.B. Burnett), *Sioux City Herald* (on the Glenn Pool), *Wisconsin State Journal* (Beatrice Fairfax), and appellate opinions in numerous civil and criminal cases involving the Burnetts. See Sources.

CHAPTER 6: THE CIGAR GIRL

Tales of Tulsa and Zeo's scandals there were found in Englert (for the quotes attributed to Arthur and Zeo Wilkins), Forbes (on oil boom towns), O'Donnell, Rister (on the Tulsa strike), and the *Ogden City Standard-Examiner* (Louise Fazenda), *Oklahoma Leader* (on James Gang gold), *Tulsa Daily World* (on Zeo's adventures in Tulsa), and *Tulsa Tribune* ("brunette of dazzling beauty").

CHAPTER 7: GOODBYE ZOE, FOREVER

The resources relied on for this chapter include Bloom (Kipling) and Adams (on Claremore's radium wells). It was difficult to find any confirmation, specific date, or details of the widely reported suicide of Leonard Smith. O'Donnell relayed a slightly different account. "Her lover was accidentally shot dead during a street fracas while going to his bank for further money to squander on his beloved. In this case Zeo must be absolved from direct responsibility for her lover's tragic fate." Most sources, however, identify Mr. Smith as a suicide. See, e.g., the *Lima News* and *Washington Post*.

CHAPTER 8: THE OLD MAN'S DARLING

The resources relied on for this chapter include Englert ("a dingy, crummy place"), Clifford ("this evil"), Clifford and Martin (957 bawdy-house arrests), Mary Kelley (on millionaires), Quinn ("extended, if not"), Randolph, and the *Arkansas City Traveler, Chillicothe Constitution, Fresno Bee* (Dorothy Dix), *Joplin News-Herald, New York Times, and Wall Street Journal*. Zeo may have owned or rented a number of places in Kansas City. The 1915 Kansas City telephone book includes a listing for "Wilkins, Zella Z., osteopath," and gives her address as 2507 Peery Avenue.

CHAPTER 9: PLUCKY OLD MRS. CUNNINGHAM AND THE SIREN

The resources relied on for this chapter include Green and the *Chicago Daily Tribune, Chillicothe Constitution, Denver Post, Joplin Globe, Joplin News-Herald, Kansas City Journal, Kansas City Post, Kansas City Times, Lima News, Mansfield News, Sandusky Star-Journal,* and *Washington Post*. The account of the litigation between Tabitha Taylor and Zeo Cunningham is based chiefly on a collection of press accounts of the scandal, primarily from Joplin and Kansas City newspapers. Zeo's lawyer, Frank P. Walsh, clipped and mounted dozens of articles in a scrapbook. After his death in 1939, it was included in the donation of his papers to the New York Public Library. Because of the way he constructed it, the scrapbook cannot be copied but is available for viewing in the Manuscripts and Archives Division.

CHAPTER 10: LOVE MAKES TIME GO, TIME MAKES LOVE GO

The details of Zeo's adventures as Mrs. Marksheffel were found in Englert (for the quotes attributed to Arthur Wilkins), Hemingway, Kimes (on early Ford race cars), Sprague (on the history of Colorado Springs, its "playboys," and Marksheffel's motor wreck), and the *Chicago Daily Tribune, Colorado Springs Gazette, Des Moines Capital, Durango Democrat,*

Emery County Press, Frederick Post, Joplin News-Herald, Oakland Tribune, and *Waterloo Times-Tribune.*

A photograph of Al's monument to Zeo is available online at http://www.newsblab.com/4_26_05.htm (scroll down).

CHAPTER 11: WILES AND MACHINATIONS

The resources relied upon for this chapter include Englert ("for years and years"), Sprague, and the *Colorado Springs Gazette, Denver Post* ("finale to her career"), *Kansas City Star* ("one of the most sensational"), *Lowell Sun, New Castle News* (John D. Mueller), and *Rocky Mountain News.*

Zeo Wilkins Marksheffel was served process in the *McNamara v. Marksheffel* case at 3805 The Paseo, which presumably was once the address of the Paseo Hotel. She also kept hours at 3010 Tracy Avenue, First Floor, according to the suit papers. John McNamara's saloon was at 1700 Main Street, Kansas City.

CHAPTER 12: SOMEONE WILL BE ADMITTING LIGHT INTO YOUR BODY

Resources relied upon for this chapter include Englert (for the quotes attributed to Arthur Wilkins) and the *Kansas City Star* (Buckner). In the days following Zeo's murder, several of her brothers and sisters repeatedly spoke to the press about her slow decline into alcoholism and their efforts to help her. The Fort Worth police chief also described her suicide attempts to several reporters. See the *Kansas City Star, Kansas City Times, San Antonio Light,* and *Fort Worth Star Telegram.*

CHAPTER 13: THE TRYSTING PLACE

Resources relied upon for this chapter include the archives of the Still National Osteopathic Museum (on Albert Abrams, D.O.), and the *Kansas City Star* and *New York Times.* The details of Zeo's final years in Kansas City and the observations of neighbors, friends, and lovers were rendered from testimony at the coroner's inquest into her murder. The direct quotes contained in this chapter constitute the testimony of those quoted except as noted. See the notes following Chapter 20.

CHAPTER 14: TIM HOWARD'S REAL NAME

Details of Jesse James's childhood are found in Breihan, Croy, Love ("Here in Kearney"), James, Ottenheimer (on cousin marriage), Steele (on James genealogy), Stiles, Yeatman, and the *Atlanta Constitution, Chicago Herald, Fort Wayne Daily Gazette, Indiana Weekly Messenger, Kansas City Star, Kansas City Times, Manitoba Morning Free Press,* and *New*

York Times. Curiously enough, Stiles's 2002 biography of Jesse James was the first book in print to divulge the slave-holding habits of the James clan.

Jesse E. James cannot be called the only son of Jesse James. When he was two years old, his mother Zee gave birth to twin boys. They were named for the doctors who attended her, Gould and Montgomery. The babies died a few days after birth. See Yeatman.

CHAPTER 15: A GOOD REPUTATION EXCEPT IN POLICE CIRCLES

The resources relied upon for this chapter include the biography of William Rockhill Nelson (on the "gang in control"), Patterson in Old West ("In Missouri, the name"), Yeatman, and the *Boston Daily Globe, Chicago Daily Tribune, Kansas City Journal, Kansas City Star, Los Angeles Times,* and *Washington Post.*

CHAPTER 16: THE LOST CAUSE

The resources relied upon for this chapter include Fink (on Frank Walsh), Patterson in Old West ("The feelings of suspense"), Patterson in Train Robbery Era ("For his concluding"), Redding (on Frank Walsh), Williams, Yeatman, and the *Chicago Daily Tribune, Fort Wayne Sunday Gazette, Fresno Weekly Republican, Kansas City Journal, Kansas City Star, Los Angeles Times, Marion Daily Star, New York Times, Oshkosh Daily Northwestern,* and *Washington Post.*

Most James scholars who have studied the Leeds holdup and the evidence in the case believe, despite the verdict, that Jesse E. James did indeed commit the robbery, though this hasn't always been the popular view. See Patterson.

CHAPTER 17: JESSE JAMES KIDNAPS BABY

The resources relied upon for this chapter include James, Harry S. Truman ("When I finished"), Yeatman, and the *Bedford Gazette, Chicago Daily Tribune, Chillicothe Constitution, Davenport Daily Republican, Fort Wayne Sentinel, Frederick News, Indiana Evening Gazette, Indianapolis Star, Iowa City Daily Press, La Crosse Tribune, Kansas City Times, Kansas City Star, Monessen Daily Independent, Nebraska State Journal, Newark Daily Advocate, New York Times, Racine Daily Journal, Oshkosh Daily Northwestern, Oakland Tribune, San Antonio Light, Statesville Semi-Weekly Landmark,* and *Washington Post.*

The only civil cases handled by Jesse James for which records were available were those which resulted in an appeal, of which there were several. See Sources. The description of the trial of Albert Crone is based on a review of the pleadings and trial transcript in the Missouri State Archives.

The four children of Jesse and Stella James were Lucille, Josephine Frances, Jessie, and Ethel Rose. The direct descendants of Jesse Woodson James now number in the dozens (and unrelated namesakes perhaps in the tens of thousands). For more on the genealogy of the James family, see Stray Leaves, a website maintained by Eric James, at http://www.ericjames.org.

CHAPTER 18: UNDERWORLD MONEY

The resources relied upon for this chapter include Hartmann, Howard, Schirmer (targeted for "destruction"), Yeatman, and the *Elyria Chronicle Telegram*, *Kansas City Post*, *Kansas City Star*, *Modesto News-Herald* (Minott Saunders), *Oakland Tribune*, *Ogden City Standard-Examiner*, and *Washington Post*.

The description of the trial of Mattie Howard is based on extensive press coverage and a review of the pleadings and trial transcript in the Missouri State Archives. The direct quotes attributed to Mattie appeared in her autobiography, which was written in the third person and published under a pseudonym.

Special Prosecutor James Aylward's prediction that Jesse James would represent Mattie Howard's boyfriend came true. In a later trial, James represented Sam Taylor for the murder of Diamond Joe. Taylor was also convicted and went to prison.

CHAPTER 19: UNDER THE BLACK FLAG

Details about Jesse's film and the Kansas City Ku Klux Klan came from Bell (on the Kansas City Klan), Crittenden (on Jesse's poor acting), George ("curious, thrilling meetings," "thousands believed,"), Gotham (on population and race relations in Kansas City), Green (on Kansas City politicians), Stella James, Kirkendall (on the Kansas City Klan), MacLean (on the Ku Klux Klan), Mitchell (on Truman and the Klan), O'Connell (on Eva Evans), Petrone ("Frank wouldn't have"), Reddig (on the Kansas City Klan), Rice (on the Ku Klux Klan), Schirmer (on the Kansas City Klan), Margaret Truman in Harry S. Truman ("bed sheet variety," "cheap un-American," "walked off the platform"), Underhill (on Truman's last Klan appearance), Yeatman, *Moving Picture World* ("we are not making"), and the *Chillicothe Constitution*, *Danville Bee*, *Edwardsville Intelligencer*, *Excelsior Springs Standard*, *Kansas City Post*, *Kansas City Star* ("no amount of money"), *Plattsburg Leader* (on the Black Flag premiere), *Riverdale Pointer*, and *San Antonio Light*.

CHAPTERS 20 THROUGH 25

The details of Zeo's last days emerged under oath during the coroner's inquest, which is presented here as the press redundantly reported it. In those instances in which there was room for doubt in the reporting, the specific source has been identified in the text. The most thorough and accurate coverage came from the *Kansas City Star*, *Kansas City Times*, *St. Louis Post-Dispatch*, and the independent office of the Associated Press in Kansas City.

For original coverage of the Wilkins murder investigation see the *Atlanta Constitution, Colorado Springs Gazette, Denver Post, Durant Daily Democrat, Fort Worth Star Telegram, Kansas City Call, Kansas City Journal, Kansas City Post, Kansas City Star, Kansas City Sun, Kansas City Times, Kirksville Daily Express, Kirksville Weekly Graphic, Lima News, New York Times, Rocky Mountain News, St. Louis Post-Dispatch, Tulsa Daily World, Tulsa Tribune,* and *Washington Post.*

For wire coverage see the *Billings Gazette, Chicago Daily Tribune, Clearfield Progress, Chillicothe Constitution, Colorado Springs Gazette, Coshocton Tribune, Danville Bee, Decatur Review, Fayetteville Daily Democrat, Gettysburg Times, Henryetta Daily Free-Lancer, Iowa City Press Citizen, Lincoln State Journal, Los Angeles Times, Mansfield News, Marion Daily Star, Mexia Daily News, Nevada State Journal, The Oklahoman, Port Arthur News, Sapulpa Herald, Sheboygan Press-Telegram,* and *Zanesville Times Recorder.*

The original records and transcripts of the Wilkins death inquest, if any were produced, proved elusive. Dr. Wilkins's death certificate is viewable online, as are the death certificates of many others mentioned in this book, at the Missouri State Archives' Death Certificate Database.

Details on the very brief history of scopalamin as a "truth serum" came from *Opportunity: A Journal of Negro Life.*

O'Donnell set forth the allegations concerning Dr. Wilkins's dabblings in abortion and blackmail. He did not identify his sources, and no other account of her life or death refers to either.

CHAPTER 26: STALKED TO THE GRAVE BY THE GHOSTS OF HER WILD CAREER

The resources relied on for this chapter include Randolph and the *Frederick Post, Lima News, Kansas City Call, Kansas City Star, Ogden City Standard-Examiner, St. Louis Post-Dispatch, Syracuse Herald,* and *Washington Post.*

Though there were many hints that Dr. Zeo Wilkins had dealings in the underworld, few details could be uncovered beyond those reported. One writer did elaborate. Said Vance Randolph: "Zoe [*sic*] has been credited with major crimes in Dallas and Houston and San Antonio; it is said that she financed bankrobbers, and helped in the commission of two murders, but nobody in Texas ever produced sufficient evidence to justify prosecution." This allegation, like the one O'Donnell made connecting Zeo to abortion and blackmail, was neither repeated nor substantiated by any other known source.

EPILOGUE: JESSE JAMES ON CARPET

The resources relied on for this chapter include Angel (on Paso Robles), Bell ("Every klansman"), Croy, Crittenden ("the writer understands"), Cochran (on Vance Randolph),

Stella James, Margaret Truman in *Harry S. Truman* ("vicious, hate-filled"), Yeatman, the archives of the Jesse James Farm & Museum ("I am so very discourage" [*sic*]), and the *Atlanta Constitution, Brownsville Herald, Charleston Gazette, Chillicothe Constitution, Decatur Daily Review, Excelsior Springs Daily Standard, Excelsior Springs Daily Herald, Independence Examiner, Iowa Recorder, Kansas City Journal, Kansas City Post, Kansas City Star, Lincoln State Journal, Long Beach Independent, Los Angeles Times, Lowell Sun, Manitoba Morning Free Press, New York Times, Oakland Tribune, Port Arthur News, Syracuse Herald-American,* and *Waterloo Daily Courier.*

After Jesse E. James passed away, his heirs donated two handguns and a shotgun to the Jesse James Farm & Museum. Jesse had always said they belonged to his father. A recent inquiry based on their serial numbers demonstrated that the handguns were manufactured after the 1882 murder of Jesse James and could not have been the outlaw's guns (though the shotgun proved to be of the correct vintage). The real McCoys were apparently stolen at some point in Jesse Jr.'s life. The whereabouts today of the pair of pistols wielded with legendary skill by the most feared and admired bandit in American history are another James riddle.

INDEX

ACKNOWLEDGMENTS

I am grateful for the assistance of many people. Some helped with the research, some with the prose, and others saved me from making embarrassing errors. I thank the staff of the Colorado State Archives; the staff of the Missouri State Archives, Jefferson City; the staff of the Missouri Valley Special Collections, Kansas City Public Library; the staff of the Oklahoma Historical Society; the staff of the University of Michigan Harlan Hatcher Graduate Library; the staff of the Still National Osteopathic Museum; Lori A. Bain; Ana Brazil; Evie Bresette; Mary Beth Brown; Tim Carroll; Harold Dellinger; Glenna Dunning; Steve Galbraith, Bobbie Gosnell; Cheryl A. Gracey; Gordon Gray; Steve Huff; David W. Jackson; Gary Maize; Liz Murphy; Patrick K. Robb; Jay Shouse; Peter Skutches; Debra Loguda-Summers; H. Morley Swingle; Nancy Thaler; Deborah Orth; Doug Smith; Patterson Smith; and Jeri Westerson. At Sterling Publishing, I would like to thank my editor Iris Blasi, production editor Scott Amerman; interior designer Chris Welch, cover designer Karen Nelson, and copyeditor Kalista Johnson. I owe a special thanks to my literary agent, Rick Broadhead, who showed an interest in the story just as I was considering chucking eight years of research into a garbage can.

ABOUT THE AUTHOR

Laura James (no relation to the James Gang) is an attorney and crime historian in Detroit. She is the proprietor of *Clews*, one of the top true crime sites on the Internet. James has been interviewed or consulted as an expert in historic crimes and the true crime genre by PBS/*Nova*, the *BBC World NewsHour*, and the History Channel, among others. Her articles and book reviews have appeared in the *On the Spot Journal* (devoted to gangster-era crime) and *The Lizzie Borden Quarterly*.